Theology Dept

In Search of Christian Unity

In Search of
Christian Unity
Basic Consensus / Basic Differences

Joseph A. Burgess, editor

Fortress Press   Minneapolis

IN SEARCH OF CHRISTIAN UNITY
Basic Consensus/Basic Differences

Scripture quotations unless otherwise noted are from the Revised Standard Version of the Bible, copyright ©1946, 1952, and 1971 by the Division of Christian Education of the National Council of Churches.

Cover design: Pollock Design Group
Internal design and typesetting: Peregrine Publications

Library of Congress Cataloging-in-Publication Data
In search of Christian unity : basic consensus/basic differences, Joseph A.
  Burgess, editor.
      p. cm.
    Includes bibliographical references.
    ISBN 0-8006-2302-9 (alk. paper)
    1. Christian union. 2. Christian union conversations.
  I. Burgess, Joseph A. II. Title: Basic consensus/basic differences.
  BX9.I49   1991
  262'.001 – dc20   90-32433
                                                                        CIP

The paper used in this publication meets the minimum requirements of American National Standard for Information Sciences—Permanence of Paper for Printed Library Materials, ANSI Z329.48-1984.   ∞™

Manufactured in the U.S.A.   AF 1-2302
95   94   93   92   91   1   2   3   4   5   6   7   8   9   10

Contents

v

Abbreviations

AELC   Association of Evangelical Lutheran Churches

ALC   American Lutheran Church

Ap   Apology of the Augsburg Confession

ARCIC   Anglican-Roman Catholic International Commission

BC   *The Book of Concord. The Confessions of the Evangelical Lutheran Church* (tr. and ed. T. Tappert; Philadelphia: Fortress, 1959)

BEM   *Baptism, Eucharist and Ministry* (Faith and Order Paper 111; Geneva: WCC, 1982)

CA   *Confessio Augustana* (Augsburg Confession)

CTCR   Commission on Theology and Church Relations (LCMS)

DS   *Enchiridion Symbolorum* (33rd ed.; ed. H. Denzinger and A. Schönmetzer)

DV   *Dei Verbum*

FC Ep   Formula of Concord. Epitome

FC SD   Formula of Concord. Solid Declaration

GiA   *Growth in Agreement* (Ecumenical Documents 2; ed. H. Meyer and L. Vischer; New York/Ramsey; Paulist, 1984)

LCA   Lutheran Church in America

LCMS   Lutheran Church—Missouri Synod

LCUSA   Lutheran Council in the U.S.A.

LED   Lutheran-Episcopal Dialogue

LG   *Lumen Gentium*

L-RC 6   *Teaching Authority and Infallibility in the Church* (Lutherans and Catholics in Dialogue 6; ed. P. C. Empie, T. A. Murphy, and J. A. Burgess; Minneapolis: Augsburg, 1978)

L-RC 7   *Justification by Faith* (Lutherans and Catholics in Dialogue 7; ed. H. G. Anderson, T. A. Murphy, and J. A. Burgess; Minneapolis: Augsburg, 1985)

LW   *Luther's Works* (general eds. J. Pelikan and H. Lehmann)

LWF   Lutheran World Federation

PG   *Patrologiae cursus completus. Series Graeca* (ed. J. P. Migne)

SA   Smalcald Articles

UR   *Unitatis Redintegratio*

WA   *Dr. Martin Luthers Werke* (Kritische Gesamtausgabe; "Weimarer Ausgabe"; Weimar: Böhlau, 1883 to the present)

WARC   World Alliance of Reformed Churches

WCC   World Council of Churches

In Search of Christian Unity

Background Material

1

Introduction

WHAT IS fundamental consensus? If two committees find a fundamental consensus and their sponsors still disagree, is the problem simply how one defines "fundamental consensus"? Hundreds of ecumenical dialogues have produced statements of clarification, convergence, and consensus, yet in most cases the churches involved have made little progress toward unity. Some progress could be expected anyway in a world growing smaller, with better transportation, faster communication, natural mergers because of cultural affinities and local pressures, and the breakdown of traditional distinctions as the result of rapid change. Have the dialogues treated symptoms, not the underlying disease?

Metaphors such as "fundamental" and "basic" have been useful in sorting out what "consensus" or "difference" means. Yet even such metaphors need definition. On the one hand, fundamental consensus seems to presuppose that a fundamental difference is not possible. Historically speaking, did not the first assembly of the World Council of Churches in 1948 at Amsterdam covenant to stay together? And, even though not all churches are members of the World Council of Churches, who would claim that the sacraments of baptism and the Eucharist in another's church are not truly sacraments in that church?

Further, a long list of fundamental differences has been suggested, such as the relationship between gospel and church, the understanding of "person," the conflict between faith alone and faith plus works, and the like. Does not such variety prove that "fundamental" differences is not the real issue? Instead, it has been suggested, one should think of "types" of the church reflecting a fundamental consensus differentiated through history but complementary.[1] Therefore at most one might speak of a "fundamental question."[2] It is, after all, notoriously difficult to demonstrate real contradictions in historical matters. For example, if one were

3

convinced that the fundamental difference between Lutherans and the Reformed lies in their differing use of Scripture,[3] how could this be demonstrated historically because ample historical evidence could undoubtedly be cited for the same use of Scripture by both Lutherans and the Reformed? So-called nontheological factors also complicate the picture. The church before the eschaton is inextricably caught up in culture and, more seriously, is a mixture of wheat and tares (Matt 13:24-30).

On the other hand, a fundamental difference seems to presuppose that fundamental consensus does not exist. The trouble with ecclesial "types" is that "the various Christian traditions do *not* correspond to basic 'types.'"[4] Nor is it possible to claim that differences are merely differences in thought structure, for scholars "learn more than one language and more than one system of conceptuality. It is possible to discern incompatible meanings under the conditions of a plurality of thought structures."[5] What happens is that those who participate in dialogues have had the experience of pressing one point that moves to a second, decisive point that dissolves into a third, until finally one is aware of being up against "a matrix, a form of life . . . so basic and deep that it seems like a Kantian *a priori*" and is nevertheless different for each side.[6] Or, as also happens, when a difference is considered so fundamental that it could only be overcome by a "profound change" in one or both parties, a "conversion" — as Tillard describes it in quotation marks, it may qualify as a fundamental difference.[7]

Yes, we are one in Christ. To ask, however, Where is this fundamental consensus? is also to ask, Where is the true church? Is not salvation at stake? It makes a fundamental difference.

As part of the ongoing discussion of these questions,[8] the Division of Theological Studies of the Lutheran Council in the U.S.A., New York City, and the Institute for Ecumenical Research, Strasbourg, France, held a conference on "Fundamental Consensus and Church Fellowship" from January 30 to February 6, 1987, at La Ceiba y La Fuente, Rio Grande, Puerto Rico. The greater part of the participants was made up of Lutheran leaders and theologians, but the Episcopalian, Methodist, Orthodox, Reformed, and Roman Catholic traditions were also represented.[9]

Before the conference the staff of the Institute for Ecumenical Research in Strasbourg prepared "The Task: Questions and Definitions." These are not intended to be exhaustive, but an aid in delimiting the issues. In the months before and after the conference a study process made up of participants named by the Division of Theological Studies produced their report, "Fundamental Consensus — Fundamental

Differences." It brings out the tension, though not polarity, between "hermeneutical" and "ecumenical," which is not unlike the more familiar question of the relationship between gospel and church.[10]

Thanks and appreciation are due especially to the Aid Association for Lutherans, Appleton, Wisconsin, whose generous grants made it possible to hold this conference and publish its findings. Thanks are also due to the Institute for Ecumenical Research, Strasbourg, France, the Lutheran Church in America, New York City, and the Lutheran Council in the U.S.A., New York City, for their helpful and substantial contributions.

Notes

1. Cf. the branch theory of unity and diversity in the church; Nikolaus von Zinzindorf's idea of the *"tropoi"* of the church (M. Schmidt, "Einigungsbestrebungen. II. Einigungsbestrebungen in Europa vom 16. bis 18. Jahrhundert," *Religion in Geschichte und Gegenwart* [3rd ed.; Tübingen: Mohr, 1958] 2:384); Walter Kasper, "Das Petrusamt in ökumenischer Perspektive," *In der Nachfolge Jesu Christi* (ed. K. Lehmann; Freiberg: Herder, 1980) 103-4, 113-14.

2. W. Kasper, below, 37.

3. Cf. J. L. Leuba, "Die Union als ökumenich-theologisches Problem," *Um evangelische Einheit. Beiträge zum Unionsproblem* (ed. K. Herbert; Herborn: Oranien-Verlag, 1967) 296-97, 307, 316; G. Ebeling, "The Significance of Doctrinal Differences for the Divison of the Church," *Word and Faith* (Philadelphia: Fortess, 1963) 168; as cited in H. Meyer, "Fundamental Difference — Fundamental Consensus," *Mid-Stream* 25 (1986) 254.

4. S. Mark Heim, "Modes and Levels of Confession: A Protestant Perspective on 'Basic Differences'" *Mid-Stream* 25 (1986) 289. Emphasis in text.

5. Carl Braaten, "Justification," in *Lutherans in Ecumenical Dialogue: A Reappraisal* (ed. J. Burgess; Minneapolis: Augsburg, 1990) 97.

6. Heim, "Modes," 288.

7. J. M. R. Tillard, "We are Different," *Mid-Stream* 25 (1986) 286.

8. The questions, though using different terminology, go back at least as far as the Reformation; see the discussion of "fundamental articles" in Martin Schmidt, "Einigungsbestrebungen," 382-84; W. Joest, "Fundamentalartikel," *Theologische Realenzyklopädie* (Berlin, New York: de Gruyter, 1983) 11:727-32; E. Schott, "Fides implicita," *Religion in Geschichte und Gegenwart* (3rd ed.; Tübingen: Mohr, 1958) 936-37. As an ecumenical issue the term "fundamental difference" can be found as early as J. G. Walch, *Historische und Theologische Einleitung in die Religions-Streitigkeiten ausser der Evangelisch-Lutherischen Kirche* (Jena: Johann Meyer, 1733-36; facsimile reprint, Stuttgart-Bad Cannstatt: Frommann, 1972) 714-15; cited in Hans Jörg Urban, "Die Frage nach den konfessionellen Prinzipien vom 17. bis 19. Jahrhundert," *Handbuch der Oekumene* (ed. H. J. Urban and H. Wagner; Paderborn: Bonifatius, 1987) 3,1:205-6. For the history of the debate about "fundamental consensus" and "fundamental differences," see Hans Jörg Urban

5

and Harald Wagner, "Die konfessionellen Prinzipien: Grundübereinstimmung — Grunddissens," *Handbuch der Oekumene* (ed. H. J. Urban and H. Wagner; Paderborn: Bonifatius, 1987) 3, 1:195-260; and, particularly for more recent literature, André Birmelé, *Le Salut en Jésus Christ dans les Dialogues Oecuméniques* (Paris: du Cerf, 1986) 277-315; Meyer, "Fundamental Difference — Fundamental Consensus," (n. 3 above) 247-59; Comité mixte catholique-protestant en France, *Consensus oecuménique et différence fondamentale*. Paris: Le Centurion, 1987.

9. The participants, with titles and addresses as of the date of the conference, are listed at the close of this volume. During the latter part of the conference most of the European participants plus a small number from the United States met separately under the auspices of the Institute for Ecumenical Research, Strasbourg, to discuss the following essays: "Möglichkeit und Umfang ökumenischer Konsense. Eine historisch-theologische Studie zur 'Grundkonsens'-Problematik," by Professor W. Beinert; "Grundkonsens und Kirchengemeinschaft," by Professor W. Kasper (printed in a revised form as "Grundkonsens und Kirchengemeinschaft," *Theologische Quartalschrift* 167 (1987) 161-81 and translated for this volume from the revised text); "Grundkonsens. Ein Konzept heutiger ökumenischer Theologie im Spiegel der Erfahrungen der Kirche des Augsburgischen Bekenntnisses," by Professor Dr. G. Kretschmar; and "Grundkonsens und Kirchengemeinschaft aus lutherischer Sicht," by Professor H. Meyer (included here in a condensed English version). Three essays from the general conference have already appeared in print: Gerhard O. Forde, "Justification by Faith Alone. The Article by which the Church Stands or Falls," *dialog* 27 (1988) 260-67; Carl J. Peter, "Justification by Faith Alone. The Article by which the Church Stands or Falls. A Reply," *dialog* 29 (1990) 55-58; Archbishop Methodios, "Fundamental Consensus and Church Fellowship," *Ekklesia kai Theologia* (London) 7-8 (1986-87) 609-19.

10. A study process on "Basic Consensus — Basic Differences" conducted by the Division of Theological Studies (LCUSA) met June 2-3, 1986, at Techny, IL; November 7-8, 1986, at Des Plaines, IL; and April 10-11, 1987, at Techny, IL. The Standing Committee of the Division of Theological Studies included itself in the study process and added: Eric Gritsch, Gettysburg, PA; Marc Kolden, St. Paul, MN; Robert Jenson, Gettysburg, PA; Michael Root, Columbia, SC; Wayne Stumme, Columbus, OH; and Dean Wenthe, Fort Wayne, IN. The following were discussed: (June 2-3, 1986) Robert Jenson, "The Relevance of Justification to Ecclesiology and Sacramentology"; Eric Gritsch, "Basic Differences as Seen in the Volumes of the U.S. Lutheran-Catholic Dialogue"; Marc Kolden, "Basic Differences: How 'Basic' and How 'Different'?" (printed as "Lutherans in Dialogue: Basic Differences?" *Word and World* 7 (1987) 302-15); (November 7-8, 1986) Robert Jenson, "The Christological *Differenzen*" (a later version of this essay was presented at the conference and is included in this volume); Wayne Stumme, "A Discussion of Unity and Diversity in the New Testament according to Dunn and Käsemann"; Joseph A. Burgess, "Probe einer Problemskizze"; (April 10-11, 1987); the final report of the study, printed as part of the background material in this volume.

The North American Academy of Ecumenists also took up this question. On September 27-29, 1985, in Washington, D.C., at its annual meeting the theme was "Fundamental Differences — Fundamental Consensus." Along with the translation of the description of the problem by Harding Meyer (which appeared in German as "Grundverschiedenheit — Grundkonsens. Problemskizze zu einem Studienprojekt des Strassburger Instituts für Oekumenische Forschung," *Oekumenische Rundschau* 34 [1985] 347-59), the three essays at the annual meeting were published as a special volume of *Mid-Stream* through the partnership of the Council on Christian Unity of the Christian Church (Disciples of Christ) with LCUSA (*Mid-Stream* 25 (1986) 247-98): Harding Meyer, "Fundamental Difference — Fundamental Consensus," 247-59; Anton Ugolnik, "Unity and the Orthodox Sensibility," 260-75; J. M. R. Tillard, "We are Different," 276-86; S. Mark Heim, "Modes and Levels of Confession: A Protestant Perspective on 'Basic Differences'," 287-98. A shortened form of these four essays appeared as "Fundamental Difference — Fundamental Consensus," *Ecumenical Trends* 15 (1986) 37-49.

On September 26-28, 1986, in Chicago, IL, the North American Academy of Ecumenists at its annual meeting took up the cognate question: "Doctrine Unites, Culture Divides. The Non-Theological Factors." The essays were: Donald W. Dayton, "Non-Theological Factors: An Evangelical Perspective"; George Lindbeck, "Non-Theological Factors: A Lutheran Perspective" (printed as "Non-Theological Factors and Structures of Unity," *Einheit der Kirche. Neue Entwicklungen und Perspektiven* [Festschrift H. Meyer; ed. G. Gassmann and P. Nørgaard-Høyen; Frankfurt am M.: Lembeck, 1988] 133-46); James Coriden, "Non-Theological Factors: A Roman Catholic Perspective."

2

The Task:
Questions and Definitions

THE MAIN TASK of this book is to reflect upon the relationship between consensus and church fellowship, focusing particularly on the concept of "fundamental consensus" as this concept or its equivalent terms has emerged in some of the recent ecumenical dialogues. In this respect three preliminary clarifications are necessary:

a) The term "church fellowship" refers to the "unity of the church" (*unitas*; *communio*) and does not simply mean a preliminary stage of unity.

b) It is assumed that doctrinal consensus is an important, but not the only presupposition or reason for church fellowship.

c) "Fundamental consensus" here may provisionally be defined as the extent and the kind of consensus (whether it is in one single doctrine, or in the totality of the church's teaching) which enables and permits church fellowship to exist as unity in diversity and not as uniformity.

The whole problem can be broken down into the following questions and clusters of questions. Not all these questions have the same status or value. Consequently not all of them need to be discussed in detail. What is needed is not only to develop areas of priority but also to raise and deal with additional questions.

Theological-historical evidence

Does the idea or term "fundamental consensus" (or its equivalents) have a place in the theological tradition of our churches?

In what context (occasion, reason, intention) is it encountered and what is its significance (difference from and rapport with "partial consensus" and "individual consensus")?

To what extent is the idea of "fundamental consensus" considered problematic and for what reasons?

Does the idea of "fundamental consensus" have biblical grounds?

Ecumenical evidence

Are we aware of the phenomenon and the idea of "fundamental consensus" within our own churches (with regard to their internal coherence and their own communal life and work)?

How far does the idea of "fundamental consensus" play a role in the ecumenical thinking of our churches (understanding of unity; ecumenical methodology)?

In which interconfessional dialogues is the notion of "fundamental consensus" being encountered today and how is it understood and applied?

In what areas and with which partners does it seem that a "fundamental consensus" has been achieved in the dialogues? What conclusions have been drawn from this?

Clarification of the terms and their relationship to one another

What are the definitions, distinctions, and interrelationships among terms like: "consensus," "partial consensus" (*Teilkonsens*), "individual consensus" (*Einzelkonsens*), "fundamental consensus," "agreement," "substantial agreement," "substantial consonance"?

In view of the preceding relationships, how is the term "convergence" to be looked upon and categorized ("partial consensus" or "fundamental consensus")?

What is the significance of the fact that the term "fundamental consensus" can be used both in the singular and the plural ("fundamental agreements" on individual issues)?

Does the use of the term "fundamental consensus" in the singular mean a comprehensive common expression of faith or doctrinal formula (analogous to the creed of the early church)? Or does it rather mean a constellation of "fundamental agreements" on individual issues which would embrace the necessary extent of consensus in faith for church fellowship? Can and should the term "fundamental consensus" be used in both senses? If so, do distinctions need to be made in using the term?

9

Consensus; "fundamental consensus"; church fellowship

If "consensus" is the goal of interconfessional doctrinal conversations, does one then not need to determine more precisely, in light of ecumenical experiences and insights, what kind of and to what extent consensus is needed for church fellowship? Does the notion of "fundamental consensus" represent a more precise definition of the consensus needed for church fellowship and thus of the goal of doctrinal conversations?

Does the notion of "fundamental consensus" correspond to a specific concept of unity or church fellowship, and, vice versa, does a specific concept of unity require a more specific understanding of consensus or a more precise definition of the notion of consensus, as provided by the notion of fundamental consensus?

What kind of specific confessional differences does one have to expect in determining the kind and extent of consensus needed for church fellowship and consequently in the understanding and the use of the notion of "fundamental consensus"? To what extent does this have an effect on the dialogues between the different partners? To what extent does this impair the usefulness of the term "fundamental consensus"?

Are there "levels" or "stages" of consensus which have or should have their equivalents in different "levels" of church fellowship?

Fundamental consensus and difference

To what extent is "fundamental consensus" defined by its relation to ongoing differences between the partners?

What does the attainment of a "fundamental consensus" mean in view of such ongoing differences? Does it mean that with the attainment of a "fundamental consensus" (in the singular) these differences lose their divisive character and that former doctrinal condemnations become immaterial? Put another way: Does it follow that the acknowledged existence of remaining church dividing differences and the continued pertinence of doctrinal condemnations are indications of a lack of "fundamental consensus"?

Or could it be that an achieved "fundamental consensus" and still-dividing differences can at least temporarily co-exist?

In what sense and under what prerequisites would it be meaningful to talk simultaneously about a given "fundamental consensus" and a "fundamental difference" which still exists among the partners?

3

Fundamental Consensus / Fundamental Differences

ECUMENISM IN recent years has been an anomaly of progress and frustration. Bilateral and multilateral dialogues appear to have resolved many of the issues that have long divided church from church. Some influential participants and commentators have suggested that we have moved beyond a consensus on isolated issues toward a deeper and more complete consensus, a fundamental or basic consensus about the Christian message itself.[1]

This optimistic picture is marred, however, by seemingly recalcitrant yet central problems (e.g., ministry and authority) and by widespread official inaction on proposals that have emerged from the dialogues. With some important exceptions new ecumenical reports simply lengthen the already long shelf of dialogue statements and essays. The frustration of those who have invested their careers in ecumenical dialogue is easy to understand.

More difficult to understand are the causes of this anomaly. Can the problem be attributed to what have come to be called "non-theological factors," such as institutional inertia or the self-interest of church leaders? While such explanations are tempting and often may partially account for the anomaly, few find such an explanation completely convincing. Is there some problem in the dialogues themselves? Have they really addressed and resolved the most important issues that have separated the churches? Will one or two more dialogues overcome the remaining difficulties?

Some voices, voices which one can hear in this volume, have said that the problem does lie in the dialogues but that it will not be solved by yet another discussion that looks at individual issues in isolation. Rather, the problem lies in deeper divisions that are expressed in but not identical with individual themes or issues. The individual topics are only symptoms, not the disease itself. A focus only on the symptoms and not the disease will produce an endless series of dialogues; the deeper division will always reappear in a new form demanding further discussion. A sense that the truly fundamental, encompassing differences have not been addressed lies behind the inaction of the churches, or so the suggestion goes.

If there are unaddressed fundamental differences, what are they? Unfortunately, suggestions are multitude.[2] For the last few years various ecumenical study groups, such as the one writing this report, have been analyzing the various proposals about fundamental differences and their relation to ecumenical consensus. The essays in this volume from the Puerto Rico ecumenical conference on "Fundamental Consensus and Church Fellowship" are also products of this discussion.

I

As is true with many such discussions, clarity about the central issues and concepts is not present at the beginning but is only achieved within the process of study. Initially the issue was defined as fundamental *difference* and its relation to the lack of church fellowship. A subtle shift may have taken place, however, to a focus on fundamental *consensus* and its relation to church fellowship.[3]

This shift may be seen in the diversity of the essays presented here. At least three types of essays can be differentiated. Some essays address the issue of fundamental difference. The essays by Walter Kasper, Robert Jenson, and Gerhard Forde are the clearest examples of this focus. A second group addresses the question: What would constitute a fundamental consensus? The essays by Pierre Duprey, Paul Fries, and Archbishop Methodios typify this approach. A third group, closely related to the second, deals with the question of levels of fellowship and their relation to levels of consensus. The essay by Samuel Nafzger would be the clearest example of this focus. All essays do not fall simply into one group or another. The essay by James Dunn, for example, addresses the nature of both fundamental consensus and fundamental difference.[4]

This shift in focus my be important. The differences of focus among the essays are paralleled to a large degree by different, "implicit definitions" of the central terms. Unless these differences are noted, significant confusion can result. Most importantly, the term "fundamental difference" is used in at least two different ways, which then affects the meaning of its presumed contradictory, "fundamental consensus." A brief, highly formal outline of the different way these terms are used can help the reader keep the issues clear.

On the one hand, "fundamental difference" can be defined as a "hermeneutical" concept:

> A difference which interprets and explains the nature of the comprehensive and systematic difference between two traditions.

This hermeneutical sense of "fundamental difference" predominates in essays of the first type listed above. Such a difference is fundamental not necessarily because it is important in itself. Rather, it is hermeneutically fundamental; it explains other differences. For example, Kasper and Jenson claim that the differences they highlight explain other differences. The search for a fundamental difference is the search for a difference at some crucial nexus that will explain the comprehensive and systematic difference between traditions. Thus the difference Kasper locates in differing understandings of the relation between word and church is a fundamental difference only if it can explain the comprehensive and systematic differences between Lutheran and Roman Catholic understandings of the faith. Any proposed fundamental difference of this sort is then a comprehensive interpretive proposal about how to interpret or understand the differences between traditions and to a degree about how to understand the traditions themselves.[5]

If "fundamental difference" is understood in this way, then "fundamental consensus" could be understood simply enough as its contradictory:

> A consensus that excludes fundamental or basic differences.

Note that fundamental consensus in this hermeneutical sense may or may not be required for church fellowship. Whether the difference between two theological traditions can be explained in terms of some hermeneutically fundamental difference may be entirely irrelevant to the question of whether the traditions can co-exist in full fellowship with each other. With sufficient interpretive skill one might find a hermeneutically fundamental difference that will explain the systematic difference between the theologies of Aquinas and Bonaventure. That is, one might find a single difference that explains all the other differences between them. Nevertheless, the success or failure of this interpretive enterprise would not affect the judgment whether these two forms of theology can co-exist in full fellowship. In his essay Robert Jenson explicitly argues that the fundamental difference he elaborates is *not* in fact church dividing.

On the other hand, one might understand "fundamental difference" as an "ecumenical" concept:

> A difference incompatible with the full visible unity of the church.

13

"Fundamental difference" in this ecumenical sense is precisely a difference that is church dividing. Whether or not it is explanatory of other differences is irrelevant. Such a difference is fundamental in relation to ecumenical rather than hermeneutical considerations.[6] "Fundamental consensus" could again be understood as what is contradictory to "fundamental difference":

(A consensus sufficient for the full visible unity of the church.

We have achieved fundamental consensus in this ecumenical sense when we have achieved the consensus necessary for full fellowship. These ecumenical senses of the terms predominate in the second type of essay noted above.

The differing senses of "fundamental difference" and "fundamental consensus" thus form two matched pairs: a hermeneutical pair defined by the presence or absence of a single difference that interprets and explains other differences and an ecumenical pair defined by the presence or absence of a difference incompatible with the full visible unity of the church. These differing senses of the terms must be kept distinct. If they are confused, the false conclusion can be drawn that a hermeneutical fundamental difference must also be an ecumenical fundamental difference or vice versa. Even more damaging is confusing the two senses of "fundamental consensus." Such a confusion would lead to the assumption that an ecumenical fundamental consensus must also be a hermeneutical fundamental consensus. Impossible and inappropriate goals are set for ecumenical discussion if hermeneutical fundamental consensus is seen as the condition of church unity. The plurality of theological perspectives that we have come to appreciate and that has always characterized the church would be seen as incompatible with the visible unity of the church.

II

The ecumenical definitions of "fundamental consensus" and "fundamental difference" offered above are, of course, utterly formal without some further specification of just what kind of consensus is needed for the full visible unity of the church and what sort of difference is incompatible with that fellowship. The essays in this volume give a variety of more precise specifications of the needed consensus and the differences it must exclude. At least four groups of questions can be differentiated in this discussion.

First, what is the visible unity of the church? The sort of unity deemed appropriate to the church will influence conclusions about the sort of consensus this unity requires. An investigation of this question must be careful to consider the assumptions made in the use of such a phrase as "full visible unity." Does this phrase, for example, assume a sacramental view of the church in opposition to the eschatological perspective of a Reformation doctrine of justification?

Second, are there levels or degrees of visible unity and if so, what are they? All participants seemed to assume that there are such levels.[7] If there are such levels, then division is not simply from the church, but within the church. The nature of such levels needs thorough and concrete examination from both theological and practical perspectives.

Third, what sort of consensus is required for what sort of visible unity; or, conversely, what sort of difference creates what sort of disunity? As the famous "*satis est*" of Article 7 of the Augsburg Confession shows, proposals answering these questions are not new. Nevertheless, they need to be developed and justified in the contemporary ecumenical situation.

Fourth, what role does what authority play both in the formation of consensus and in the declaration that consensus has been achieved? This meta-question lurks behind much of the discussion of the previous questions.

These are some of the most important and difficult ecumenical questions the churches face. All of them are addressed in the essays included in this volume. The proposal of this report is that the more general questions of fundamental difference and fundamental consensus can be more adequately answered if correlated with these four more precise and specific ecumenical questions.

III

The recent discussion of fundamental difference and fundamental consensus has been educational. The recommendations and reports of ecumenical dialogues must strive for greater clarity. If "substantial agreement" or "fundamental consensus" is declared, the precise meaning of these phrases must be defined. In addition, attention in the near future needs to focus on the nature of the visible unity of the church. Discussion of consensus and difference, fundamental or otherwise, is rudderless without a sense of the sort of unity we are seeking. Without such a sense we cannot say what consensus is sufficient and what differences are important and in what way.

In seeking clarity some awareness of similar terms used in the past may be helpful. Perhaps useful as background for the contemporary discussion would be an investigation of the traditional concepts of heresy, schism, and apostasy. While these terms overlap in differing ways with the ecumenical sense of "fundamental difference," none is simply identical with it. Closest to it is heresy, often defined as the obstinate rejection by a Christian of some fundamental aspect of Christian truth.[8] In practice "fundamental" appears here to have been understood as "church dividing." [9] While this understanding of heresy was developed in the context of church discipline rather than ecumenical relations, heresy was seen as one possible cause of schism. Although schism has also often been defined in the context of church discipline,[10] questions about the nature of schism are closely related to questions about levels of unity. That heresy has been traditionally distinguished from apostasy, i.e., "the total repudiation of the Christian faith," indicates that distinctions were drawn between sorts of church dividing differences.[11]

Inseparable from a concrete discussion of unity is a discussion of authority. What is the authority of past decisions and definitions by the churches in the formation of present consensus? Who must be consulted in the formation of consensus? Who has the authority to say consensus has been achieved? What means, if any, are to be used to preserve consensus once achieved? Lutherans in particular need to ask about the authoritative function of the doctrine of justification as a criterion of the gospel. As the essay by Kasper shows, these questions about authority are fundamental in both a hermeneutical and an ecumenical sense. One conclusion of the recent discussion of fundamental consensus and fundamental difference is that such questions require continuing attention.

The progress of the many bilateral and multilateral dialogues created an optimism that the slow progress of reception has now dampened. The reception process has brought to light questions about the nature of consensus that the dialogues themselves did not address. That the reception process raises new theological questions should not be cause for undue frustration, however much such frustration is understandable. New theological questions can be taken as a sign that the ecumenical process is proceeding with the rigor that is needed if progress is to be enduring.

Notes

1. See a summary of such statements in Harding Meyer, "Roman Catholic/ Lutheran Dialogue," *One in Christ* 22 (1986) 155-68.

2. See the survey by Harding Meyer, "Fundamental Difference — Fundamental Consensus," *Mid-Stream* 25 (1986) 247-59.

3. The shift in focus can be seen by comparing the essay by Harding Meyer in this volume with his earlier statement of the problem in "Fundamental Difference — Fundamental Consensus."

4. That Dunn's essay, the only presentation to deal extensively with New Testament material, received little discussion is worth reflection.

5. That these are primarily interpretive proposals may explain the multitude of proposed fundamental differences. A variety of *loci* may legitimately be taken as interpretive vantage points for understanding the encounter between two Christian traditions. While all such vantage points will not be equally valid or helpful, more than one such vantage point may produce a plausible interpretation.

6. A proposed fundamental difference may, of course, meet both definitions. It may be both an explanation of other differences and a church dividing difference. The fundamental difference proposed by Kasper would seem to meet both definitions.

7. Note that even Archbishop Methodios seems to imply such a differentiation of levels in the different ways he speaks about Orthodox relations with Roman Catholics, Anglicans, and Protestants. See J. M. R. Tillard, O. P., "We Are Different," *Mid-Stream* 25 (1986) 280, for a Roman Catholic consideration of levels of unity in this context.

8. Cf. *Code of Canon Law: Latin English Edition* (Washington: Canon Law Society of American, 1983), canon 751, p. 285; Karl Rahner, "Heresy," *Sacramentum Mundi* (New York: Herder and Herder, 1969) 3: 16-25; Wenzel Lohff, "Heresy and Schism," *Encyclopedia of the Lutheran Church* (ed. J. Bodensieck; Minneapolis: Augsburg Publishing House, 1965) 1006; S. W. Sykes, "Heresy," *A Handbook of Theological Terms* (ed. V. A. Harvey; New York: Macmillan, 1964) 249.

9. See Rahner and Lohff (note 8).

10. See J. G. Davies and A. T. Hanson, "Schism," *A Handbook of Theological Terms*, 523; and "Schism," *The Oxford Dictionary of the Christian Church* (2nd ed.; ed. F. L. Cross and E. A. Livingstone; London: Oxford University Press, 1974) 1242.

11. For definition, see *Code of Canon Law*, canon 751, p. 285. The distinction between heresy and apostasy is at least as old as Aquinas, although it was denied by some early modern Roman Catholic theologians; see Louis Bouyer, *Dictionary of Theology* (trans. C. U. Quinn; Tournai: Desclée, 1965) 32.

In Search
of Christian Unity

4

Basic Consensus
and Church Fellowship:

The status of the ecumenical dialogue between the
Roman Catholic and Evangelical Lutheran Churches*

Walter Kasper

I. The new way of stating the ecumenical question

The ecumenical movement starts with the basic premise that the separation between churches does not reach to the core. Protestant and Catholic Christians do not call each other separated brothers and sisters casually; in this way they acknowledge each other as Christian. They know they are bound together in their common confession of Jesus Christ and in their common baptism confirming this confession. The real difference does not lie between separated churches, but between them and non-Christians. Between Christians, to the contrary, there is a basic consensus; it consists in the fact that they together confess Jesus Christ on the basis of Holy Scripture, as do the early baptismal formulas, among which the Apostles' Creed has a major role. In order to spell out this basic consensus, one can, in addition to the creed of the early church, point to the Confessional basis of the World Council of Churches, referred to by Vatican II (cf. UR 1).

This basic consensus is not something that we search out and "create," for we find ourselves already in it. On the basis of their common faith in Christ and their common baptism, Protestant and Catholic Christians not only jointly confess Jesus Christ, they are also jointly "in Jesus Christ." They participate together in the one Spirit of Christ; they are a new creation together in Jesus Christ. Thus one can, to use the terminology of Vatican II, speak of an already existing, incomplete church fellowship among communions (UR 2-3). The great gift of the ecumenical movement is experiencing and becoming aware of this fellowship

*This is a revision of a lecture given at a consultation held by the Lutheran Council in the U.S.A. and the Lutheran Institute for Ecumenical Research, Strasbourg, on "Basic Consensus and Church Fellowship" at Rio Grande, Puerto Rico, from January 30 to February 6, 1987. It was also a guest lecture at the Gregorian University, Rome, on December 5, 1987.

that already exists in spite of all the differences. As a consequence, the ecumenical task is to reach full church fellowship, including eucharistic fellowship, on the basis of and by expanding this basic consensus of the already existing, though incomplete, church fellowship.

A variety of ways to reach this goal have been tried in the last two decades:

1. The most common way has been through numerous doctrinal discussions between the churches in the last two decades.[1] These have reached a broad consensus or at least astonishing convergence on many of the previously controversial questions. Negotiations on the mutual condemnations of the sixteenth century have confirmed this result.[2] Many contradictions proved to be merely apparent; others could be "reworked" using modern biblical and historical research so that many of the condemnations from the past no longer apply to one's dialogue partner today. That is why many theologians consider full church fellowship to be already possible in the foreseeable future.[3]

Nevertheless, as yet no adequate consensus can be foreseen in a number of questions, especially the question of ministerial office and certainly the question of papal primacy. That is one reason why up to this point no decisive steps toward full church fellowship have been or could be undertaken at the institutional level. The methodology of consensus and convergence used thus far has somehow become ineffective. At present the ecumenical movement seems to be at a stalemate. To put it rather pointedly: What has been a cold war — which at times has also been hot — seems at the moment to be leading to a state of peaceful coexistence rather than to a peace treaty.

2. In view of the high hopes the general public often has for ecumenical progress, it is understandable that this situation has provoked considerable frustration and many expressions of discontent. Moreover, if the public were to grant any validity to the remaining controversial questions, it would not be because they are church dividing. As a consequence, for many the way out of this impasse is to substitute a program of pragmatic unification using the "basic Confession" instead of painstaking theological discussions, which are in fact difficult to understand for those using the "basic Confession." At the same time to ask about truth frequently becomes suspect and those asking about truth are thought to be promoting an ideology; to ask about truth is taken to mean one is uninterested in, if not actually opposed to, unity.

This point of view has a legitimate side, for faith and life belong closely together. Lived faith can and even must precede theological reflection. But it must be a lived faith that responds to the heard truth of the gospel. Therefore both the Catholic and Protestant churches consider untenable a unity achieved purely by pragmatic means. Indifference to the question of truth can never be acceptable to the church. If only to be humanly acceptable, unity presupposes agreement. Finally, any church unity that does not arise from obedience to the truth of the gospel, but is instead put into operation arbitrarily "from below," would actually have an apocalyptic dimension opposing God and could only be called the worst perversion of what is ecumenical. Unity can only be unity in the truth. Above all, one cannot do the same thing together during worship and yet think differently. Such pretended unity would be deeply dishonest and could not last for long.

3. Thus it is understandable that at the other end of the spectrum the question of truth is once again given emphatic, if not overly emphatic, prominence. The existing consensus and convergence documents are accused of dealing only with the superficial and with healing symptoms, and of not even glancing at the actual and more deeply seated causes of separation. Although agreement is certainly possible on individual questions of substance, the formal principles of the communions differ, making it inevitable that we make statements differing in content. And we also see the whole differently even while saying the same thing. Indeed, it is precisely because we differ (*aliter*) when seeing the whole that we also see different things (*alia*).[4] Therefore one frequently speaks of a basic disagreement or of contradictory basic decisions rather than of a basic consensus.[5]

Until now, to be sure, no one has successfully defined this basic difference unequivocally and acceptably enough so that Confessional partners feel themselves truly understood rather than completely misunderstood from the beginning. Because churches have tied their differences to specific issues, never to basic differences, it is likely that the basic differences formulated in any specific era are based less on a church's Confession than on the systematic and theological stance of that era. The churches can explain existing disagreements using the theological viewpoint of a particular era, but they cannot provide adequate grounds for these disagreements. Understanding such theological systems can be helpful for understanding the disagreements better and more deeply. For it is legitimate to have different starting points as long as they do not affect the unity of the church itself. Theological systems are church divisive only as long as they interpret and systematize creedal issues divisively. If that is not the case, they represent legitimate differences between theological schools within a larger unity. Then one should speak of a basic problem in theology rather than basic disagreement.

4. Here is where the majority of more recent ecumenical reflections begins. In order to find a way out of this impasse, this majority asks

about the unity necessary in diversity and the diversity possible in unity.[6] Thus it accepts what is legitimate in discussions about basic differences by declaring that no communion can be adequately described by the points of controversy separating it from others. Rather, each church represents a relatively independent expression of the church, that is, its own type of the church. The Eastern churches, for example, could be described as each having its own rite. By rite is meant not only a particular form of liturgy, but the totality of specific liturgical, theological, spiritual, and disciplinary expression in a church. Thus rite means a particular way of being church. Church unity is then not to be understood as monolithic uniformity, but as the "communio-unity" of differing "rite-churches."[7] That cannot happen, it goes without saying, merely at the level of juggling terminology. To the contrary, true ecumenism presupposes conversion and change. Only on the basis of such change can previous contradictions be mutually recognized as legitimate possibilities within a total conception of the church.

The issue for the communio-model is, of course, whether the model based on relationships among the Eastern churches as well as on the relationship between Rome and the Eastern churches can be applied automatically to the relationship between the Catholic Church and the Protestant churches. For the Eastern churches have the same basic hierarchical structure of the church. But it is precisely this episcopal constitution of the church, based on apostolic succession, which is a basic problem in the relationship between the Catholic Church and the churches of the Reformation. Thus this more recent major ecumenical effort is faced with the same concrete difficulty which created unresolved problems for the previously mentioned methodology of consensus and convergence. There is one decisive difference, to be sure. The question of ministerial office can no longer be considered an isolated, independent problem. It must be seen within a diversified yet total view of what it is to be Christian and what it is to be church. The continuing difference on the question of ministerial office points to a deeper difference, and a solution can only be reached within a larger context.

In order to escape the ecumenical impasse, we must therefore start with what is fundamental. We must ask what we mean specifically by the presupposed ecumenical consensus, how far it goes, how it is related to the differences that are church dividing, and how much diversity it permits. This way of stating the question leads then by itself to the second question, of the relationship between basic consensus and full church fellowship within the framework of a communio-unity of the churches.

II. The question of the content of the basic consensus — the material principle of the Reformation

1. The content of the basic consensus

We shall begin again with what has been established as the accepted basic consensus: the common Confession of Jesus Christ on the basis of Holy Scripture and the interpretation of the early Christian creeds. But the problem that has been discovered from the present state of the discussion already sketched in Part I is how this basic consensus is related to the distinctive doctrines of each church. If these are not merely supplements to the common Confession, but developments from it, then the question arises: If such different conclusions are drawn from one and the same basic truth, does this not suggest that the differences are already contained in a different understanding of the consensus here presumed? Does our difference thus not indeed point to a different understanding of the common core?

We shall deal with the problem first from the standpoint of Catholic theology. More recent Catholic theology distinguishes between a model of revelation based on information theory or instruction theory and a model of revelation based on communication theory.[8] The first understands revelation to be the revelation of individual truths and realities (plural!) which are not accessible to human reason on its own. The second understands revelation to be God's self-revelation and self-communication, in which God reveals to human beings not "something" but himself and the mystery of his will (singular!). According to this second model there are ultimately very few revealed truths, but instead only one single truth: God's revelation of himself through Jesus Christ. This one truth discloses itself, of course, in many individual historical words and deeds, summed up and completed in Jesus Christ (DV 2). For this reason there can and even must be for this model talk of truths of revelation (plural). Yet the many statements of revelation are internally connected, which Vatican I calls the *nexus mysteriorum* (DS 3016). They form an organic whole, a structural unity which Vatican II terms the "hierarchy of truths" (*hierarchia veritatum*) and which it derives from the *mysterium Christi* (UR 11).[9]

This doctrine of the hierarchy of truths is fundamental for ecumenical discussion. It is, however, misunderstood if taken quantitatively, i. e., if it is understood to mean that there are first, second, and third class truths, where the latter constitute what might be called a less important quantity. In the mind of the council the hierarchy of truths was not a principle of reduction but of concentration and interpretation. This means that all individual truths must be interpreted in light of the total context. They form a diversified total structure, whose basis and middle is the mystery of Christ.

This leads to rejecting two tendencies: On the one hand, rejecting a positivistic and objectivized concept of the faith as single, isolated, and catalogued "things to be believed" (*credenda*) and of a purely propositional understanding of the truths of the faith as truth statements; on the other hand, rejecting a spiritualized, liberal, and in the final analysis gnostic dissolving of the content of the faith into lived personalism and existentialism or truth understood as merely that which is lived or experienced.

What is positive is that every individual expression of faith mirrors the whole and points at any given moment to the totality of revelation and ultimately to God himself, who revealed himself once and for all through Jesus Christ by the Holy Spirit. Scholasticism defines the central article of faith in this sense as "the perception of divine truth going beyond itself" (*perceptio divinae veritatis tendens in ipsam*),[10] that is, as material which is understood yet which points beyond itself to the one truth of God, always greater and richer and thus only to be comprehended by analogy.

2. Basic consensus and our understanding of truth or revelation.
If one uses instruction theory, one will have a quantitative understanding of basic consensus. In that case basic consensus means agreement in most of, and the most important, articles of faith; the others will be classified as adiaphora, or theologumena, or mere "peripheral truths." In any case they will not be considered constitutive for the unity of the church. This position is represented in various ways. The starting point is often a statement stemming from the Augustinian tradition: "In essentials unity, in non-essentials liberty, in all things charity" (*In necessariis unitas, in dubiis libertas, in omnibus caritas*).[11]

This approach took on concrete form in the doctrine of fundamental articles,[12] which was represented, again in various ways, by Erasmus, Calvin, some Anglican theologians, some ecumenical irenicists (Calixt: "the consensus of the first five centuries" [*consensus quinquesaecularis*]; Leibnitz; Bossuet; and others), some ecumenists, and, most recently, to some degree, Fries/Rahner. Pius XI opposed this irenic solution to the problem of unity in the encyclical Mortalium animos (1928). His rationale was that all truths of faith are based on the same formal authority of God and must therefore be accepted with the same obedience of faith.[13] What undermines this counter argument, however, is that it is based on the same quantitative understanding of faith as the doctrine it opposes.

① have I misunderstood WK in my book?
② Is it serious on rel'ly tangential?

Basic Consensus and Church Fellowship

NB

If, on the other hand, one begins with the understanding of faith based on communication theory, one arrives at a qualitative understanding of basic consensus. Then basic consensus means agreement in the foundation of the faith. This is understood, to be sure, to mean that as the foundation it supports and includes the totality of faith. Thus in the background lies a wholistic understanding. This wholistic understanding is based on the scholastic doctrine of implicit faith (*fides implicita*). According to this doctrine, the fundamental truths of faith objectively (not, as later interpretations often said: "according to subjective intention") include all other truths. In this sense basic consensus already implies full consensus in the whole truth.[14]

As part of a long tradition of interpreting Hebrews 11:6, one can therefore say that whoever believes that God exists and that he is the salvation of humanity believes not only a part but implicitly the whole faith. That one is in invisible fellowship with the universal church, which extends beyond its institutional boundaries. According to the early church as well as according to both Catholic and Reformation traditions, the church exists in hidden form among all peoples. According to Catholic tradition something similar applies to the rustic (*rudes*), the uneducated. They cannot and need not know the total, developed faith. It is enough if they know the basic truths and, according to Thomas Aquinas, if they participate to some degree in the celebration of the principal festivals of the church year.[15] To the extent that they hold to these basic truths in the community and do so according to the meaning of the church, that is, if they remain subjectively open to the developments objectively present in these truths, they implicitly confess the total faith.

3. A proposed Catholic solution.

In the recent past frequent attempts have been made to use this Scholastic doctrine of implicit faith as a key to solving the ecumenical problem.[16] After what has been said, of course, it is evident this is only possible with reservations. For in ecumenical relationships what is at stake is not the faith of individual Protestants or Catholics, because normally they cannot be expected to know and understand all controversial doctrines and their implications for the history of theology. As far as the ecumenical problem is concerned, the issue is rather the relationship between churches, each of which has its own distinctively developed Confession, which it also must confess. Thus individual Christians can be in an uneducated state (*statu rudis*), but not the churches as such. There is, in addition, a second reservation. On the basis of their own diverse Confessional developments, churches positively rule out certain developments in other churches. Thus each of them is not exactly open to developments that, according to the conviction of the other church, are implicitly present in the one fundamental truth. As long as such exclusions are maintained, it is impossible, in all honesty, to speak of an implicit faith.

The doctrine of implicit faith is nevertheless helpful as long as it does not need to require of the other partner explicit acceptance of all distinctive doctrines beyond the basic consensus (for instance, the more recent mariological dogmas). It is sufficient if the ecumenical partner acknowledges such developments to be basically legitimate on the basis of the gospel and if they are no longer condemned as contrary to the gospel. Where this happens, it does not mean that criticism is suspended, but that there is an intentional assent to the whole truth. Former contradictions are transformed into complementary tensions. Each confesses the same faith, although in diverse expressions. Such unity in diversity does not therefore mean that there is automatically complete dogmatic harmony. Consensus in substance is sufficient; at the level of formulations difference is possible and even necessary in light of diverse cultural and historical situations.[17] Such unity in diversity corresponds to the trinitarian archetype of the church (cf. LG 3; UR 2) even better than a monolithic understanding of unity. One must, of course, be aware that for each of the separated churches such unity in diversity also represents quite an imposition and is impossible without heartfelt conversion.

One difficulty with this solution remains, however. Although it can create openness within Catholicism, as an attempt to be a bridge making contact with the churches of the Reformation it causes great difficulty. For the Reformers sharply rejected the doctrine of implicit faith and condemned it as worthless, blind faith. They suspected that, among other things, it would pervert faith in Christ into faith in the church.[18] This critique indicates not only a different definition of the relationship between basic consensus and church, but also a different understanding of basic consensus itself. Thus, after having presented the Catholic understanding of basic consensus, we must take a look at the corresponding Protestant proposal in order this way to begin to have an understanding of the basic problem between the Catholic Church and the Evangelical Lutheran churches.

4. *The Reformation proposal: the* articulus stantis et cadentis ecclesiae. For Luther the article by which the church stands and falls was the article on justification. "Nothing in this article can be given up or compromised,

even if heaven and earth should be destroyed."[19] For Luther and the Lutheran churches this is not one article of faith among others, but the center and criterion of all of faith and all of theology.[20] This is true because this article for Luther represents nothing less than the sum of the whole proclamation of Christ. Faith in Jesus Christ and justification *sola gratia* and *sola fide* are for him one and the same. For this reason Luther accepts the Christology of the early church, on the one hand, and transforms it into something new through his own interpretation, aided by the doctrine of justification, on the other. He sets the prefix "for me" (*pro me*) before the whole of Christology. By doing this he emphasizes the soteriological dimension of Christology, which today one could call the existential.[21] For him the doctrine of justification is not, however, the only way in which the faith in Christ can be formulated. Luther does not use the word justification at all in his Small Catechism. The doctrine of justification can also be expressed through other metaphors (today perhaps by liberation, reconciliation, and human dignity). It is not a matter of terminology, but rather that this all-encompassing hermeneutical function (more precisely, critical function) is in fact carried out. This applies both to the correct understanding of faith in Christ as such and especially to the understanding and the practice of the church. The issue is always whether the unconditionality of the salvation God has given in Jesus Christ is recognized and not obscured or lessened by conditions set by human beings, that is, merely by the church and canon law.

Today there is general theological consensus that because of recently successful attempts at theological clarification and convergence,[22] the doctrine of justification as such is no longer church divisive. As always, the decisive question, of course, is whether this applies also to the application, especially the ecclesiological application, of the doctrine of justification. The problem between us today is therefore no longer so much the doctrine of justification as an individual doctrine or as the framework for individual doctrines, but rather the event of justification as hermeneutical principle and critical norm for the whole Christian faith.[23]

The issue is often formulated as follows: Whether and to what extent does the unconditionality of grace permit human cooperation made possible and supported by the grace of God; or, whether God's omnipotence is an omnipotence which only allows human passivity.[24] Because of the central importance of the article on justification, this question is not to be postponed until the discussion of appropriating Jesus Christ's saving work by faith, but must be asked already in Christology and soteriology, namely, in the question of how the humanity of Jesus Christ is active in salvation.[25] This question recurs further in Mariology as the question whether and to what extent in a special way Mary has an active role in the history of salvation because she was especially elected and blessed. The question arises finally and preeminently in ecclesiology:[26] Whether and to what extent it is possible to think of the mediation of salvation through the church and its clergy understood instrumentally within and under the mediation of salvation through the exalted Lord in the Holy Spirit. To put it in more hermeneutical terms: Whether and to what extent the fact that the truth of the gospel authenticates itself, according to the Reformation emphasis, allows for the church, especially through its teaching office, to be competent in interpretation.

Thus we come to the conclusion that the questions still unresolved between the churches, especially the question of ministerial office, are not like a comparatively unimportant residue that one could perhaps ignore. Rather, they point back to *the* basic problem between the separated churches, namely, to the correct definition of the relationship between God and human beings in the event of salvation. This is, to be sure, a problem worth discussing and fighting about, especially because it deals with the basic problem of the modern world. Are therefore the still remaining disagreements, especially the disagreement on ministerial office, possibly an indication of possible disagreement in the understanding of the basic consensus itself? How unified are we really? Supposedly, or better, hopefully, more than seems to be the case after all that has been said. For Catholics do not hold that human beings cooperate independently with grace but that they cooperate simply because grace is given to them and supports them; Lutherans do not hold to a philosophical determinism, but to the freedom of the Christian. Are these then only divergent theological emphases, conceptualities, or thought forms that separate us, or are they disagreements that divide the churches? This question cannot be answered in the abstract, but only in the light of specific and concrete questions under dispute. On the following pages we shall take up this question as it applies to ecclesiological problems because the question of possible full church fellowship culminates especially in them.

III. The question of the form of the basic consensus — the formal principle of the Reformation

1. The fundamental significance of church fellowship.
The separated churches agree that the word of God and the people of God, i.e., fellowship with Christ and fellowship in the church, belong

together. God's people can exist without God's word as little as God's word can exist without God's people.[27] The community of faith is the place and arena where God's word is proclaimed, heard in faith, and received. Therefore the church is not only an external institution and organization. We together confess it to be one holy church in spite of its obvious weaknesses. For according to Paul God's mystery realized through Jesus Christ in the Holy Spirit is revealed in the church.[28] The church is the body of Christ and as such our mother in the faith. The slogan: "Jesus, yes — the church, no," therefore cannot be used by either Catholic or Protestant theology. Christology and ecclesiology cannot be separated.[29] This theological assessment, according to which the truth of the gospel can only be received in the church, is also supported by modern exegesis (form criticism). We "possess" the revelation of God in Jesus Christ only in the testimony of the earliest congregations, a testimony transmitted to us, as is Scripture generally, through the testimony of the church.

Such common agreements are important for the question of how the truth of the faith can be discovered concretely. On the basis of what has been said, a binding, basic consensus in the faith obviously cannot be constructed in the abstract while avoiding the church and its Confession. One cannot, therefore, as modern humanism does when using historical criticism, try to go back behind the Confession of the church to the original gospel of the so-called historical Jesus or of a Paul not yet involved in "early catholicism," so that only by going back one reaches the normative basic consensus absolutely necessary for unity. Apart from the questionable hermeneutics of such a process, such an attempt would betray a static and unhistorical concept of Christian truth. Only a consensus of the church in the church can determine what the indispensible basic consensus is.

2. Divergent classifications of basic consensus and church fellowship.
It was possible for the early church to make use of a concept of consensus already well-known to ancient philosophy. Consensus among the nations (*consensus gentium*) was already a criterion of truth for Aristotle and, more particularly, for the Stoics. For all people cannot be mistaken all the time.[30] The early church adapted this philosophical tradition to its own use and understood agreement in faith as a sign and result of the Holy Spirit.[31] According to Vincent of Lerins whatever is believed everywhere, always, and by everyone must be true and catholic (*quod ubique, quod semper, quod ab omnibus creditum est*).[32] This was later developed into the docine of the "consensus of the faithful" (*consensus fidelium*), "consensus of the fathers" (*consensus*

patrum), and "consensus of the theologians" (*consensus theologorum*).[33] An ecumenical council was the authorized place for discovering such a consensus.[34] For the early church the content of the apostolic tradition and thus also of the basic consensus is to be discovered only within the concrete structure of the church and through the mediation of the episcopal office standing in apostolic succession.[35]

The Reformers accepted the doctrine of consensus. The Augsburg Confession testifies to and relies on a "great consensus" (*magnus consensus*), and the Formula of Concord(!) considers itself to be a "pious and unanimous consensus" (*pia et unanima consensu*).[36] Within Reformation theology, however, consensus would have a different meaning from the one it had in existing teaching. For the Reformers the empirical church of the time seemed so very widely separated from and opposed to the gospel that they could only support the truth of the gospel by being critical of the existing church. Thus the Reformation originated in the conflict between the truth of the gospel as Luther rediscovered it in his doctrine of justification and unity with the Roman Church. Very early in his career Luther already declared that councils could err.[37] Over against the claims of the teaching office in Rome, Luther emphasized the superiority of the gospel over the church. He understood the church as "creature of the word" (*creatura verbi*).[38] "No longer is a council the representation of all believers; nor is a consensus arrived at by majority constitutive for finding theological truth. Rather, theological truth is arrived at by hearing God's salvific revelation which is bound to Scripture. The consensus of the church is based on affirming God's activity, which leads to the fellowship of faith." In this sense one can then say that consensus is "the Protestant equivalent of the Catholic teaching office."[39]

Thus, in spite of all basic agreement, the quest for consensus, or rather basic consensus, does not lead to consensus but to disagreement. The Reformers and Catholics each give a different "status" to consensus. Indeed, the concept of consensus and the place given it is a central and fundamental problem in polemic theology. The issue is not only the relationship between unity and diversity in the church, but the relationship between truth and unity, i.e., between gospel and church. More specifically, the issue is the critical function of the gospel over against the church, its consensus formulas, and the institutions of such a consensus (for instance, apostolic succession in episcopal office as well as the primacy and infallibility of the pope).

The Reformers defined the relationship between gospel and church as "over against." On this basis, and using the slogan "*sola scriptura*," they came not only to condemn individual traditions, but also to oppose a teaching office of the church that makes binding decisions about the interpretation of Scripture and tradition. At the Council of Trent the Catholic Church, on the other hand, once again lifted up the sense and consensus of the church as normative for the interpretation of Scripture (DS 1507). It taught, of course, neither then nor even less today that the church and its teaching office stands above the word of God. Already Trent characterized the gospel as the one source of all saving truth and of all moral discipline (DS1501). More precisely, Vatican II says that the teaching office does not stand over the word of God, but serves it (DV 10). The Catholic Church, however, cannot acknowledge that the word of God is ever genuinely over against the church. Because it believes that the word of God is effective through God's Spirit in the church and its tradition, it speaks of the relationship between the word of God and tradition as both "in and over against" and emphasizes the inner connection between Scripture, tradition, and church (DV 9-10).[40] According to Catholic understanding, therefore, any consensus in matters of faith that the church has discovered at a particular time remains binding (irreformable and infallible). It can, of course, be deepened and basically improved, but it must be taken into consideration in the process of discovering consensus at a later time. Up to now there has been no way of reaching full consensus on this issue.[41]

One problem, perhaps even the decisive ecumenical problem, is therefore how a basic consensus can ever be reached and how binding it can be. How is the content of the basic consensus related to the ecclesiastical form of the basic consensus?

3. Present convergences.

Today there are convergences from both sides also on this important ecumenical question. Even though the Catholic side cannot acknowledge that the gospel can ever be genuinely over against the church, or Scripture ever genuinely over against tradition, nevertheless today one recognizes the historicity of all dogmatic formulations and the necessity of reinterpreting these more comprehensively and more thoroughly on the basis of Scripture and thus to receive them anew. In this sense the interpretation of Scripture becomes the key to all proclamation and practice in the church (cf. DV 21). The Protestant side, on the other hand, because of recent exegetical insights (form criticism), today finds that a nonhistorical confrontation between Scripture and tradition is no longer possible. Scripture itself, after all, was part of the developing tradition of the early church and a valid hermeneutics of Scripture can only exist within the continuing tradition of the life of the church.

Thus today both Catholic and Protestant theology distinguish a tradition of the gospel in and over the church from purely human traditions.[42]

In this way the question under dispute is reduced from the start to the question of the competence of the ecclesiastical teaching office within the sum total of Scripture, tradition, and interpretation. That is in no way an incidental problem because what is at stake is the question: How does the church speak authoritatively? Is it even capable of speaking authoritatively?[43] The issue is not the superiority of the gospel over the church. Both churches agree on that. The issue is rather how this actually works and actually is transmitted.

There are convergences here as well. On this point "The Ministerial Office in the Church" states: "In both churches there thus exists a teaching responsibility above the level of the congregation, which, to be sure, is perceived in different ways. But one can still recognize a certain parallelism between the two churches. Teaching authority in both churches is tied to the witness of the whole church to the faith. Both churches know that they are subject to the norm of the gospel. But both churches also know that the question of the methodology and binding character of doctrinal decisions by the church needs further investigation. Dealing with this problem is a common task, in the course of which the question of infallibility, in particular, will also require further discussion. Today Catholics and Lutherans can already join in saying that the church is unceasingly guided into and upheld in the truth by the Holy Spirit. 'The church's abiding in the truth should not be understood in a static way, but as a dynamic event which takes place with the aid of the Holy Spirit in ceaseless battle against error and sin in the church as well as in the world.' "[44]

In short, both churches acknowledge that the truth of the gospel prevails again and again in the church. Both realize that they made use of ecclesiastical offices in this process, but both also know that these offices are no guarantee of the unadulterated transmission of the gospel. Yet neither do Protestant churches think that the whole tradition needs to be revised.[45] Therefore the question is: Practically speaking, are the differences that remain merely differences in how one emphasizes the irreformability of church doctrine and the way the teaching office concretely interprets Scripture and tradition, or does a still unexamined difference in principle remain?

4. The understanding of the church: the still unexamined problem.
To me the actual question does not seem to be a matter of details. Such still unsolved, or rather not yet completely solved, questions of detail do exist, but with sufficient goodwill on each side agreement on these

can be reached through extensive discussion. But the real problem lies deeper. The issue is the understanding each side has of the church.

As a matter of fact, the problem of the church stood between us from the start. The Reformation began, after all, as a rebellion against an overpowering church institution, against which Luther set his understanding of the gospel. Burning the book of canon law in front of the Elster gate at Wittenberg was a symbolic act of some consequence for the self-understanding of the Reformation; later generations impressed this act on their memory with good reason. The result of this controversy was Luther's doctrine of the hiddenness (not invisibility!) of the church, according to which the church is not bound to specific times, places, or persons.[46] The Counter-Reformation (especially Bellarmine) countered this by firmly insisting on the visibility of the church concentrated in the papacy.[47]

This question, however, was never taken up explicitly either in the Confessional writings of the Reformation or at Trent. One highly significant allusion, to be sure, can already be found in the sixteenth century. According to the Augsburg Confession a ministerial office does exist in the church by divine law (*iure divino*) (CA 5). But for the unity of the church it is sufficient (*satis est*) to agree on the right proclamation of the gospel and administration of the sacraments according to that gospel (CA 7). As a matter of course, this includes an office for publicly proclaiming the gospel, but recognition of this office is limited by the requirement that it permit the freedom of the gospel understood according to the Protestant doctrine of justification. Thus even present convergence texts declare that fellowship with the office of bishop in apostolic succession is both desirable and worth striving for, for the sake of symbolic completeness, but it is not constitutive for the being of the church.[48] The Catholic tradition, on the other hand, when addressing the question of what elements are constitutive for the unity of the church, follows and elaborates the Lukan description of the first congregation in Jerusalem, which had three bonds (*ligamina*) for full church unity: fellowship in the same faith, in the same sacraments, and with the one ministerial office in the church (LG 13; UR 2-3). Only against this background does the full significance of speaking of the "defect in the sacrament of order" (*defectus sacramenti ordinis*) in the Reformation churches become evident (UR 22).

It was, to be sure, not until the nineteenth century that these differences were dealt with thematically. A difference in fact became a difference in principle. F. Schleiermacher and J. A. Möhler did this most clearly. F. Schleiermacher put up the well-known thesis: Protestantism makes one's relationship to the church depend on one's relationship to Christ, Catholicism makes one's relationship to Christ depend on one's relationship to the church. J. A. Möhler definitely agreed with this antithesis.[49] If one considers the origin of the Reformation to be rebellion against the church in the name of the gospel, this sharp antithesis has a certain plausibility. The question remains, however, whether a conflict in fact has to be a conflict in principle.

Ecumenical dialogues in our century have up to this point unfortunately undertaken almost no explicit discussion of the question of the church. A rare exception is the bilateral document: "Church Fellowship in Word and Sacrament" (1984). It states: "There are, of course, clear differences in the traditions of our two churches on how precisely to determine the relationship between the visible, institutional form of the church and the hidden, spiritual being of the church which can only be grasped by faith. . . . Whether in the future it will be possible to regain the church fellowship broken at that time will depend precisely on the resolution of this disputed question."[50] As long as clarity has not been reached here, ecumenical dialogue cannot escape the bind it is in. For the question of the church not only forms the decisive background to the still unresolved points on ministerial office, it is in fact behind all questions. That is to say, as long as we do not know what church is and therefore what church fellowship or church unity means, we cannot decide whether or to what extent existing ecumenical results are sufficient for full church fellowship.

There is now undoubted progress in this question also. Vatican II has expanded again the limits to the visible, institutional, hierarchical church set by the Counter-Reformation and renewed the sacramental understanding of the church found in the first millennium. According to this understanding the visible church is only a sign and instrument of the spiritual reality of the church (LG 1, etc.);[51] the church is a unique, complex reality composed of visible and invisible elements (LG 8). This sacramental-symbolic meaning of the visible elements is also emphasized in more recent ecumenical documents (especially Uppsala, 1968), after New Delhi (1961) had already highlighted visible unity. Thus a certain convergence exists.[52]

It is, however, precisely at this point that a profound, still unresolved difference shows up. In Catholic understanding the sacramentality of the church means not only that the church is the place and sign of salvation, but also that it is the instrument of salvation. As a matter of comparison, the document on doctrinal condemnations in the sixteenth century notes that Protestant doctrine also holds that "mediation" of the doctrine of justification happens *in* the church, but Protestants have reservations about speaking of "mediation" *through* the church.[53] In a certain sense, of course, Protestant theology also has to speak of a mediation of salvation in the church through word and sacrament as means of salvation (CA 5). The unanswered question therefore is what kind of mediating function the church has in salvation. Does the church, under its head who is the actual subject of the church's activity in word and sacrament, have its own active role as subject made possible and supported by Jesus Christ?[54]

The answer to this question will, of course, affect the precise understanding of sacraments and ecclesiastical offices and of their instrumentality in salvation, particularly their competence as teaching offices. in relation to the truth of the gospel and how it is self-evident. The question of the church's significance as instrument is ultimately the basic question of the doctrine of justification: the question of human institutions in mediating salvation. The question of ministerial office is thus a part of the problem of the doctrine of justification functioning as the article by which the church stands and falls.

In spite of the fundamental character of this question, I would not like to speak of a basic difference in the church, but merely of a basic problem that has not yet been adequately discussed. It had not surfaced until now, until such a high degree of consensus has been reached on so many individual problems, higher than we would have even dared dream of before. To approach the individual disagreements that still remain in this fundamental manner does not have the aim of confirming them and in this way making them permanent, but of elucidating them in a larger context and thus making them more easily solvable. For supposedly, or better, hopefully, we are also closer in this basic question than had seemed possible until now. What has been said thus points to the basic question of our theme: "Basic consensus and church fellowship." That question is: Is there basic consensus on the meaning of church fellowship? What is the place and meaning of church fellowship for fellowship in Christ? To what extent is the concrete form of church fellowship in the office of bishop in apostolic succession a constitutive part of the basic consensus?

5. Prospects for future dialogue.
In conclusion, it is at least possible to indicate both a possible answer for the Catholic point of view and the future course of ecumenical discussion between Catholic and Evangelical Lutheran theology. The starting point and framework is the ecclesiology of *communio*, of unity in diversity and diversity in unity.

As far as the basic definition of the relationship between God and human beings is concerned, consensus seems to exist that the model of negation is unsuitable. According to it, everything that is attributed to God must be withdrawn from human beings, and everything that is attributed to human beings must be withdrawn from God. That God is totally real and totally powerful does not mean that he alone is real and he alone is powerful. According to Catholic teaching precisely the radical and total dependence of human beings on God is the basis for their infinitely qualitative difference and, as a consequence, their relative independence from God. Independence and dependence therefore do not increase in an inverse, but a synonymous relationship. This is true in a special and unique way also within Christology.[55]

This fundamental understanding has, however, been expressed very differently within the Catholic tradition itself. Along with the Augustinian, more unitarian, conception, in which human freedom in the saving event is considered rather insignificant (cf. for instance, Augustine's doctrine of predestination), stands the Thomistic view, which emphasizes more relative human independence within theonomy. Both viewpoints have a place within the Catholic tradition. Both must be rethought in light of modern challenges. The basic Reformation concern formulated in the article on justification, i.e., the unconditional sovereignty of God, does not at all have to be understood as that which cannot be assimilated by the Catholic tradition. To the contrary! But it cannot be the only and exclusive Catholic concern. For the temptation to idolatry rejected by this doctrine, i.e., the idolizing of created objects because the distinction between God and world has not held, is not the only temptation. Opposed to it stands the other, equal temptation to blasphemy, i.e., disparaging the holy by radically secularizing, instrumentalizing, and functionalizing signs and means of salvation instituted by God himself.[56] Thus ecumenical discussion is essentially more open than it at first might appear, and it does not have to reach uniform theological answers if the basic concern is kept in mind.

In like manner, greater variety than is commonly supposed is possible concerning the precise method of defining the mediation of salvation through the church. Here also there are significant differences within schools of thought in the Catholic tradition, differences not decided by the teaching office between the Augustinian-Franciscan-Bonaventurean-Scotist view and the Thomistic view.[57] Therefore the ecumenical discussion can also here be carried on in a relatively open manner that does not look backward but forward. In so doing, it can be helpful to include the Eastern churches and their pneumatology, mostly forgotten in the dialogue of the Western churches. If one, for example, as in the Eastern churches, does not shift immediately from Christology to ecclesiology, if one realized more clearly than is generally the case in the Western tradition that it is the work of the Holy Spirit to make present the salvation Jesus Christ gives, then one recognizes that the basic pattern for mediating salvation in the church is the *epiclesis*.[58] The church does not control salvation, but it can and must pray with authority for the Spirit of Jesus Christ who mediates salvation, and it can be certain this prayer is heard on the basis of the promise made by Jesus Christ. Such an understanding of the mediation of salvation through the church could decrease the basic problem between the separated churches of the West and lead toward a solution.

Such a solution does not have to be uniform for specific, concrete questions either. For the Catholic tradition has very considerable and even breathtaking variability in the concrete shape and exact understanding, for example, of the office of bishop, episcopal succession, and, even more, the papacy. Therefore there is no reason not to grant the separated churches the greatest measure of freedom within a future "communio-unity" as long as basic consensus exists in what is essential.[59]

What then is the sum of what has been said? To me it seems to be two things: (1) The most important theme for the next phase of ecumenical dialogue must be the church. Ecclesiology is the framework within which all the remaining dialogue results can finally be evaluated. We have hardly talked about this theme until now. (2) Ecclesiology has to be discussed from the perspective of the basic theological problem that stands between the separated churches of the West, i.e., the question of the active function of human beings within, and in a certain sense under, God's gracious activity in saving us. At first glance such a basic way of asking the question makes ecumenical dialogue more difficult, no doubt. But the more profoundly we begin, the more confident we can also be, and so much the more individual disputed questions can be enriched by the power and dynamic of the basic consensus that already exists. Without trusting that the truth, who is Jesus Christ himself, takes over our churches more fully and deeply and draws us together to the middle, we cannot carry on a meaningful theological conversation anyway. In this trust ecumenical resignation and scepticism are, of course, inappropriate. In this trust we shall overcome present difficulties.

Issue ≠ C-dividing but does need clarification, acc to K.

39

Notes

1. The most important documents of the Luther-Roman Catholic dialogue are: Malta Report (1972), The Eucharist (1978), Ways to Community (1980), All Under One Christ (1980), The Ministry in the Church (1981), all to be found in *Growth in Agreement. Reports and Agreed Statements of Ecumenical Conversations on a World Level* (ed. H. Meyer and L. Vischer; New York/Ramsey: Paulist; and Geneva: WCC, 1984); Bilaterale Arbeitsgruppe der Deutschen Bischofskonferenz und der Kirchenleitung der Vereinigten Evangelisch-Lutherischen Kirche Deutschlands, *Kirchengemeinschaft in Wort und Sakrament* (Paderborn: Bonifatius; and Hannover: Lutherisches Verlagshaus, 1984); Roman Catholic/Lutheran Joint Commission, *Facing Unity. Models, Forms and Phases of Catholic-Lutheran Church Fellowship* (Geneva: LWF, 1985). André Birmelé, *Le salute en Jésus Christ dans les dialogues oecuméniques* (Paris: du Cerf, 1986) is an excellent theological evaluation of these dialogues; I only came to know it after completing this lecture, but his thorough presentation of the material supports my conclusions.

2. *Lehrverurteilungen — kirchentrennend?* Volume 1: *Rechtfertigung, Sakramente und Amt im Zeitalter der Reformation und heute* (ed. K. Lehmann and W. Pannenberg; Freiburg: Herder; and Göttingen: Vandenhoeck and Ruprecht, 1986).

3. Heinrich Fries and Karl Rahner, *Unity of the Churches. An Actual Possibility* (Philadelpia: Fortress; and New York/Ramsey: Paulist, 1985).

4. Cf. Karl Barth, *Die Kirche und die Kirchen* (Theologische Existenz Heute 27; Munich: Kaiser, 1935).

5. This debate, that ultimately goes back to F. Schleiermacher and J. A. Möhler, has recently been revived, although with very different intentions and methods, by both Protestant (P. Tillich, G. Ebeling, E. Herms, R. Frieling, H. M. Müller, and others) and Catholic (Y. Congar, J. Ratzinger, K. Lehmann, and others) theologians. Cf. the surveys in W. Beinert, "Konfessionelle Grunddifferenz. Ein Beitrag zur ökumenischen Epistemologie," *Catholica (M)* 34(1980) 36-61; P. Neuner, "Der konfessionelle Grundentscheid — Problem für die Oekumene?" *Stimmen der Zeit* 202(1984) 591-604; H. Meyer, "Fundamental Difference — Fundamental Consensus," *Mid-Stream* 25 (1986) 247-59; Birmelé (n. 1 above), 277-302.

6. Especially Y. Congar, *Diversity and Communion* (Mystic, CT: Twenty-third Publications, 1985). From a very different perspective: O. Cullmann, *Unity through Diversity* (Philadelphia: Fortress, 1988). Cf. note 16 below.

7. Cf. W. Kasper, "Kirche als communio. Ueberlegungen zur ekklesiologischen Leitidee des II. Vatikanischen Konzils," *Theologie und Kirche* (Mainz: Grünewald, 1987) 187-99, especially 192-95; *idem*, "Die Kirche als Sakrament der Einheit," *Internationale Katholische Zeitschrift* 16 (1987) 2-8.

8. Cf. especially M. Seckler, "Der Begriff der Offenbarung," *Handbuch der Fundamentaltheologie* (ed. W. Kern, H. J. Pottmeyer, and M. Seckler; Freiburg: Herder, 1985) 2:64-67; also, A. Dulles, *Revelation Theology* (New York: Seabury, 1969); R. Latourelle, *Théologie de la Révélation* (Paris: Desclée de Brouwer, 1963); R. Eicher, *Offenbarung. Prinzip neuzeitlicher Theologie* (Munich: Kösel, 1977).

9. Cf. U. Valeske, *Hierarchia veritatis* (Munich: Claudius, 1968); Congar (n. 6 above), 126-33.

10. Cited from Thoman Aquinas, *Summa Theologiae.* I-II q.1 a.6. Similarly q.1 a.2 ad 1: *"Actus autem credentis non terminatur ad enuntiabile, sed ad rem."* Cf. L. Hödl, "Articulus fidei. Eine begriffsgeschichtliche Arbeit," in *Einsicht und Glaube* (ed. J. Ratzinger and H. Fries; Freiburg: Herder, 1962) 358-76.

11. Cf. Congar (n. 6 above), 107-8.

12. Ibid., 108-25.

13. DS 3683.

14. Cf. Thomas Aquinas, *Summa Theologiae.* II-II q.1 a.7 and the commentary in *Die Deutsche Thomas-Ausgabe* (ed. Albertus-Magnus-Akademie; Heidelberg: Kerle; and Graz: Pustet, 1950) 15:438-43; Congar (n. 6 above), 131-32.

15. Cf. Thomas Aquinas, *Quaestiones disputatae de veritate* q: 14 a. 11 c. a.

16. Cf. especially Congar (n. 6 above), 168-77, and the Catholic authors cited there, such as M. Villain, Th. Sartory, A. de Halleux, G. Dejaifve, P. Duprey, E. Lanne, L. Bouyer, A. Dulles, J. M. R. Tillard, H. Muehlen, and others; also, W. Kasper, "Erneuerung des dogmatischen Prinzips," in *Theologie und Kirche* (Mainz: Grünewald, 1987) : 19-20; also, the articles by N. A. Nissiotis, L. Klein, A. Dulles, and H. Meyer in *Theologische Quartalschrift* 166 (1986), number 4. Of special importance is the similar statement of the Gemeinsame Synode der Bistümer in der Bundesrepublik Deutschland in its resolution "Pastorale Zusammenarbeit der Kirchen im Dienst an der christlichen Einheit" 3.2.3 (*Gemeinsame Synode der Bistümer in der Bundesrepublik Deutschlands. Beschlüsse der Vollversammlung* (Offizielle Gesamtausgabe; ed. L. Bertsch et al.; Freiberg: Herder, 1976) 1:780-81. The proposal by H. Fries and K. Rahner also goes basically in this direction. But in various formulations it goes further in that in the present spiritual situation it permits openness in intellectual judgments not only to individuals but also to churches and thus runs the danger of relativizing the question of truth. But can a church be "in an uneducated state" (*in statu rudis*)? Can it be satisfied with withholding judgment? Would it be itself any longer if it would no longer hold to its confession clearly and unambiguously? Cf., however, how in his response to the debate H. Fries delimits the proposal, in the special edition of H. Fries and K. Rahner, *Einigung der Kirche-reale Möglichkeit* (Quaestiones Disputatae 100, Sonderausgabe; Freiburg: Herder, 1985) 157-89, and in *Theologische Quartalschrift* 166 (1986) 302-12.

17. This way of reaching unity has already been officially used by Pope Paul VI and the Coptic Pope-Patriarch Shenouda III in their common declaration on Christology in 1973 (*L'Osservatore Romano,* 5 May 1973) and between Pope John Paul II and the Syrian Patriarch Moran Mar Ignatius Zakka I. Iwas in 1984 (*L'Osservatore Romano,* 29 June 1984). In both cases an agreement was reached with these non-Chalcedeonian churches on the Chalcedonian Christology that had divided the churches since that time without using the complete terminology of the Council from 451.

18. A. von Harnack, *History of Dogma* (3rd ed.; tr. N. Buchanan; New York: Dover, 1961) 6:165-66, makes clear, to be sure, that the Reformers did not reject this doctrine totally, but only criticized the postivist, nominalist version. On the issue itself, cf. the commentary in *Die Deutsche Thomas-Ausgabe* (ed. Albertus-Magnus-Akademie; Heidelberg: Kerle; and Graz: Pustet, 1950), 15:438-43.

19. SA 2,1, 5; BS 415; BC 292.

20. Cf. the well-documented survey in O. H. Pesch, *Theologie der Rechtfertigung bei Martin Luther und Thomas von Aquin* (Mainz: Grünewald, 1967) 151-59.

21. Cf. P. Althaus, *The Theology of Martin Luther* (tr. R. C. Schultz; Philadelphia: Fortress, 1966) 181-93. Cf. note 25 below.

22. Cf. *Justification by Faith* (Lutherans and Catholics in Dialogue 7; ed. H. G. Anderson, T. A. Murphy, and J. A. Burgess; Minneapolis: Augsburg, 1985) and *Lehrverurteilungen* (n. 2 above), 35-75. See the survey of the discussion in Birmelé (n. 1 above), 45-105.

23. Thus *Justification by Faith* (n. 22 above), 56-57, 69-70; *Lehrverurteilungen* (n. 2 above), 75. Cf. the important and well-founded critical reflections on this by Carl J. Peter, "Justification by Faith and the Need of Another Critical Principle," *Justification by Faith*, 304-15.

24. See especially E. Przywara, "Gott in uns und Gott über uns," in *idem, Das Ringen der Gegenwart* (Augsburg: Filser, 1929) 543-78, especially 547-52; with application to the doctrine of justification, see. H. Küng, *Justification: The Doctrine of Karl Barth and a Catholic Reflection* (tr. T. Collins, E. E. Tolk, and D. Granskou; New York: Nelson, 1964) 265-67. H. Volk, "Die Lehre von der Rechtfertigung nach der Bekenntnisschriften der evangelisch-lutherischen Kirche," *Gesammelte Schriften* (Mainz: Grünewald, 1966) 2:31-64.

25. Y. Congar, "Regards et réflexions sur le christologie de Luther, " in *Das Konzil von Chalkedon* (ed. A. Grillmeier and H. Bacht; Würzburg: Echter-Verlag, 1954) 3:457-86, held that Luther teaches that God alone acts, which is, to be sure, not monophysitism, but a monergism, monopraxis, or monophysitism of God's plan of salvation. Later he modified this thesis and granted that in Luther Jesus' humanity has a kind of active function in salvation; cf. "Nouveaux regards sur la christologie du Luther," in *idem, Martin Luther. Sa foi, sa réforme* (Paris: du Cerf, 1983) 105-33. On this question, see especially M. Lienhard, *Luther: Witness to Jesus Christ* (Minneapolis: Augsburg, 1982), esp. 195-98, 235-40, 296-98. Th. Beer, *Der fröhliche Wechsel und Streit. Grundzüge der Theologie Martin Luthers* (Einsiedeln: Johannes-Verlag, 1980), especially 439-40, 441-53, has repeated the thesis: Luther teaches that God alone acts, but Beer does this in a pointed and very onesided manner, and without taking more recent literature into account. Cf. Birmelé (n. 1 above), 298-302.

26. G. Maron, *Kirche und Rechtfertigung. Eine kontroverstheologische Untersuchung ausgehend von den Texten des Zweiten Vatikanischen Konzils* (Göttingen: Vandenhoeck and Ruprecht, 1967), asks this question in a very polemic fashion; E. Jüngel, "Die Kirche als Sakrament?" *Zeitschrift für Theologie und Kirche* 80 (1983) 432-57, is much more nuanced and basically more open.

27. Cf. M. Luther, "On the Councils and the Church" (1529); WA 50:629; LW 41:150.

28. Cf. G. Bornkamm, "*mysterion*," *Theological Dictionary of the New Testament* (ed. G. Kittel; tr. G. W. Bromiley; Grand Rapids: Eerdmans, 1964) 4:819.

29. Augustine's thesis: "Christ is all, head and members" (*Christus totus, caput et membra*), must not be given up, but also must not be confused with the thesis that the church is "the extended Christ" (*Christus prolongatus*), which

Protestant theologians often unjustly accuse Catholics of holding. Whereas the first stresses the distinction between Christ as head and the church as the body of Christ and subordinates the body to the head, the second extends Christology into ecclesiology. The second is expressly rejected by LG 8, for the council finds an analogy (which always includes difference at the same time) between the divine Logos and the human nature of Christ, on the one hand, and the Spirit of Christ (!) and the social structure of the church, on the other hand. Cf. Y. Congar, "Dogme christologique et Ecclésiologie. Vérité et limites d'un parallèle," in *Das Konzil von Chalkedon* (ed. A. Grillmeier and H. Bacht; Würzburg: Echter-Verlag, 1954) 3:240-68.

30. Cf. L. Koep, "Consensus," *Reallexikon für Antike und Christentum* (Stuttgart: Hiersemann, 1957) 3:295-98; M. Suhr, "*Consensus omnium*," *Historisches Wörterbuch der Philosophie* (ed. J. Ritter; Darmstadt: Wissenschaftliche Buchgesellschaft, 1971) 1:1031-32; G. Sauter, "Consensus," *Theologische Realenzyklopädie* (Berlin/New York: de Gruyter, 1981) 8:182-83.

31. Cf. Irenaeus of Lyons, *Adv. haereses* I, 10,2; V, 20, 1.

32. Cf. Vincent of Lerins, *Commonitorium* 2, 3; cf. 29, 41.

33. Cf. H. Bacht, "Consensus," *Lexikon für Theologie und Kirche* (2nd ed.; Freiberg: Herder, 1959) 3:43-46.

34. Cf. J. J. Sieben, *Die Konzilsidee der Alten Kirche* (Konziliensgeschichte, Series B; Paderborn: Schöningh, 1979).

35. Cf. J. Ratzinger,"Primacy, Episcopate, and apostolic succession," in Karl Rahner and Joseph Ratzinger, *The Episcopate and the Primacy* (Quaestiones Disputatae 4; New York: Herder and Herder, 1962) 37-63, especially 51-54.

36. Further examples in Sauter (n. 30 above), 185-86.

37. Cf. M. Luther, "*Ad dialogum Silverstri Prieratis de potestate papae responsio*" (1518); WA 1:656, and elsewhere.

38. Cf. M. Luther, "The Babylonian Captivity of the Church," (1520); WA 6:560-61; LW 36:107-108. On the relationship between tradition and innovation in the Lutheran understanding of the church, cf. W. Kasper, "Das Augsburger Bekenntnis im evangelisch-katholischen Gespräch," *Theologische Quartalschrift* 160(1980) 87-90.

39. Sauter (n. 30 above), 185-86.

40. Cf. the commentary by J. Ratzinger in *Lexikon für Theologie und Kirche* (Freiburg: Herder, 1967), Ergänzungsband 2:523-28; *idem*, "Luther und die Einheit der Kirche," *Internationale Katholische Zeitschrift* 12(1983) 572-73; similarly K. Lehmann, "Worüber jetzt zu sprechen wäre. Luther und die Einheit der Kirchen heute," *Herder-Korrespondenz* 37(1983) 559-60.

41. Cf. *Lehrverurteilungen* (n. 2 above), 31.

42. Cf. the declaration of the World Conference on Faith and Order in Montreal (1963) on "Scripture, Tradition, and Traditions," *The Fourth World Conference on Faith and Order, Montreal 1963. The Report* (Faith and Order Paper No. 42; ed. P. C. Rodger and L. Vischer; London: SCM, 1964) 50-60.

43. Cf. Deutscher Oekumenischer Studienausschuss, *Verbindliches Lehren der Kirchen heute* (Beiheft zur *Oekumenischen Rundschau* 33; Frankfurt am Main: Lembeck, 1978).

44. The Ministry in the Church (1981), in GiA 266, #58.

45. Cf. *Lehrverurteilungen* (n. 2 above), 31.

46. Cf. Ap 7 and 8:17-22; BS 238-39; BC 171-72.

47. Cf. Y. Congar, *Die Lehre von der Kirche. Vom abendländischen Schisma*

bis zur Gegenwart (Handbuch der Dogmengeschichte; Freiburg: Herder, 1971), 3/3d:54-55, 60-62.

48. Cf. *Baptism, Eucharist and Ministry* (Faith and Order Paper No. 111; Geneva: WCC, 1982), M 28-31, 51-55.

49. Cf. F. Schleiermacher, *The Christian Faith* (ed. H. R. Mackintosh and J. S. Stewart; Edinburgh: T. & T. Clark, 1928), Section 24, p. 103; J. A. Möhler, *Die Einheit in der Kirche oder das Prinzip des Katholizismus* (1825) (ed. J. R. Geiselmann; Darmstadt: Wissenschaftliche Buchgesellschaft, 1957) 405; Sec. 64.

50. Bilaterale Arbeitsgruppe (n. 1 above) 14.

51. Cf. W. Beinert, "Die Sakramentalität der Kirche im theologischen Gespräch," *Theologische Berichte* (ed. J. Pfammatter and F. Furger; Zürich: Benziger, 1980) 9: 13:66; W. Kasper, "Die Kirche als universales Sakrament des Heils," in *idem*, *Theologie und Kirche* (Mainz: Grünewald, 1987) 162-74.

52. Cf. *Die Sakramentalität der Kirche in der ökumenishen Diskussion* (ed. Johann-Adam-Möhler-Institute; Paderborn: Bonifatius, 1983), especially G. Gassmann, "Kirche als Sakrament. Zeichen und Werkzeug," 171-201. Especially important is the critical essay by E. Jüngel (n. 26 above), which nevertheless opens up the discussion; Birmelé (n. 1 above), 203-53, has a survey of the discussion.

53. *Lehrverurteilungen* (n. 2 above), 63.

54. The document of the combined Catholic-Protestant Commission in France takes up precisely this thesis: "Consensus oecuménique et différence fondamentale," *Documentation catholique* 69(1987) 40-44. What is at stake is summarized as follows: "Is the church sanctified in such a way that it becomes itself a sanctifying subject?" (page 43).

55. Cf. W. Kasper, "Autonomie und Theonomie. Zur Ortsbestimmung des Christlichen in der modernen Welt," *Theologie und Kirche* (Mainz: Grünewald, 1987) 99-117.

56. Cf. Peter (n. 23 above), 309.

57. Cf. textbooks in theology, for example, J. Auer, *Kleine katholische Dogmatik 6* (Regensburg: Pustet, 1971) 79-83.

58. Cf. Y. Congar, *I Believe in the Holy Spirit* (New York: Seabury; London: Chapman, 1983), 3:267-74.

59. Cf. W. Kasper, "Das Petrusamt in ökumenischer Perspektive," *In der Nachfolge Jesu Christ* (ed. K. Lehmann; Freiburg: Herder, 1980) 93-122; *idem*, "Der apostolische Sukzession als ökumenisches Problem," in *Lehrverurteilungen — kirchentrennend?* III *Materialien zur Lehre von den Sakramenten und vom kirchlichen Amt* (Dialog der Kirchen 6; ed. W. Pannenberg; Freiburg: Herder; and Göttingen: Vandenhoeck & Ruprecht, 1990) 329-49.

5

Basics and Christology

Robert W. Jenson

I

IT HAS BEEN for decades the regular experience of ecumenical dialogues that each particular matter that divides the churches proves amenable of resolution, but that after each such agreement the churches remain as mutually disapproving as before. Thus Roman Catholics and Lutherans have found it possible to agree even on "justification by faith" or on the desirability of the papacy, yet having done so find themselves little if at all advanced toward restored fellowship. It has equally been the experience that no amount of such frustration seems able to convince those involved in the conversation, whatever may be the conviction of more distant officials, that such frustration should be understood as appropriate.

Such experiences, often repeated, have led ecumenists to the supposition of our conference, that there must be, between each pair of separated churches, some "basic difference(s)" underlying and transcending the particular practices and theologoumena which are apparently divisive, and some "basic consensus" underlying and transcending these in turn. Any two of the great churches can seemingly achieve common statements on any of the questions that had been thought to divide them, without thereby achieving greater spiritual commonality. It indeed seems likely that if two of the great churches should reach agreement about *all* the items on their list of traditional disputes, the very discussion that achieved this would generate some new question in order to continue the division. It thus has come to seem that the particular theological occasions of separation between any two of the great churches must be only symptoms and manifestations of differences hidden at some level deeper than that occupied by the traditional matters of controversy.

Equally it has come to seem that there must be a consensus of the great churches at the same level, of which the possibility of resolving the traditional controversies is the manifestation.

Since it is the church's persisting *divisions* which occasion our conference and its linguistic usages, a hermeneutical strategy is dictated. I will always first consider "basic *differences*" and only thereupon interpret "basic *consensus*."

I will suppose that the communities we here represent are not divided in *faith*; I will not argue this supposition. A "basic difference" among us must then be some other difference than any which runs between faith and unbelief. In order not to foreclose the question of whether the differences among us ought to be church divisive, I will stipulate that the differences to be considered are those which *explain*, but may or may not *justify* our divisions. A *basic* difference will then be one that *compendiously* explains our existing divisions; it may or may not justify them now or have once justified them.

What then would be a "basic *consensus*"? Again, I will suppose that we here are united in Christ and that this unity is therefore not just by itself the consensus we are trying to discover. I see three possibilities. A basic consensus might be a consensus that *explains* why those divided by "basic differences" continue to recognize unity in the faith. Or it might be a consensus that would *overcome* our divisions, should we have achieved or achieve it. Or it might be a consensus that made the *difference* between "explain" and "justify" in the previous discussion of "basic differences."

I assume that in our discussions here all of these uses of "basic consensus" will appear and intermingle. There is nothing the matter with that so long as we are aware of the situation and poised to avoid sheer equivocation. In this essay, however, I will try to remain clearly with the *third* stipulated sense of "basic consensus." I choose this because I think its problematic the most interesting and the discussion thereof the most likely to generate new thinking among us.

II

I turn to more material discussions. In accord with the hermeneutic situation I must begin with *differences* rather than with consensus. I have a proposal to lay before you. The divisions of Christ's church can be compendiously accounted for in my judgment by the *incompletion* of Christianity's primary theological task: the *interpretation of God* by what happened and will happen with Jesus Christ. I will argue that in consequence of an interpretation of God only partly bent to the gospel, dialectics are generated within the practice and understanding of the faith which *compel* Christianity's repeated division into polar communities which can neither be reconciled nor leave one another alone. One such binary pair is made by the Eastern and Latin bodies. And within the latter Catholic and Protestant wings repeat the pattern.

People do not first begin to think of God when Christian evangelists come to them. Thus Christian interpretation of God is always the reinterpretation of antecedent understanding. In our theological history the antecedent interpretation is that which came of Greece's experience within the religious world of Mediterranean antiquity and of the reflection which that experience generated. The direct fruit of the gospel's struggle with Hellenic worship and theology is the doctrine of the Trinity, which affirms about God nearly everything that Plato was concerned to deny of God, but does so in language continuous with that of Hellenic reflection and at Hellenic reflection's level of sophistication. Thus the Fathers asserted that a *temporal figure* is "one of" God and thereupon asserted that God's "*ousia*" is *infinite*, that this infinity is that of a *life* and its motion, and that deity is *not* a predicate susceptible of degrees, so that there can be *no* almost-gods.[1]

Antecedent religion naturally does not meekly accept such reinterpretation. Christian reflection's weapon over against such resistance is the reflective mode we call "Christology." Christology, I suggest, is to be the reflection involved in *getting over* the self-evidences about God which antecedent religion has deposited in the structures of our apprehension: e.g., within *our* heritage, "*Surely* God cannot suffer?" A christological proposition is adequate precisely insofar as it comprehensively and ingeniously *offends* what "everybody" at a time and place "of course" knows to be true of God: "The Invisible is seen . . . , the Ungraspable is laid hold of . . . , the Impassible suffers . . . , the Deathless dies . . . ."[2]

It has been suggested before that the divided church's "basic differences" are christological.[3] In making the same suggestion, I do not renew the discussion of whether e.g., Lutherans are "monophysitic"or the Reformed "Nestorian." For one thing, such mutual exchanges of compliments are unlikely to advance the ecumenical cause. But for another and more interesting thing, in my judgment *both* of such paired compliments are almost always *right*. Our traditional christological anathemas occur within a *common* christological tradition which itself harbors the flaw we should seek and cure; so long as that flaw is not cured, Antioch and Alexandria must evoke and anathematize one another sempiternally.

Some history telling is inevitable. I must apologize for dragging some of you through territory you know far more intimately than I. Moreover, I have the systematician's always slightly skewed reading of theological history; I can only plead that occasionally just this skewing can find truth. It is platitudinous that the ancient christological battles were fought between two great centers of scholarship and speculation. I suggest a *reading* of their opposition that may not be quite so platitudinous.

Antioch, we must remember, had been the home of that commonsensicalized Origenism we have anathematized as "Arianism." The one concern of Antioch was to allow no thought to pass which might sully the deity of God, and this deity was self-evidently understood by the canons of late antique reflection as constituted in *apatheia*, "impassibility." Already Justin Martyr had taken it as obvious that full-fledged *God* could not, e.g., have lunched with Abraham[4] — and as for emerging from a womb or hanging on a cross. . .! Since in the early fourth century it was still remembered that "the Logos" was a title of *Jesus*, Arius' question was Antioch's inevitable question: "How can the Logos be God since he sleeps like a man, and weeps, and suffers?"[5] The outcome of the Nicene controversy was an initial victory for Alexandria, whose position may be bluntly summarized: We have no idea how the suffering Jesus can be God, who to be sure must be impassible, but somehow he is or salvation is undone.

"The Logos," said Nicea and Constantinople I, "is *homoousios to patri.*" Antioch agreed to the Nicene position and indeed quickly became super-Nicene, but what this meant for *Antioch* was that the Logos in turn became incapable of wombs and crosses. Thereupon the pressure of the *apatheia* axiom simply shifted; Antioch now had to ask, "How can Jesus be the Logos, since Jesus sleeps like other men, and weeps, and suffers?" *This* was the question that tore apart the Eastern church from 381 on, and it remains to this day the question that concretely defines Christology. The actual christological question has been simply Arius' question shifted a notch.

Antioch has had a good press from the great liberal historians of dogma for its supposed attention to the human Jesus. But what the texts in fact show (except in the case of Theodore himself!) is the old anxiety that this humanity not contaminate God. The great controversy, after all, was precipitated by Nestorius' sheer horror at his new congregation's delight in the Logos' occupancy of a womb.[6] To be sure, no more than in the first round could Alexandria provide explanations either of *how* it could be true that Mary is *Theotokos* or, as it was insisted in the last decisive controversy, that "one of the Trinity died."

But for the sake of salvation Alexandria had to insist that *somehow* such propositions are true.

The motive of all Antioch's christological dialectic was to establish two subjects of what happens with Christ. The one agent must be divine, to do the empowering. This agent does not suffer, for suffering was understood as merely the deficiency of agency and therefore in any case inapplicable to a divine agent. The other agent must be human, to do the suffering. The terminology was never the point and could be negotiated.

Conversely, the motive of Alexandria's formulations was to establish *one* agent of what happens with Christ. There is, Alexandria insisted, but one subject available for whatever we want to attribute to the Savior. As, famously, Cyril wrote: "We teach that the one who is the Son begotten of the Father and is God only-begotten . . . did himself suffer in the flesh on our account. . . ."[7]

The Council of Chalcedon has been regularly praised for settling the issue between Antioch and Alexandria not by constructing new solutions to the disputed questions but by setting limits and within those limits declaring a truce. Doubtless Chalcedon's method was in the circumstances wise, but the strategy also has its limitations, exactly the limitations which now plague the ecumenical movement's use of the same method. It was perfectly possible for each party to proclaim a victory and thereafter approve the others as little as before. Thus Chalcedon confessed "one and the same Lord Jesus Christ" as "one *prosopon* and one *hypostasin*" — for Alexandria, though Antioch had its own use of "*prosopon*," which made "one *prosopon*" affirm exactly what Cyril denied. And Chalcedon confessed "two natures" which are unmixed, unadulterated," — for Antioch, though Cyril had his own use of "nature," which made "two natures" say exactly what Antioch denied.

What appeared in the vacuity of Chalcedon's formulas, besides ecumenical strategy, was the ecumenically *shared* failure to overcome the old *question*: "How can the Logos/Jesus be God, since he suffers?" Within the doctrine of the Trinity itself a mighty spiritual and intellectual feat had been done: the gospel had successfully and fundamentally reinterpreted Mediterranean antiquity's antecedent understanding of deity. The feat was at least equal to the greatest achievements of the Hellenic religion and theology with which the trinitarian theologians struggled. But the old question, expelled from the doctrine of God proper, or at least from the trinitarian part of it, merely moved to take up residence in the new christological reflection, and there it was never overcome.

III

Since faith has lacked energy fully to reinterpret God by the gospel, two paths, and only two, open from Chalcedon. The one path has been to accept Antioch's canons, whatever propositions may be affirmed, and leave God as one agent and the man Jesus as a second. I will argue that this was the path taken by the West.

I hesitate to discuss Eastern Christianity's path since my knowledge of it is external. But let me risk the following. Abstractly considered, the other path open from Chalcedon must be rigorous interpretation of the story about Jesus by the given definition of deity. I think this to be by far the preferable path, for such interpretation cannot help, even against its own intention, but become reciprocal, so that theology's task of reinterpreting the antecedent understanding of God must also be furthered. Eastern Christians often claim that, precisely because they have been more immediately related to the Greek heritage, they have never accepted that heritage so uncritically as did the West; surely the claim is very plausible.

Nevertheless, it must be said that the incompleteness of Christology's task can be seen also in Eastern reflection. Perhaps I may take Gregory Palamas as one in whom specific Eastern tendencies become acute. Then a way to bring out the problem I want to raise is to ask what that strange divine "*ousia*" is *for* within his thinking. Gregory of Nyssa himself can be read as equating the "infinite" and so ungraspable divine "*ousia*" simply with *infinity* as such, the infinity *of* the life among the three hypostases. On this reading not only does "God" and all other names for the same reality get its meaning as it conceptualize the energies, but it is this hypostatic divine life that is the *referent* of "God," the transcendence of God being established sheerly as the infinity of this life.[8] With Gregory Palamas, however, the impression is unavoidable that he uses the "*ousia*" as a sort of sanctum for deity as antecedently defined: "God himself neither becomes nor suffers, so far as concerns his *ousia*."[9]

Palamas taught that the "*hypostasis*" of the Logos, the *in* and *with* of the divine life, the "energy" which he lives with the Father in the Spirit, is directly present to *our* hypostatic individuality and plurality, as one of us is hypostatized in him.[10] And that, I think, is exactly what must be said and what the West never *quite* says. But then the dogma that the "natures" are "unmixed," etc., is preserved by saying that the divine "nature," "*ousia*," is in any case inaccessible and thus also is not touched by the Logos' hypostatic involvement with us.[11] *Insofar* as this "*ousia*" is then retained as the chief referent of "God" and thus as an *other* than the hypostatic life also called "God," precisely the inaccessibility of the "*ousia*" must make it immune to interpretation by Jesus' human story.[12]

Should this analysis be correct, the result of Eastern Christology's heroic and right effort to follow Cyril could be deeply ironic: a drastic interpretation of Jesus' story by the antecedent Hellenic interpretation of deity, still tucked away in that "*ousia*." Therein would be located a compulsion to freeze also the story about Jesus and indeed history generally into a timelessly established image of the atemporal. Western observers regularly think they perceive just such a phenomenon in the life and thinking of the Eastern church. The following questions may at least be asked.

Does not the East indeed maintain separation from the West by finding in every situation some reason to denounce "innovation"? Is it not finally the sheer fact that Western Christianity *has* a history — which always undoes attempts to restore fellowship, which is the East-West "fundamental difference"? That innovation is often wrong and in Western theological history sometimes has been wrong is indisputable. But why should "You Westerners have innovated!" not sometimes be a *compliment*?

IV

I turn to that branch of this history whose division in turn is the preoccupation of the modern ecumenical movement. Key Chalcedonian phrases were present at the insistence of Pope Leo I, and his so-called Tome in which he did the insisting was appended as authorized commentary. And it has been Chalcedon taken *as* a statement of Leonine Christology that has been the operative christological authority of the West. I cite the key passage of the Tome: "Each nature does its own work, in cooperation with the other...."[13]

Two great forces maintained the Leonine Christology through the history of Western Christianity. One was Augustine's exceptionally uncritical reception of the axiom that God is above all "*apathos*."[14] From Augustine on, it was unquestioned that no theological proposition could be true from which it could follow that God is in any way different on account of his actual relations to creatures than he would have been without them; applied to the analysis of the hypostatic union, this meant that no way of conceiving the union could be entertained from which anything would follow about the Logos himself.

The second force was the Anselmian doctrine of atonement. According to Anselm, the atoning *work* of Christ was solely of the human nature because only humans owed the debt and only a human could pay it. Christ had also to be God in order that the merit of the human's work be infinite and thus available to all the race. That "each nature does its own thing in cooperation with the other" is the very motto of this soteriology.

Scholasticism performed a brilliant analytical work on meager matter. The starting analysis is an undialectical distinction between a "hypostasis" and the "nature(s)" hypostatized, which, if several natures are hypostatized together, nothing follows about those natures. Thus that Christ's divine and human natures are of but one hypostasis is made to be a purely (in modern terms) logical assertion: that *somehow* propositions can be true that attribute acts or characteristics of either nature to the same real subject.[15] Consideration of *how* this may be is postponed to another doctrine altogether, the doctrine of the "communication of attributes."

But also this doctrine is ruled by Leo. In such propositions as "Jesus will rule" or "The Logos was born of Mary," "Jesus" and "the Logos" are analyzed as merely alternative phrases to denote the same reality, the one hypostasis. About Jesus *as* a human person or about the Logos as he is "*homoousios to patri*," they say nothing at all. Moreover, they are further to be analyzed as true "*in verbo*" but not "*in re*":[16] although they are true, they do not conform to the facts that verify them. To obtain a proposition conforming to the fact that is stated, "The Logos was born of Mary," e.g., it must be translated into "The man Jesus (who is hypostatically one with the Logos) was born of Mary."

This pair of doctrines verges on vacuous circularity. The hypostatic union is but permission to speak of Christ in the ways stipulated by the doctrine of the communication of attributes. But such speech can be true only by way of the hypostatic union. Vacuity is avoided by using the doctrine of "created grace." Christ's humanity is said to be gifted with the virtues and capacities needed for his role in salvation, which gifts are not different in character from the graces otherwise given to saints, being unique only as the gifts appropriate to Christ's unique role. What makes Christ savior is not granted *by* the hypostatic union, but rather to the human *picked out by* the hypostatic union.[17]

In turning now to display how this Christology creates the divisions of the Western church, I must avoid a misunderstanding. I do not mean that church people divising a liturgy or establishing a canon look up formulae in christological tracts and deduce practice and ideology from what they find. Technical Christology at once expresses and enforces an entire way of interpreting Christ and therein an entire way of interpreting church and world *by* Christ; to understand a technical christological formula one must always be thinking of that way of interpreting Christ.

My thesis at this second juncture is: the Christology of the West will not support the Christian religion. So long as it is not fixed, we are driven either to assign properly christological functions elsewhere or to give up pieces of the faith. Catholicism does the one, Protestantism the other. There are many cases by which one might demonstrate the dialectics; I choose two, the second the more obvious.

The first case. It is ecumenical teaching that the risen Christ speaks in the church and by the church to the world. The gospel is not merely the word of the believer who speaks but the word of Christ. But precisely when the risen Christ speaks, is this the word of *God* or the word of a creature? By the restrictions Western doctrine places on the communication of attributes, exactly *in that* the risen Christ's servants speak the word of the human united to the Logos, what they say may be inspired and even infallible information *about* the word of God, but not God's own word.

In consequence, Catholicism, which Protestants usually accuse of authoritarianism, may better be accused of the opposite error. Consider the famous doctrine of Trent: that "none can know with the authority of faith...that one has obtained the grace of God,"[18] — whatever their pastors tell them! Catholicism has not dared to think that the church's word can bear that unconditional certitude which is the soul's inner correlate to grace. It has thought that to found the certitude of faith, the church's message must refer away from itself to something more reliable.

Perhaps it may be accepted for something more disinterested than sheer Protestant prejudice if I note that Catholicism's besetting temptation surely does seem to be semi-(or hemi- or hemi-demi or...) Pelagianism. It is in the space opened by the above referral that this temptation has its ineluctable home. If I hear the gospel promise of grace and am by that promise directed *elsewhere* as to the actual place of that grace, there is a move I now have to make upon which my sanctification depends. There is no way to avoid this conditioning of the gospel's promise so long as the church's speaking of the gospel and actual participation in grace are thought to be two events.

Trent again: "If anyone says that one is absolved of sin...because one believes firmly that one is..., *anathema sit*."[19] What we can *hear* and thereupon *believe* is one thing, saving grace yet another thing still to come. According to Trent the gospel call is indeed utterly a matter of prevenient grace, involves no initiative of the sinner, and occurs in that hearers, "conceiving faith by hearing. . . ," believe "those things to be true which are divinely revealed and promised." But what this hearing and believing *do* is "dispose" those thus "stirred up" to *turn to grace* for "justification itself," which is available in the sacraments.[20] Of the sacraments Catholicism can say what it cannot bring itself to say of the word, that they "contain the grace that they signify."[21]

But what if we decide to overcome this structural Pelagianism *without* questioning the traditional reading of Christ's reality? Without acknowledging the human Christ's word in the church as God's own creative word? How on those terms will we eliminate the Catholic space between hearing of grace and sacramentally receiving it?

Since the space in which the Catholic turn is to be made has two poles, there are two moves to be made. We will depose the sacraments from their Catholic position, whether we retain them in churchly routine or not. We will then relocate sanctifying power closer to the word, but as long as we remain faithful to Leo we will not be able to attribute such power to the word *itself*. Given the Christian repertoire, only one move is open: to locate sanctifying power in an "internal," i.e., unsacramental work of the Spirit, and to suppose that this work of the Spirit, though it accompanies the speaking and hearing of the gospel, is ontically independent thereof. For this position, let me cite a hero of mine lest I quote *in malam partem*: "Means," of which "the glorious gospel" is chief,[22] "have no influence to produce this grace either as causes or instruments. . . ."[23] "The word of God is only made use of to convey to the mind subject matter" of "saving intervention."[24]

Therewith the position of Protestantism. Nor can Protestantism move an inch from this position without simply ceasing to be Christian. For, if it decides to "reemphasize" the sacraments, these can now only reappear as religious ceremonial extraneous to the gospel and in this way as in fact the pagan magic at the church's heart which Protestants have often suspected in Catholicism. And, if it abates the *testimonium internum* by a single jot, it has no grace left at all.

Each of these positions cannot fail to see what is wrong with the other. And both critiques are right.

The second case. The Western church has been continuously torn by controversy about Christ's presence in the Eucharist. The question itself, to be sure, is decisive: How *can* the bodily risen man be present as loaf and cup?

Strict conceptual limits have bounded all Western attempts to answer this question. It has been thought definitive for the reality of a *body* to have its own distinct place. Then Scripture and creed appear to tell us what that place is: the right hand of the Father, in heaven. It was too mythological also for the pre-Enlightenment church to think of Christ moving spacially between heaven and the altars. On all this there is beautiful agreement between Catholic and Protestant. Calvin: "For this is the hope for our own resurrection and ascension into heaven, that Christ rose and ascended. . . . And this is the eternal truth of any body, that it is contained in its place."[25] Thomas: "Plainly, the body of Christ does not come to be in the sacrament by spatial motion."[26]

As to the *fact* of the presence Thomas can thus speak for all: ". . . the body of Christ is not in the sacrament as a body is in the place by whose dimensions it is itself measured, but in a special way unique to the sacrament. . . . "[27] But that only poses the question the more urgently: How can it be *true* that such a presence occurs? And to that question, Leonine *Christology* can provide no answer. For it can "really" attribute nothing of God's freedom over against space to body and blood. Therefore the Catholic tradition must find another sort of answer. There is only one move to make: the fact of Christ's presence as bread and cup is said to be "altogether supernatural, effected by the special power of God."[28]

Also the last proposition may be ecumenically very acceptable. But if Christ's presence is in *such* fashion supernatural, the event must be, as it were, a *reliable* supernatural event, for we cannot be left wondering at each celebration if this time it is really happening. Catholicism provides the needed assurance by making the church itself the guarantor, gifted with power to say "This is my body" knowing that it is true because it is thus said.[29]

None of the Reformers could accept such a grant of power to the church, though their reasons varied greatly. But where does that leave us? Again two paths are open! We may abandon the ancient doctrine that the bread and cup are Christ's bodily presence, or we may look for some other ground of the presence. Typically Protestantism has done the first, with whatever bad conscience or protestations. The sacramental elements are said to supplement the word in creating consciousness of the sacrament's *res*. Whether this consciousness then has grace for its content depends on a second movement whereby this consciousness becomes or does not become faith. Thus the Leonine restrictions are fully operative for both word and element.[30] What Catholicism attributes to the church's sacramental structure, Protestantism attributes to the individual's faith.

The Lutheran Reformers are those who for better or for worse took the second mentioned path. If the ground of sacramental presence is in neither the church nor individual believers, we can only return to

Christology to find it. Notoriously, that is what the Lutheran Reformers did, breaking through Leo's restrictions in the process.

V

Every church group supposes it is the exception to the scheme by which it classifies the other groups. Since this conference is called by the Lutherans, it may be permitted me to indulge our version of this supposition. There is, to be sure, a problem about who the "Lutherans" may be. If we mean the denominational group labeled this way, then in my judgment there is no important difference at all between them and other Western Christians; most of us are, in the terms I have been using, Protestant, and the remainder of us are in those terms Catholic. But if the "Lutherans" are Luther and those enlightened by his insights, also as these have found place in the Lutheran Confessional documents, then the fundamental difference between them and other Western Christians is that the Lutherans advanced or were driven beyond the standard Christology.

The deed was done in two documents: the 1526 *Suevian Syntagma*, by the young Johannes Brenz and his friends, and Luther's 1528 *Confession Concerning Christ's Supper*. As is notorious, the technical occasion of Luther's christological reflections in the latter document was Zwingli's christological explanation for his denial of Christ being bodily present as the elements: his doctrine of "*alleosis*." This doctrine was in fact nothing remarkable; it was merely a simplistic statement of the standard Western understanding of the communication of attributes. Luther, however, was outraged; perhaps Zwingli's naiveté let Luther recognize what he would have been reluctant to recognize in one of the Fathers. "Beware, Beware, I say, of this alleosis, for it is the devil's mask since it will finally construct *a kind of Christ* after whom I would not want to be a Christian."[31]

And we quickly learn what is wrong with the tradition's Christ: in both directions, the communication of attributes is puny. On the one hand: "For if I believe that only the human nature suffered for me, then Christ would be a poor Savior for me...."[32] On the other hand, and centrally for the sacramental controversy:

> And if you can say, "Here is God," then you must also say, "Christ the man is present too."
>
> And if you could show me one place where God is and not the man, then the person is already divided and I could at once say truthfully, "Here is God who is not man...." *But no God like that for me!*[33]

For Luther the traditional doctrine that "thus we should ascribe to the whole person whatever pertains to one part of the person. . ."[34] has as its content that suffering is "really" communicated to the Logos, also as God, and God's infinite energies (?!) really communicated to the man Jesus. We may, indeed, take a very "Eastern" question to make clear Lutheranism's divergence from standard Western Christology: Is the "flesh" of Jesus "life giving" by virtue of the "created graces" bestowed on the one united to the Logos, or by virtue of the union itself and the divine attributes thereby shared with this flesh? Does God save by the *instrumentality* of a specially equipped man or by *being* that man? The Scholastics said the one, Lutherans the other.[35]

Luther and his followers pressed forward to a Christology which finally amounts to the proposition that "one of the Trinity suffered" *because* the man Jesus who suffered *is* personally one of the Trinity and that, where we hear or see or touch the man Jesus, we hear or see or touch God the Logos, *as* God the Logos. It is such a Christology and only such a Christology that overcomes the antinomies which drive Western Christianity to division and mutual condemnation. Whether the Lutherans therewith pressed beyond, e.g., Gregory Palamas, is hard to say; in application at least the same ambiguity I claimed to see in Palamas has regularly afflicted also the Lutherans.

VI

Where then are we with respect to a "basic *consensus*"? Let me first say a few words to and for those "Lutherans." Should my glorious claim of Lutheran insight be at all accurate, the Lutheran fundamental difference within Western Christendom would be precisely the theological position from which its divisions may be healed; I know, of course, that every group says something similar. It would be the Lutheran ecumenical calling to descry the *christological vantages* from which particular controversies between Catholic and Protestant may be transcended.

Our divisions can be transcended, even by Lutheran Christology, only, of course, if a basic consensus (and that exactly in the third of the senses I analyzed at the beginning) indeed obtains. I will conclude by proposing that there is such a consensus and what it is. Again in accord with my opening analyses, it is our basic difference as just described which must provide the horizon of our basic consensus.

I suggest: Our basic consensus beyond shared faith is precisely *the shared historic and continuing effort to reinterpret Mediterranean antiquity's interpretation of God*, and a limited but real history of success. In what do we agree? We agree *in the presupposition of our disagreements*: that God must be understood by what happens with Jesus and that this must be possible since we have partly already done it. For us to affirm the basic consensus which in my view in fact joins us would be to declare that this effort is both our common heritage and our present common task.

I suggest further: Since our fundamental differences are precisely the perhaps inevitable manifestations of the fact that our historic common task is not finished, they cannot be considered "church divisive." The consensus suggested is exactly of my third sort: it states why our basic differences explain but do not justify our division.

It does not follow that other differences which are *not* "basic" in the sense of our conference may not indeed be just so divisive, may not indeed justify some or all of the existing division. When we see what is the basic division between Catholics and Protestants, we come to understand *why* they dispute specifications as, e.g., Christ's presence in the Eurcharist; and, when we see how this division is caused by the historicity of a basic consensus, we come to understand what work must be done to transcend the dispute. It does not follow that the dispute, as long as it is not itself resolved, is not itself legitimately church divisive.

But what good does it then do to identify basic differences and a basic consensus? As just noted: We thereby identify *what* thinking is to be done if actually church divisive disputes are to be transcended. Or, reverting to two final strands of my initial analysis: We thereby acquire the ability *so* to adjudicate particular occasions of division that the division does not merely find other occasion. We do not necessarily and immediately acquire common concepts, but we do acquire a focus toward which such concepts may move.

Henry Chadwick

PROFESSOR JENSON has asked why, when so much agreement in faith can be uncovered by mutual listening, the communions which split off from Rome in the sixteenth century remain as far apart as before. He does not resort to psychological or social causes, but insists that theological divergences remain primary. If divided communions, setting aside malice and group rivalry (or at least wishing to be granted grace to do so), can agree on a list of particular dogmatic areas where they have understood themselves to occupy traditionally incompatible positions, are these latent and still very deep set divergences so profound that we are unaware of them until brought to the surface by "deep sea diving" into the past history of dogmatic formulation?

To reinforce this distinction between the conscious and evidently visible divergencies and the hidden underlying differences of essential premises, the essay makes an important and convincing distinction between disagreements which *justify* a state of separation and disagreements which *explain* how it came about. The contentions which rationalize division may overlap with the factors that explain the division's existence, but observation suggests that the explaining causes are not simply identical with the overt justifications for separateness. Hence the immense interest of attempts (such as those surveyed in Harding Meyer's article in *Mid-Stream*, 1986) to account for the present impasse of ecumenism by looking for "unidentified submarines," for differences of basic presuppositions in, e.g., the role of the church as guardian and witness of divine revelation, *or* the nature of the church as mediator of divine holiness and healing, *or* in the interpretations of justification by faith, *or* in Christology. (It is perhaps a regrettable feature of some of these explanations to repeat old misrepresentations and stereotypes of the group from which the writer dissents.) Congar saw the near monophysitism of Luther as cause for his disparagement of the human and for his desacralization of the empirical church.

Professor Jenson acutely proposes to see in the weakness of Western Christology, embodied in the Tome of Leo I, an explanation why the medieval West was beset by controversies concerning eucharistic presense, whereas the Byzantine East was not much troubled. It is suggested that Western two nature Christology was deeply akin to that of the School of "Antioch" (i.e., Theodore of Mopsuestia and Theodoret of Kyrrhos) and that this insufficiently affirmed the unity of Christ; that in consequence the word of Christ is but the word of a human being united to the Logos, putting distance between God's word and human testimony about God's word; that this lies behind the Augustinian refusal to allow total assurance of election to salvation except in rare cases of special revelation; that because the gospel proclaimed by the church is therefore less than utterly reliable, Catholicism has a perennial weakness for wanting to supplement grace with good works independent of grace; and that, although Catholicism is unqualified in its affirmation of God's fidelity to his promise in sacramental presence, it hesitates about the power of the preached gospel to contain the grace which the words spoken signify.

Protestantism, similarly dogged by the legacy of Leo, is seen to locate sanctifying power exclusively in an inward psychological operation of the Spirit which accompanies the words of the gospel, yet is distinct from them. The sacraments then become magic or at best a visual aid to the spoken word, less than a direct means of grace.

Professor Jenson sees Lutheran Christology as breaking out of Leo's framework. There must be historical problems here in regard to the ultra-Cyrilline exegesis of Leo and Chalcedon commonly called Neo-chalcedonianism. But we are now concerned with dogmatics. I confess to problems with this fascinating and, on any showing, illuminating endeavor to trace causes in the story of Christian thought. There is no question that Cyril of Alexandria (prince of exegetes of St. John's Gospel chapters 6 and 15) combined an aversion to two nature Christology with a strongly articulated doctrine of eucharistic presence. On the other hand, his doctrine of eucharistic *offering* is more reticent than that of Theodore and "Antioch" generally, where the Eucharist is the presence of Christ's sacrifice to which the Lord joins his people. Some of the sixteenth century antitheses on eucharistic belief are anticipated in the fifth century debate, but only some.

Nevertheless, the line of *filiation* in ideas is complex. Leo had read Augustine and often echoes him verbatim without acknowledgment. His Christology in the Tome has some direct debt to Augustine's writings. It is more probable that we should look for the point of the sixteenth century division in Augustine, though he seldom integrates his strongly exemplarist Christology with a belief in the presense of Christ and his sacrifice at "God's altar," the *mensa domini*, which he expressly denies to be a Levitical or Aaronic cultic act or to be a kind of bribe to persuade the Father to be propitious.

Is the root question: What kind of relationship between God and this world of time, space, and matter is possible? The Platonic/Plotinian tradition contained two evaluations of the visible cosmos, the one pessimistic, the other seeing it as a mirror of higher glory. Augustine the Platonist interprets the sacraments and the humanity of Jesus as steps on a Jacob's ladder up to heaven. Augustine came to allow that there can be times and places which God can use as media of holiness. He did not think the receiving of grace merely a matter of intellectual contemplation, though the *mens* is the place of understanding. Yet the Platonism in him was uncomfortable with the realism which stemmed from the realized eschatological language of the New Testament. It was a natural step to see in a Platonic framework New Testament language about testing the powers of the world to come.

That the split between the pre-Chalcedonian churches and those great churches which have accepted the fourth and fifth councils was grounded in Christology is obvious. To what degree was Christology a latent source of the gradual growing apart of Greek East and Latin West? I would think not at all. The root there was ecclesiology and the question of universal Roman jurisdiction. In the sixteenth century Christological questions have again moved and substantially in consequence of rather than as a cause of the continuing eucharistic controversy.

If I think the cart is sometimes put before the horse, that does not qualify my admiration and gratitude for a brilliant paper.

Notes

ROBERT W. JENSON

1. Robert W. Jenson, *The Triune Identity* (Philadelphia: Fortress, 1982).
2. Melito of Sardis, *Antonius Caesar*, 13.
3. So, notably, Yves Congar, "Regards et réflexions sur le christologie de Luther," *Das Konzil von Chalkedon* (ed. A. Grillmeier and H. Bacht; Würzburg: Echter-Verlag, 1954) 3:482-86.
4. Justin Martyr, *Dialogue with Trypho*, 127.
5. Arius as cited by (pseudo?) Athanasius, *Discourse against the Arians* III.
6. E.g., Nestorius, *Sermon XVI*, 286. Nestorius was a perfect Zwinglian: "Who could think deity susceptible to beastly hands?" *Sermon X*, 271.
7. Cyril of Alexandria, *Third Letter to Nestorius*,
8. Jenson, 103-14, 161-67; there documentation. My own work with Gregory of Nyssa doubtless pushed him as far in this direction as possible, or probably a bit further.
9. Gregory Palamas, *Chapters* 133: PG 150:1213c.
10. E.g., Gregory Palamas, *Triads*, I,3,9-17: ". . . the Son of God has united his own divine hypostasis (*ten heautou theiken hypostasin*). . . not only to our nature (*te kath humas phusei*). . . , but. . . also to our human hypostases themselves (*kai autais tais anthropinais hypostasesin*). . . , associating himself with each believer by participation in his holy body. . . ." Or see *Homily V*: PG 151:64d-65a. To this whole subject, John Meyendorff, *A Study of Gregory Palamas* (tr. G. Lawrence; Leighton Buzzard: Faith Press, 1964) 182-83, 208-10. For later reference, we should note the radical "communication of attributes" involved in this: the *man* Jesus "receives in himself the fullness of highest deity" so that his "flesh" is "the inexhaustible fount of holiness"; *Homily XVI*: PG 151:193b.
11. It is all neatly sorted out. Gregory Palamas, *Chapters* 75: PG 150:1173 b-c: "There are then three in God: 1) being, 2) energy, 3) the triune hypostases. . . . Since. . . according to his being God cannot be participated in at all, and since union according to hypostasis is reserved to the divine-human Logos, it remains that others found worthy to be united with God are united according to energy." See Meyendorff (n. 10 above), 182-83.
12. Palamas positively harps upon it. E.g., in the *Triads*: III,1,10-13; III,1,16-19; III,3,26-27.
13. Leo of Rome, "*Agit enim utraque forma cum alterius communione quod proprium est. . . ,*" *Letter to Flavian of Antioch*.
14. Jenson (n. 1 above), 114-31. There documentation.
15. Thus, for example, the doctrine of Duns Scotus: the Logos, as a purely "relative" hypostasis, has, *as* hypostasis, no efficacy. Thus, since it is the Logos as hypostatically other that the Father or the Spirit that is incarnate, the Logos' union with a human nature has no effect on that nature. Nor, of course, is the Logos affected by the union, since as a divine hypostasis, the Logos cannot be affected by anything. That the Logos as hypostasis is the hypostasis of the human nature therefore means only that it is the "*suppositum*" of that nature, i.e., that it is what is denoted by the subject of true predications appropriate to the nature. See, e.g., "*The Oxford Manuscript,*" III, I. To this whole subject, in the presentation of one who thoroughly approves the Scholastic

doctrine, see Léon Seiller, *L'Activite humaine du Christ selon Duns Scot* (Paris: Editions françiscaines, 1944).

16. To this, let me for variety use Bonaventure as evidence. Re, e.g., the communication to Jesus of divine ubiquity, *Four Books of Sentences*, III, XXII, 1,2. Or in the other direction: "the Son of God is said to have died, because he was the man in whom occurred the suffering of death" (*unde Filius Dei dicitur fuisse mortuus, quia fuit homo, in quo fuit passio mortis*)" ibid., III, XXI, 2,3. In general, by the communion of attributes, *nothing* is communicated to the human nature "formally, as a property. . .inhering substantially **or** accidentally (*sicut forma, et proprietas———inhaerens substantialiter **vel** accidentaliter*). . ." III, XIV, 3,3. Emphasis added.

17. Bonaventure again. The grace which as a "*habitus*" disposes Christ's soul for union with the Logos, and his "personal grace," and the grace which equips him to move his members to sanctification and so is "the grace of the (church's) head (*gratia capitis*)," are all the *same* grace; ibid., III, XIII, 2,2. To the whole matter in principle, ibid., III, XIV, 1,1-2.

18. ". . .*cum nullus scire valeat certitudine fidei, cui non potest subesse falsum, se gratiam Dei esse consecutum.*" *Canons and Decrees of the Council of Trent*, Sess. VI, Cap. IX; DS 1534.

19. "*Si quis dixerit, hominem a peccatis absolvi ac justificari ex eo quod se absolvi ac justificari certo credat. . . .*" ibid., "De Justificatione," XIV; DS 1564.

20. Ibid., Sess. VI, Cap. V-VII; DS 1526-31.

21. Ibid., "*De Sacramentiis in Genere*," VI; DS 1606.

22. Jonathan Edwards, Sermon, "A Divine and Supernatural Light," Doctrine, I, 2; *The Works of President Edwards* (New York: Leavitt and Allen, 1843) 4:444.

23. Jonathan Edwards, *Miscellanies*, 534.

24. Jonathan Edwards, "Light. . .," Doctrine II, 3; *Works* 4:444.

25. John Calvin, *Institutes of the Christian Religion*, 1536, iv, 122.

26. Thomas Aquinas, *Summa Theologiae*, iii, 75, 2: "*Manifestum est autem quod corpus Christ non incipit esse in hoc sacramento per motum localem.*"

27. Thomas Aquinas, ibid., iii, 75, 1 and 3.

28. Thomas Aquinas, ibid., iii, 75, 4.

29. Thomas Aquinas, ibid., iii, 78, 4-5; 82, 1-3.

30. See, e.g., the doctrine of Theodore Beza, as brought together by the fine interpretation of Jill Raitt, *The Eucharistic Theology of Theodore Beza* (Chambersburg: American Academy of Religion, 1972).

31. Martin Luther, *Confession Concerning Christ's Supper* (1528); WA 26:319; LW 37:209. Emphasis added.

32. Ibid., WA 26:319; LW 37:210.

33. Ibid., WA 26:332; LW 37:218. Emphasis added.

34. Ibid., WA 26:332; LW 37:211.

35. This was clear very early. Johannes Brenz, *De personalis unione duarum naturarum in Christo*, 5b (1561): "If there is to be talk of 'grace,' there could be no more perfect grace than that the Son of God poured out all his majesty into that son of man whom he in gratuitous mercy. . .by a hypostatic union assumed into unity of person (*si autem sermo est de gratia, profecto fieri non potest, quin filius Dei effundat omnen suam maiestatem in filium illum hominis, quem in unitatem personae unione hypostatica. . .gratuita clementia assumpsit*). . . ." The standard presentation of Lutheran Christology is doubtless that of Martin Chemnitz, *De Duabus Naturis in Christo* (1578).

6

Justification by Faith Alone
The Article by Which the Church Stands or Falls?

Gerhard O. Forde

I HAVE BEEN ASKED to reflect on justification by faith alone as the article by which the church stands or falls and then perhaps to conjecture as to what such reflection might mean for questions about consensus and fundamental differences. I prefer to say reflection because I think that is what is needed at this juncture in ecumenical discussion. Historical research is necessary and helpful, but we are not likely to find all the answers to today's questions "back there" somewhere. Reflection, construction, venturing of new interpretations, and further frank and open dialogue along the way is what is necessary now. It is in this spirit that what follows is offered.

I

It is obvious first of all that ecumenical discussion about justification has not issued in unanimity about the nature or degree of consensus arrived at. Reactions to the recently completed round on justification in the Lutheran-Roman Catholic dialogue in the USA demonstrate this rather clearly.[1] One must say at least that there appears to be no consensus even on whether or not we have arrived at a consensus! Why is this? Perhaps the Common Statement is itself somewhat imprecise. Consensus is claimed with reference to the gospel, but only convergence when one comes to justification by faith. Further complication arises from some ambiguity about the difference between justification by faith as a doctrine on the one hand and its use as a critical principle on the other. Thus on the one hand justification by faith as a doctrine will be treated as but one way of stating the gospel and therefore more or less relativized. On the other hand, if used as a critical principle, it functions to help determine what is gospel and what is not. The ambiguity needs further sorting out.

The sticking point continues to be not so much the doctrine of justification by faith itself but its place and function as *the* article by which the church stands or falls. There is a sense, of course, in which all Christians agree on the doctrine of justification by faith. It is a biblical teaching. One could hardly deny it, at least formally, without some consequence. Even Pelagius considered himself a champion of justification by faith. In our common statement in the U.S. dialogue, we were also able to talk about "prior and fuller convergence on the doctrine itself" which was then to provide the basis for convergence (not consensus here!) on the *use* of justification by faith as a *criterion*. Even so, the best we were able to do in common was to speak of "increasing accord" on criteria (plural!) of Christian authenticity and of "justification" as *an* [not *the*] *articulus stantis et cadentis ecclesiae* protective of the *solus Christus*.[2]

There is many a slip 'twixt the cup and the lip. The move from the doctrine to the *usus* and back again seems to be the locus of the difficulty. Proponents of justification by faith alone seem to have a difficult time convincing others about the nature and necessity of this move. There seems to be considerable haziness in the discussion surrounding particularly the question of what doctrine is for both as to what it signifies and how it is to be used. This in turn prompts the question as to whether there is real consensus or even convergence on the doctrine if agreement on what it is for is not forthcoming. Thus the Lutheran Church in America in its response to the common statement of the U.S. dialogue maintains that "If the consensus on . . . application [of justification as a criterion] cannot be broadened, *then the agreement on the doctrine itself will need to be reconsidered.*" Furthermore, it is asserted that "Testing the consensus on the doctrine of justification will reveal the extent to which there is fundamental consensus on the gospel."[3] That is a most searching chain of consequences. If the consensus on the use of justification cannot be broadened, then the claimed agreement *on the doctrine itself* is called into question. If that happens, then the claimed consensus on the gospel itself is threatened. This raises a fundamental question: Can there be consensus on the doctrine itself where there is only limited agreement on its use? The issue seems still to be in doubt.

The Lutheran claim that justification by faith alone is *the* article by which the church stands or falls continues to be the storm center, it seems, even after all the dialogue. Further reflection and dialogue is necessary on just this point. Why is it so difficult to arrive at understanding at least, if not consensus, here? Speaking personally, this was the biggest disappointment in the recently concluded discussions in the U.S.

dialogue. I think it is necessary now to be quite frank about that. Not only was it difficult, if not impossible, to arrive at mutual understanding of the issues involved here, but there appeared to be considerable reluctance even to discuss them directly. Why is that? Is it because it is a point so neuralgic it undermines the drive to consensus itself? If so, how can one proceed here? I have come to think that there is no way through this problem other than *through* the differences and a frank discussion of them. The constant drive for consensus particularly in this instance deters understanding by attempting to minimalize the differences and thus inhibits discussion and finally genuine understanding. I expect that only a more frank and open discussion of the *differences* will lead to progress on these matters.

Perhaps a modest way to begin is to suggest that part of the answer may lie in differing presuppositions about the nature and particularly the uses of doctrine. Much standard objection to justification by faith alone as *the* article of the standing or falling church seems to arise because it supposedly gives one "doctrine" preeminence over all others and consequently also narrows the understanding of salvation to the experience of guilt and the anxious conscience. Are there not many different biblical metaphors, images, or models, all of which are equally legitimate? Is the anxious conscience normative for all Christian experience? So the question goes. But such an objection presupposes that doctrines are for the most part descriptive words *about* God and his doings, metaphors, images, symbols, etc., culled from the Scriptures under appropriate authorization. Faith will be understood as acceptance of such properly authorized doctrines and as such is not *alone* sufficient to save. The Scriptures are looked upon as the source book for such descriptive words about God. Since each word is likely to be only partial and not exhaustive of the infinite deity, it could even be held advantageous to have as many and various words as the "revelation" affords. One or the other will predominate at the very most only where it answers to a particular context or human predicament, where it seems to describe the God we need. To exalt one such doctrine over all the rest would be arbitrary to say the least (even though almost everyone does it!).

Justification by faith alone, however, both presupposes and imposes a different understanding of the nature and use of doctrine. Faith comes by hearing the word *from* God. This presupposes that in essence Scripture conveys a word *from* God and authorizes the speaking of such a word. Whatever else one may want to say of its containing words *about* God, it is in essence a word *from* God for faith (*was Christum treibet*). Doctrine in this vein is concerned with fostering and guaranteeing the delivery of this word from God in the living present. "How shall they hear without a preacher?" (Rom 10:14). Doctrine therefore drives to the preaching of the word of God and insists that such preaching, rightly done, *is* the word from God for faith. Faith here, of course, is not simply acceptance of doctrine but the trust engendered by that word from God. It is the purpose of doctrine therefore to see to it that the preaching of the word from God is rightly done. Doctrine, that is, will be more like rules for preaching the word from God, whatever words, metaphors, images, etc., one uses, than compilations of authoritative descriptions of God and his doings.

Justification by faith alone is thus seen as the "article by which the church stands or falls" because it directs and drives toward speaking that word which calls forth faith and to which faith alone is the only possible answer. It insists that where the church no longer speaks this word, it has lost its reason for being. It has been said again and again but apparently still needs to be said yet one more time that justification by faith alone does not function to exclude other metaphors, symbols, images, or what have you, but only to insist that they must be used so as to speak the unconditional gospel which creates faith.

To say that justification by faith alone is the article of the standing or falling church or, with Luther, to say it is the plumb line (*Richtschnur*) by which all teaching is to be measured *is* therefore already to say that when used as a criterion of judgment it functions hermeneutically, or as has lately been suggested, metalinguistically,[4] to direct and foster the speaking of the unconditional gospel. In other words, there is no intention among those who hold it to exclude other salvation words, nor is there most certainly any concern to limit preaching to the dimensions of the anxious conscience. If any progress is to be made in the discussion, we must simply get beyond such simplicities. There *is*, however, the overriding concern that what is spoken in the church, *at all costs*, be the unconditional gospel. As the article of the standing or falling church it simply says that there is no point in perpetuating the church at all, however united it might be, where that is not its aim and goal.

It was been my experience, again to be frank, that trying to make this point in the U.S. dialogue was most frustrating and difficult. The very mention of "hermeneutics" seemed to drive some up the wall. In the end, references to "the Lutheran hermeneutical understanding of justification" were reduced to a bare minimum as a more or less troublesome point of view which "in some ways heightens the tension with Catholic positions."[5] "Metalinguistic proposal" did not fare any better. It did not even get mentioned! For a time there was some discussion of "metatheological" criteria, but that did not survive either. In the end we were able to speak only about "a fundamental affirmation" which admittedly was not "fully equivalent" to the Reformation *justificatio sola fide*[6] or about "criteria of Christian authenticity."[7] The frustrating aspect of the dialogue over these matters was simply the *lack of fruitful dialogue* about them, the seeming reluctance to engage the issues in a useful or helpful manner. We seem to grope for formulations which obscure rather than reveal the issues.

Why is this? Are we here pushing up against a "basic difference" which we have not managed even to articulate yet? One wonders. Is it not perhaps the case that justification by faith alone as the criterion by which all is to be judged entails an understanding of the nature and workings of authority in the church quite different from if not opposed to authority structures where it is not accorded that function? Is the authority structure of a word *from* God not radically different from that of our words *about* God? One cannot overlook the fact that the assertion of justification by faith alone moved immediately to an argument about ecclesiastical authority. Where justification is by faith alone, the church's authority is radically limited under the office of fostering and preaching a word which evokes faith and sets people free. Where it is not by faith alone, but rather by works, even grace-wrought works, the authority structure will be quite different. I have a different authority over you if I can only say you are justified by faith alone than if I say you must produce works with the grace tendered.

In the common statement of the U.S. dialogue it was admitted that a hermeneutical interpretation of justification by faith alone "in some ways" makes matters more difficult because it raises more Lutheran questions about "Catholic descriptions of justification as a process of ontological transformation," on the one hand, and Catholic questions about whether Lutherans "do justice to God's respect for human freedom and to the idea of real change wrought by the Holy Spirit," on the other. The "differing thought structures" both within and between the two theological "camps" were alluded to as the source of these as yet unresolved issues. The "naive" critic is likely to ask: "What other issues are there?" The need for further dialogue was duly noted.[8] But the difficulty in virtually all ecumenical dialogues as far as I can see is that with few exceptions there appears to be a general unwillingness even to discuss such issues.

Thus we arrive at a strange and marvelous impasse as far as justification by faith being the article of the standing or falling church is concerned. On the one hand, one complains that it is much too narrow and parochial an article to serve as the *only* criterion. It is only one among many biblical concepts, at best limited to one strange and supposedly unrepeatable historical aberration, the late medieval anxious conscience, and so on and on. On the other hand, one refuses even to entertain or discuss the grounds on which it could establish its claim. History and exegesis are used to abort their own theological significance. The lion, so to speak, is caged so it will not do any harm while its claim to be "King of the beasts" is ridiculed.

II

It seems imperative that efforts be made to discuss the matters involved here. This is surely borne out by the fact that the official responses of both the Lutheran Church in America and the American Lutheran Church indicate considerable uneasiness, not to say dissatisfaction, with the Common Statement of the U.S. dialogue on its treatment of the criteriological significance of justification by faith alone.[9] Nor will it be enough simply to do historical research at this point. It would be necessary to take into account the ways in which justification has actually functioned, or failed to function, among us as a critical principle to shape the life of Lutheran churches. Much water has flowed over the dam since the Reformation! Where questions remain, further constructive effort will no doubt be necessary to put the principle to the test. An essay of this scope is not the place to attempt all that, but in what follows in this section some indication of what I have in mind will, I hope, become more apparent.

One of the happy exceptions to the general reluctance to discuss the issue of the criteriological significance of justification by faith alone is the essay by Carl Peter, "Justification by Faith and the Need of Another Critical Principle," in the volume on *Justification by Faith* containing the results of the recently completed U.S. dialogue.[10] Unfortunately that essay was completed in its final form only after the dialogue was over. An earlier form was distributed at one of the last meetings of the dialogue, but there was no serious or prolonged discussion of the issues it raises. Nevertheless, it affords a good entry into the problems we face. Peter takes a rather different and in many ways more open approach to the question. Instead of the usual attempts to restrict justification as a critical principle, he welcomes its usefulness as a safeguard against misuse and idolatry, i.e., placing ultimate trust in the church, its teachings, usages, or one's own achievement, faith, etc., rather than in God and his Christ. Yet Peter too challenges the place of justification as the *sole* criterion of judgment by suggesting that we need to add another principle to safeguard essential Catholic substance. Using

Tillich's distinction between Catholic substance and Protestant principle, Peter suspects that, if the Protestant principle stands alone, Catholic substance is in danger of being mutilated or abused. The Protestant fear of substituting the conditioned for the unconditioned as the object of ultimate concern can lead to a rejection, despising of, or even blasphemy against God's action in and through the conditioned.

"Be not so prone to expect sin and abuse that you fail to recognize grace where it is at work."[11] That is one way, according to Peter, to formulate this other critical principle. Peter is quite candid about the fact that he is worried about the unexamined and "unpacked" use of the language of unconditionality among those who champion justification as the only criterion for judgment in the church. Justification and unconditionality work together to threaten all consideration of necessary conditions, however penultimate they may be. The suggestion that we need another principle such as the one indicated enables Peter to protect elements of the Catholic substance threatened by uncritical and indiscriminate talk of the unconditionality of the gospel promise. The promise is indeed unconditional. But Peter asks whether the unconditional promise excludes *all* conditions: antecedent, simultaneous, and subsequent.

Elements of the Catholic substance that Peter wants to protect by the added principle and whose role he finds "unquestionably similar to what in other contexts is that of conditions"[12] are such things as the sacraments, the forgiveness of sins, faith in the preserving activity of divine grace, traces of the divine image and remnants of free choice not totally effaced in a fallen world, human dignity, the promise that life is endowed with a meaning, and the like. In short, the trustworthiness of the church according to divine promise, the preservation of at least some degree of freedom and goodness in creation in spite of the fall, and the place of grace-wrought acts of charity are to be safeguarded by the new principle.[13]

What are we to say about this? Does the addition of yet another principle help us in the search for consensus? One can certainly agree that many of the elements of Catholic substance Peter wants to protect deserve to be and indeed that too ruthless an application of "the Protestant principle" can produce merely negative and "anti-Catholic" results. Yet wariness is evoked by the fact that some of those same elements of "Catholic substance" which Peter wants to safeguard with this new principle are precisely those that justification by faith alone wants to subject to more careful critical examination. Tillich's distinction between Catholic substance and Protestant principle is much too formal to be of much help to us in this instance. What is Catholic substance? Who is to determine that and how? If justification by faith alone is the plumb line, does that not mean precisely that it is supposed to help us in answering such questions? Perhaps our constant talk of using justification as a criterion of judgment or a critical (metalinguistic, metatheological, and the like) principle has led us too easily to operate as though its function were strictly formal over against an already existing "substance" and that it had, presupposes, or brings no material considerations of its own to the deliberations. The same should be said, I have come to think more and more of late, about the tendency to speak too hastily and uncritically of Lutheranism as a "confessional movement within the church catholic." Who or what is the church catholic? Is that not precisely the question? Does the Confession of these Lutherans not have something to say about that?

Peter's contention that justification by faith alone as a critical principle leaves certain aspects of the "catholic substance" unprotected does, however, raise many of the right questions and deserves response. It would be encumbent upon those who espouse justification by faith to show that catholic substance rightly delineated is precisely not endangered where justification is used even as the sole critical principle. But such a demonstration would involve moving to what the dialogue tends to call a "different thought structure" and which, given the circumstances, would probably have to be referred to as a "different *faith* structure." Quite naturally justification by faith alone works as the article of the standing or falling church only within the structure it presupposes and calls into being. The situation seems virtually to be tautologous: where justification is not by faith alone, it alone is not likely to be considered an adequate criterion of judgment.

Is it possible to safeguard those legitimate aspects of the "catholic substance" which Peter sees endangered within a "thought structure" called forth and normed by the *sola fide*? It is if one can think consistently from that point of view. Again, this is hardly the place to attempt a thorough reconstruction of the matter but perhaps some indication can be given in what follows as to the way the argument might move.

To begin with, to state the obvious, if we are justified *sola fide* (and here the *sola* is most important), any attempt to describe or prescribe what is necessary for Christian existence and the object with which such existence has to do so as to make it accessible or given other than to faith alone is mistaken. Does such a view somehow endanger or evoke mistrust in the church? I should think not. It simply seeks to indicate to the church what it must be about if it is to gain and maintain trust. For how does such faith come? Faith comes by *hearing*. And how shall they hear without a preacher? And how shall one preach unless he is sent? Article 2 of the Augsburg Confession is followed immediately by Article 5. To obtain justifying faith, *Gott hat das Predigtamt eingesetzt* (CA 5), that is, given the gospel and the sacraments. It is impossible to be justified *sola fide* without a preacher and consequently without the church. Precisely to be unconditional, the gospel promise must be spoken and delivered "to you." But the church and its preachers will then gain and maintain trust simply in that they deliver this unconditional gospel. If, however, the church fails to realize that this is in fact the highest exercise of its authority and source of its trustworthiness and grasps at or claims modes of exercising authority not pursuant to this end, the church fails. If one insists on speaking of the preaching of the gospel as "something similar to conditions," one may, I suppose, do so *as long as* one realizes they are conditions for the communication of the unconditional. Lutherans have preferred rather to speak of them as "means of grace."

What is a preacher? A preacher is one who knows the difference between law and gospel, one who knows the peculiar kind of speaking called gospel speaking, speaking the unconditional promise. The gift has to be given! Such a preacher knows that it is only on account of Christ that such a word can be spoken. The *sola fide* depends on the *solus Christus*. Christ is the end of the law to those of faith. Indeed, Christ is the end of the old, the death of the old being and the beginning of the new. The concrete ministry of the church is indeed necessary, but as a *gospel* ministry it is, so to speak, self-limiting. It places limits on its own claims.

Does such preaching endanger proper regard for creation, human dignity, and freedom? Apparently it has always appeared dangerous to usual views of "catholic substance." The unholy trinity of determinism, antinomianism, and Manicheanism has always dogged the trail of particularly outspoken champions of *justificatio sola fide*. Is another principle needed to prevent such disasters? I think not. For there is a "flip side" to justification by faith alone just in these cases. If we are justified by faith alone, then it would appear that there is nothing wrong with creation other than the loss of faith. This is not to belittle the seriousness of the loss by any means, but it is to indicate that the basic goodness of creation is not questioned but rather protected by the application of the *justificatio sola fide* as the criterion of judgment. To be sure, the goodness of creation is asserted, confessed, and taught by the church. It comes from the Scriptures and the creeds. It is not derived from the article on justification. But the issue here is faith, trust. Where faith and trust is lost, creation is never good enough for us. We are always on the way somewhere else according to some scheme of law

72

or system of being. One thinks in terms of a quite different structure, a structure of "works." Then creation is always questionable. It is merely the "stuff" out of which salvation by works can be fashioned. Superimpose the fall on such a structure and the place of creation becomes even more problematic. One is constantly fighting to preserve at least a bit of created integrity with which one can still "work." One rejects the consequences of the *sola fide* because it seems to threaten this last bit.

The *sola fide* cannot coexist with a structure based on works. A structure based on works implies therefore a quite different thought structure. What has been lost is faith. This is indeed desperately serious. Having lost faith, we are in bondage. Whatever is not of faith is sin. We are in bondage precisely to our schemes of works and all such. We *cannot* get out, not merely because of its impossibility but because we do not will to. We are afflicted not with the determining or forcing of the will but the *bondage* of the will. Only the unconditional promise which creates faith and grants freedom once again can put an end to this slavery and open up the possibility of the new life. But such new life is really the giving back of creation itself. That the world is *created* is after all an item of *faith*, not of natural theology. Faith in God *the creator* is, as Luther said, the summit and consummation of faith, not a premise from which fallen beings somehow *begin*.[14] The problem in the fallen state is precisely that we do not believe in creation or in our own creaturehood. And thus we are under the sway of "law, sin, and death." The *sola fide* is the plumb line also for measuring our trust *vis à vis* creation. Created life itself is given back to faith as the sheer gift it was intended to be.

Nor does this endanger human integrity and freedom. It does indeed take account of the desperate seriousness of the fallen state: It is a state of bondage from which the self can in no way extricate itself. But the gift of faith is the gift of freedom, the giving back of faith in creation itself. The *sola fide establishes* faith in creation and seeks to deliver creation from its bondage. In such a thought structure one moves from bondage to freedom. Where the scheme of "works" becomes determinative, one is always tempted to think in terms of a move from a supposed remaining bit of freedom to bondage, i.e., to this-worldly authorities, schemes of improvement, transformation, and what not. When such schemes determine and norm the church's message and practice, the church falls.

III

It will not be possible to arrive at a happy and satisfying consensus on justification by faith alone as the article by which the church stands or falls until we grapple more directly, frankly, and honestly with these different ways of conceiving the message and practice of the church. We have, I think, come a long way in our dialogues, and I do not wish to discount that. After centuries of acrimony and misunderstanding, we have been able to discover and affirm what we do hold in common. But that should also mean that we have, I hope, also arrived at the point where we can discuss the matters which still seem to divide us quite openly and candidly. We have to ask ourselves now whether the determined pursuit of consensus has not led us to the point where it begins to inhibit rather than promote such genuine dialogue. The attempt to establish consensus by forcing the issue can obscure or cover over differences. That does not bode well for the future. It simply leaves too many unhappy dissenters behind.

In this light I am convinced that we do need to proceed toward discussing "basic differences." The something less than satisfactory outcome of the dialogues on justification impels us in that direction. Once again, this is not the place to attempt full discussion of such differences, but it may be appropriate to make some concluding observations along that line for future reference. There are many ways, no doubt, in which one might get at such basic differences. If justification by faith alone does affect *every* doctrine, then it is likely one will discover some differences in every locus.

One very prominent instance of how basic differences affect thought structure comes to light is in what today has come to be called eschatology. The problems here go way back in the history of the church at least to the days of the Marcionite and Gnostic crisis. Confronted with the threat of dualism, determinism, fatalism, and the like, the "great church" rightly moved to protect the unity of God, the Old and New Testaments, the goodness of creation and the freedom of the creature, and so on. But there has been simply too much persistent complaint throughout history to avoid the judgment that the great church overreacted at the expense of eschatology. In its fight for the integrity of what it believed to be the created order, it became something of the enemy of the new order. Words such as the following are too persistent, I believe, to be ignored.

> When the universal church excluded Marcion as a heretic, it lost for itself the category of the new. As is always the case with the exclusion of heresies, the church became united, but also poorer. Since then, God's revelation has no longer been proclaimed in terms of the claim of the new and of freedom for the future, but it has been proclaimed by the authority of what is old and always true. No longer is the *incipit vita nova* announced,

but instead a *restitutio in integrum*. The lost paradise, of which even the sinner still has a fragmentary memory, is won back through Christ and the church.... The old naturalistic notion of the eternal return of the same...dominates Christian hope.... Thus it is no longer "the new" but "the old" that now becomes the warrant for the truth of Christianity.

With Marcion, Paul also was lost for the church. It was only because she retained Marcion's "New Testament" in the canon that the church stored up for herself her own permanent revolution.[15]

In other words, the price the church paid for overcoming the threat of metaphysical dualism was simply the loss of the eschatological "dualism" of the New Testament. "Catholic substance" began to look more like a synthesis between the old and new ages. In the face of heretical *doctrina*, which was essentially a philosophy of religion, the church developed its own *doctrina*, an antitype, but still something like a philosophy of religion. The word as the bearer of the eschatologically new was lost. The sacraments remained the only instance in which the new could somehow break in upon us, but within the framework of the restitution of the old suffered severe handicap. They could at best be considered rather strange *interruptions* of the old order, authorized and administered by a church and a priesthood specially endowed with the power to do this. In such a scheme the church appears to borrow as much from the power structures of the old age as from those established in Christ and manifest in the new.

From this perspective one could say that it has been the constant struggle of the church to arrive at an appropriate understanding of Christian eschatology and consequently a proper exercise of the church's power. The Reformation was the major epoch in this quest. Justification by faith alone as the article by which the church stands or falls recalls the church to the realization that its true power is simply the power of the gospel, the unconditional promise of the new eschatological kingdom. The doctrine of the church is intended to foster the delivery of such a promise through the preaching of the word and the giving of the sacraments which end the old and begin the new. Doctrine so conceived will bear an unmistakable eschatological stamp in every locus, signaled by the distinction between law and gospel, God hidden and revealed, theology of the cross vs. theology of glory, revelation *sub contrario* in Christ, the *communicatio idomatum, genus maiestaticum*, Christ as the end of the law, the dialectic of bondage and freedom in anthropology, the "two kingdoms," and so on. The very *structure* of the whole is altered. One might say that the house (the content of the faith) is not derived from the plumb line, but the plumb line does indicate where and when the house must be rebuilt lest it fall. Many things are simply dismantled and discarded. The "plumb line" of justification by faith alone imposes an eschatological stamp in every instance to foster a proclamation which creates faith and brings new being. Yet amazingly enough *virtually none of these things* has ever been discussed thoroughly in ecumenical dialogue. Instead, the agenda has for the most part been set in the light of the difficulties which one encounters in attempting to arrive at a "consensus" when one thinks mostly in terms of the old order of things.

There is obviously an agenda for discussion of basic and important differences here. As long as they remain undiscussed, they are bound to continue as a constant source of difficulty and suspicion, and we will not, I think, get any closer to consensus. It is time that we realized this now and got about the business of trying to get at these basic differences. It is my guess and hope that we will arrive at greater understanding if we attempt to do just that.

A ROMAN CATHOLIC RESPONSE

Carl J. Peter

THE ESSAY by Gerhard O. Forde to which I am responding is entitled "Justification by Faith Alone: The Article by which the Church Stands or Falls?" On first hearing it struck me as being a contribution at once both very much to the point of this consultation and eminently worthy of a reply. Subsequent study of the text has reinforced my initial impression.

At times one listens to good music only subsequently to hear it discussed and demeaned with faint praise challenging any grounds for the appreciation that accompanied the original experience. My hope is that my remarks, especially when they are critical, will enhance appreciation of what is a first-rate essay, one of the quality that over the years I have come to expect in Dr. Forde's work.

My reply will involve three points. I shall try to make them successively and briefly.

The first has to do with one particular consensus. Which one? The one that in their statement "Justification by Faith" the members of the Lutheran-Roman Catholic dialogue in the United States explicitly states they have reached.[1] On what precisely did those members, rightly or wrongly, claim to have reached a consensus? The answer to that question will be my first point.

The second will take up a criticism made by Dr. Forde. In his view the results reported by the U.S. Lutheran-Roman Catholic dialogue in its statement "Justification by Faith" were reached after at best scant attention to a very important and relevant theme. And that is the use of justification by faith alone as the article on which the church stands or falls. To this criticism by Dr. Forde I should like to add some recollections of my own and at the same time share a hope for the future.

My final point will take up Dr. Forde's contention that justification by faith alone, precisely as the article on which the church stands or falls, needs no other critical principle. Of this I remain unconvinced despite his impressive elucidation of what he calls the "flip side" of justification by faith alone. Why I am not persuaded to cease and desist in my urging another critical principle I shall try to explain. And there I shall conclude.

Ad primum. Dr. Forde says on page 64 of his text:

> It is obvious first of all that ecumenical discussion about justification has not issued in unanimity about the nature or degree of consensus arrived at. Reactions to the recently completed round on justification in the Lutheran-Roman Catholic dialogue in the USA demonstrate this rather clearly. One must say at least that there appears to be no consensus even on whether or not we have arrived at a consensus![2]

In response let me say I agree it is important to see ourselves as others see us. But along the way it may help to remind others of the way in which we saw ourselves and in which we invited others to know we wished to be seen. To this end it seems appropriate to recall the following passage endorsed by the dialogue in its statement "Justification by Faith."

> A fundamental consensus on the gospel is necessary to give credibility to our previous agreed statements on baptism, on the Eucharist, and on forms of church authority. We believe that we have reached such a consensus.[3]

The term agreed to was *consensus*, indeed *fundamental consensus on the gospel*. And if one wonders what was meant by *gospel* in this context, the answer is given on the previous page.

There the dialogue is speaking of an affirmation it has just made. And of that affirmation it says:

> Where this affirmation is maintained, it is possible to allow great variety in describing salvation and in interpreting God's justifying declaration without destroying unity. There may still be debate over the best way to proclaim or evoke reliance on God's gift of himself in Christ Jesus. The belief that the assurance of salvation and the certainty of hope are to be found (as Thomas Aquinas puts it) "chiefly" (*principaliter*) by looking at God's mercy, not at oneself, does not decide such disputes. But where the affirmation is accepted, Lutherans and Catholics can recognize each other as sharing a commitment to the same gospel of redemptive love received in faith.[4]

By *gospel* the dialogue meant that to which one shows commitment by accepting and maintaining an affirmation. But what affirmation? To that question the dialogue had just provided the answer when it said:

> ...our entire hope of justification and salvation rests on Christ Jesus and on the gospel whereby the good news of God's merciful action in Christ is made known; we do not place our ultimate trust in anything other than God's promise and saving work in Christ.[5]

Of this christological affirmation, whose acceptance shows commitment to the gospel, two important things are said by the dialogue: a) It is not the full equivalent of the Reformation teaching on justification by faith alone;[6] and b) agreement on it raises the question whether the remaining differences on this doctrine need be church dividing.[7]

For my part I have no regrets about a word of that! We very explicitly said we thought we had a consensus on the gospel and indicated clearly what we meant by that. We did not exaggerate and claim that the elements of our christological affirmation (cited above) matched those of justification by faith alone on a one for one basis. But we did assert that our consensus was manifested by what we called "a fundamental affirmation,"[8] one that made us wonder whether remaining unresolved differences about the doctrine of justification by faith alone need be church dividing.

That is what the dialogue said about the consensus it claimed to have achieved. *Scripta manent*; the text will bear this out.

To this, responses have been forthcoming from the Lutheran Church in America and from the Inter-Church Relations Committee of the American Lutheran Church.[9] Personally I welcome both and hope for one from my own church[10] as well as one from the Lutheran Church — Missouri Synod and the Evangelical Lutheran Church in America.

It is my intention to return to these two responses later. But for now let me say this. I read neither as *denying outright* the existence of the consensus that is claimed. However different they may be, each asks for evidence that the alleged consensus exists. What is more, each seems to suggest that certain conditions will have to be fulfilled if that evidence is to be forthcoming. But more on those conditions later!

Ad secundum. The process by which the dialogue reached its conclusion was flawed. The results show it. That is how I read Dr. Forde. In his opinion much more attention should have been given to justification by faith alone as the critical principle used to evaluate preaching, teaching, worship, and witness.

My own recollection is that the members of the dialogue discussed at length the *use* of the gospel that we thought ourselves able to affirm in common. We found at best convergences when the gospel we both accepted was *used* to judge preaching and teaching about justification as forensic or transformative, original sin, free choice, justifying faith in relation to hope and love, merit, and predestination.[11] My point is this. It is a mistake to think that the gospel, or what the dialogue called the fundamental affirmation, on which there was agreement was not applied. Precisely because it *was used* or *applied*, convergences resulted which indicated lack of consensus on the individual themes listed above. But because of the alleged consensus on the gospel, manifested through acceptance of the fundamental christological affirmation, we asked whether the remaining differences on justification by faith alone, inevitably indicated by the convergences, had of themselves to be church divisive. The gospel or fundamental affirmation was applied! But there was genuine disagreement as to the terms appropriate to describe this critical function of either the gospel or justification by faith alone.

On that disagreement Dr. Forde is surely right. To be more specific, the mere mention of hermeneutics seemed to drive some of our colleagues up a tree. But it was not along confessional lines that those on the ground were distinguished from those in the branches. Personal philosophical bend was more decisive!

Of course the process was flawed. Would any one of us have expected it to be otherwise? Each of the participants would, I suspect, have his or her own candidate for what ought to have been otherwise. I surely do. I urged (to the point of trying my colleagues' patience) that the Lutheran members clarify what they mean when they speak of the *unconditionality* of God's promise of forgiveness in Christ Jesus.[12] Would not, I asked repeatedly, the use of *unconditional* without qualification of any kind undermine for many the importance that Lutherans attribute to preaching, sacraments, church, Bible, and faith? The dialogue's statement would in my judgment have been much improved had I been successful in getting into *its* text what Dr. Forde writes so well:

> Precisely to be unconditional the gospel promise must be spoken and delivered "to you." But the church and its preachers will then gain and maintain trust simply in that they deliver this unconditional gospel. . . . If one insists on speaking of the preaching of the gospel as "something similar to conditions," one may, I suppose, do so *as long as* one realizes they are conditions for the communication of the unconditional.[13]

Precisely!

Having expressed this recollection of past processes, I am delighted to have the opportunity to say I hope the dialogue will take up Dr. Forde's agenda as well as those implied in the reactions of the Lutheran Church in America and the Inter-Church Relations Committee of the American Lutheran Church. I cannot say what the outcome might be. But with regard to the concerns expressed in the reactions of the two churches, I should like at this point to make an initial observation. Neither church endorses the dialogue's claim to have reached a consensus with regard to the gospel. Both wish to see the claim tested, hence the agenda of which I spoke. But this, I confess, perplexes me not a little. It looks to me as if both churches in their reactions are saying that the gospel of *unconditional forgiveness* can be acknowledged as being preached and celebrated only if certain *conditions* are seen to be fulfilled.[14] That in turn appears to be at least enigmatic if not inconsistent. And thus you see I have my own reason for wishing that the dialogue would make such matters part of its future agenda.

Ad tertium. In addition to holding that the *use* of justification by faith alone needed more discussion than it received in the dialogue, Dr. Forde contends that there is no need for another critical principle to be used along with it. He states that I have maintained the contrary.[15] In his view I postulate the need of that other critical principle so as to safeguard: a) the trustworthiness of the church according to the divine promise; b) the preservation of at least some degree of freedom and goodness in creation in spite of the fall; and c) the place of grace-wrought acts of charity.[16] He in turn maintains that this safeguarding can be accomplished by paying more attention to the "flip side" of justification by faith alone. What is more, some of those same elements which I propose to safeguard with the new principle are the very ones that the principle of justification by faith alone wishes to subject to more careful critical examination.[17] Therefore in Dr. Forde's view no new principle, call it whatever you like, is needed. The safeguarding can be done without one and positing one keeps justification by faith alone from doing what it is intended to do.

Let me preface my reply to both contentions by thanking Dr. Forde for the care with which he presented my position. He is right; I do regard the use of justification by faith alone as a needed safeguard against abuse and idolatry. Nevertheless, he says no additional principle is needed because the one he celebrates does what I want the other one to do and without the problems the other one causes or occasions. What about this?

Let me repeat it. I admire the way in which Dr. Forde says one ought to go beyond the "strictly formal" use of justification by faith alone as a criterion of judgment or critical principle. He suspects that ". . . constant talk. . . ." of this critical function of justification by faith alone ". . . has led us to operate as though. . . it has, presupposes, and brings no material considerations into the deliberations."[18] He goes on, in my opinion brilliantly, to show how the "flip side" of justification by faith alone brings with it, for example, the goodness of creation.[19] This section of his essay is particularly thought-provoking. My response is that however ingenious this use of the "flip side" of justification by faith alone is, I wonder why Lutherans would find it necessary to derive the goodness of creation in spite of original sin from justification by faith alone. Why would not the First Article of the Creed Lutherans share with other Christians do that? On the other hand, if Lutherans choose to regard the goodness of creation as a material consideration brought along by justification by faith alone, why would other Christians have to do so? The latter might regard the First Article of the Creed as sufficient. Or they might think that a second critical principle does the job more effectively.

As for Dr. Forde's second ground for challenging the need for another critical principle, there may be some misunderstanding here. That second critical principle *in no wise* keeps justification by faith alone from subjecting to a "more careful critical examination" the same elements that second principle is intended to safeguard. Far from it! Indeed I say:

> Have at it. Those elements need criticism conducted in the light of justification by faith alone. But do not expect other Christians to play dead theologically while this is going on. Expect some of us to bring to bear another critical principle to prevent justification by faith alone from making one ". . . so prone to expect sin and abuse. . . " that one ". . . fails to recognize grace where it is at work." Let Lutherans use the "flip side" of justification by faith alone. Other Christians may still say another critical principle is needed as well. Not to fence off a sacrosanct domain (e.g., papacy, purgatory, indulgences, devotion to Mary and the saints, office of bishop) that may not be touched critically by justification by faith alone! But rather to provide explicit and effective recognition of promised grace that may go unnoticed or even be rejected if justification by faith alone functions *in critical exclusivity and isolation.*

In short, Dr. Forde has advanced the discussion notably. But for the reasons given I think another critical principle is needed as well. That principle in my judgment is both catholic and ecumenical. It too commends ultimate hope and trust in God alone as it urges:

Seek in faith to recognize God's grace in Jesus Christ and through the Holy Spirit, grace that because of the divine promise has been at work, is working yet, and will work in the future in individuals and institutions despite sin and abuse.

Notes

GERHARD O. FORDE

1. The official responses of the American Lutheran Church ("A Statement of Response of the Inter-Church Relations Committee of the American Lutheran Church to the Lutheran-Roman Catholic Dialogue on Justification," *The American Lutheran Church Thirteenth General Convention: Reports and Actions: Supplement* [Minneapolis: Office of the General Secretary of the American Lutheran Church, 1986] 827-31), the Lutheran Church in America (adopted by the Lutheran Church in America, 1986 Convention, Milwaukee, Wisconsin. *A Response to Justification by Faith* [New York: Dept. for Ecumenical Relations of the Lutheran Church in America, 1986] 8 pages), unpublished responses from various Lutheran theological faculties, and editorials in *dialog* by Robert Jenson, 23 [1984] 84-85 and Carl Braaten, 23 [1984] 245-46), raise serious questions about the extent of the consensus claimed in the U.S. Lutheran-Roman Catholic dialogue.

2. L-RC 7, 70, #155. The formulation is itself significant. Justification by faith alone has to be "justified" in the light of the *solus Christus*.

3. The LCA Convention's *A Response to Justification by Faith* (n. 1 above); it occurs at the end of section II on "Evaluation." Emphasis added.

4. Eric W. Gritsch and Robert Jenson, *Lutheranism: The Theological Movement and Its Confessional Writings* (Philadelphia: Fortress Press, 1976) 42-43.

5. L-RC 7, 70, #154.

6. Ibid., 72, #157.

7. Ibid., 70, #155.

8. Ibid., 70, #154.

9. Cf. the ALC and LCA Official Responses. The ALC response questions whether the *articulus stantis et cadentis ecclesiae* has been adequately stated and held to. The LCA statement says there appears to be more agreement on the *sola gratia* than on the *sola fide*.

10. Carl J. Peter, "Justification by Faith and the Need of Another Critical Principle," L-RC 7, 304-15.

11. Ibid., 309.

12. Ibid., 311.

13. Ibid., 311-13.

14. "Preface to Sermons on Genesis, " (1527); WA 24:18, 26-33. "*Denn das is one zweiffel der hoechste article des glaubens, darynne wir sprechen: Ich gleube an Gott Vater almechtigen schoepffer des hymels und der erden, Und wilcher das rechtschaffen gleubt, dem is schoen geholffen und is widder zu recht bracht und dahyn komen, da Adam von gefallen ist. Aber wenig sind yhr, die so weit komen, das sie voeliglich gleuben, das er der Gott sey, der all ding schafft und macht, Denn ein solch mensch mus all dingen gestorben seyn, dem guten und boesen, dem tod und leben, der hell und dem hymel und von hertzen bekennen des er aus eygnen krefften nichts vermag.*"

15. Jürgen Moltmann, *Religion, Revolution, and the Future* (tr. M. D. Meeks; New York; Charles Scribner's Sons, 1969) 14-15. Moltmann is of course not the only witness here. One thinks for instance of the great historians of dogma like Harnack, Loofs, Seeberg, or perhaps even the more "heretical" but nevertheless persistent witnesses who in one way or another have complained about the apostasy of the "great church," like Gottfried Arnold, Reimarus, Overbeck, and even down to the present day such interpreters as Schweitzer, Martin Werner, and the like. Many of them saw clearly the eschatological nature of the message of the church even if they were not able to come up with an appropriate or acceptable application of it. And it goes without saying that more current "theologies of hope" also stand witness to this line of thinking.

CARL J. PETER

1. The text appeared first in *Origins* 13 (1983) 277, 279-304. It was reprinted, this time with essays by members of the dialogue, in L-RC 7, 15-74, 316-38.

2. Gerhard O. Forde, "Justification by Faith Alone: The Article on Which the Church Stands or Falls?" above, 67.

3. L-RC 7, 74, #164.

4. Ibid., 73, #159.

5. Ibid., 72, #157.

6. Ibid.

7. Ibid., 16, #4.

8. Ibid., 72, #157.

9. Cf. *A Response to Justification by Faith* (New York: Dept. for Ecumenical Relations on the Lutheran Church in America, 1986) 8 pages; and "A Statement of Response of the Inter-Church Relations Committee of the American Lutheran Church to the Lutheran-Roman Catholic Dialogue on Justification," *The American Lutheran Church Thirteenth General Convention: Reports and Actions: Supplement* (Minneapolis: Office of the General Secretary of the American Lutheran Church, 1986) 827-31.

10. A committee of the National Conference of Catholic Bishops in the United States is presently engaged in such an evaluation. Their theological advisor is Jared Wicks, S.J., professor of theology at the Gregorian University in Rome and by appointment of the Vatican Secretariat for the Promotion of Christian Unity a member of the Lutheran-Catholic Joint Commission.

11. L-RC 7, 71-72, #156.

12. See "Justification by Faith and the Need of Another Critical Principle," L-RC 7, 304-15, 376-78, and especially here 310-14.

13. Forde, "Justification by Faith Alone," 72. Here Forde is referring to Peter, L-RC 7, 311. Emphasis in the text.

14. In its text ("A Statement of Response . . . ," 831) the Inter-Church Relations Committee of the American Lutheran Church asks: "But what happens when justification by faith is applied to purgatory, the papacy, and the cult of the saints (#153)? What happens when the gospel is preached unconditionally (#154)? When it is preached that the law is not a way of salvation? When justification is made the criterion of all church proclamation and practice (#121)? Of teaching on Mary? Of the church's teaching authority in ethics, celibacy, ordaining women, the authority of bishops? Can these teachings be acceptable to Catholics when preached and practiced in accord with justification by

faith?...In conclusion: sufficient clarity concerning the gospel is not present to affirm there is consensus in the gospel." Answers to these questions appear to be conditions that must be fulfilled before one can say responsibly that there is evidence sufficient to attest to consensus in the gospel. The Lutheran Church in America in its general convention approved *A Response to Justification by Faith* (see note 9). In that text one reads on page 6: "Thus this 'fundamental consensus on the gospel' needs to be tested further....Differences over application of this criterion involve issues that divided Lutherans and Roman Catholics during the Reformation (e.g., indulgences, papacy, purgatory). If the consensus on this application cannot be broadened, the consensus on the doctrine of justification will need to be reconsidered. Testing the consensus on the doctrine of justification will reveal the extent to which there is fundamental consensus on the gospel." The consensus claimed to have been reached by the dialogue must be tested. *Unless* (a condition) it leads to a reduction of differences on hitherto disputed issues, another look will have to be taken at the claim itself.

15. Forde, "Justification by Faith Alone," 69. He is correct. I did this not only in the essay referred to above in note 12 but earlier as well in "Justification and the Catholic Principle," *Lutheran Theological Seminary Bulletin* (Feb. 1981) 16-32. This has been reprinted in *Encounters with Luther* (Gettysburg: Lutheran Theologican Seminary; Institute for Luther Studies, 1986) 3:19-35. Recently Avery Dulles, S.J., has written in favor of "the Catholic principle"; cf. *The Catholicity of the Church* (Oxford: Clarendon, 1985) 6-7.

16. Forde, "Justification by Faith Alone," 70.

17. Ibid.

18. Ibid., 71.

19. Ibid., 72-73.

7

Consensus in the Gospel

Ralph A. Bohlmann

I AM PLEASED that this important conference is taking place and delighted to have the opportunity to visit again with the many friends and fellow Lutherans from North America and Europe with whom I have become acquainted during more that twenty years of theological study and inter-church discussions and dialogues as we have participated in the quest for a deeper and closer relationship to each other and to other Christians.

This ongoing ecumenical quest is particularly meaningful this year for us in The Lutheran Church — Missouri Synod as we mark important anniversaries in the life and work of our first president, Dr. C. F. W. Walther. One of his dreams, expressed in 1856, was that free conferences would enable American Lutherans to achieve a "unity of faith and Confession" that would lead to establishment of "one single Evangelical Lutheran Church of America." That dream of "unity of faith and Confession" or "consensus in the gospel," if you prefer, remains a goal that I pray we will all continue to pursue with diligence and patience whether we exist in multiple structures or in a single church body.

There are three supremely important reasons for pursuing that dream with urgency and with relentless vigor. Of prime importance is the sobering fact that approximately three out of every four persons in the world today do not know Jesus Christ as their Lord and Savior. In this world of more than five billion people the evidences of sin and its ugly consequences are overwhelming; everywhere there are war and famine, inhumanity and injustice, fear and oppression, and the tragic bloodshed of the innocent, including even our unborn children. Surely the achievement of greater consensus in the gospel among Christians would strengthen our efforts to bring Jesus Christ and the forgiveness of sins, life, salvation, and eternal hope that he promises to this darkling world.

Another compelling reason is the need to assist our nearly seventy million Lutheran Christians worldwide to achieve a greater understanding and enjoyment of the gospel itself. Statistics from 1982 as well as 1972 provide the most unwelcome information that an alarming percentage of American Lutherans, nearly forty percent, are oriented more toward the law than toward the gospel in their understanding of salvation. In the church of "grace alone" fifty-five percent of Lutheran laymen polled in 1982 (down from fifty-nine percent in 1972) agreed that the main emphasis of the gospel is on God's rules for right living! Is this perhaps the case because we have simply assumed a common understanding of the gospel among us while neglecting to preach and teach it as effectively and forcefully — and purely — as we could and should? And if such statistics give us American Lutherans pause, is it presumptuous to assume that the evidence from our European Lutheran churches, with their often disappointing church attendance and lay involvement, would be any different? Surely the quest for consensus in the gospel is one that must begin and continue close to home — within our own church bodies and congregations!

A third reason is the need for all Lutherans to achieve greater clarity and strength in the confession of our faith before other Christians. Differences within the Lutheran family are well known and deep. Bishop James Crumley of the Lutheran Church in America was surely correct in 1983 when he expressed concern to The Lutheran Church — Missouri Synod about our "diverging courses." For our differences in the areas of doctrine, ecumenical activity, and social-political questions often threaten to obscure what we hold in common. At a time when Lutherans seek to speak with a common voice to non-Lutheran Christians, is it not a tragedy that our structural separateness must bear witness to our diverging courses? Moreover, the pain of our being on divergent courses is made especially acute when we acknowledge, as we must in all candor, not only that we differ on substantive issues but that we even differ on the significance of differing! Nowhere is this more apparent than in our contrary approaches to inter-communion with non-Lutherans, a practice that some understand as underscoring the basic unity of all Christians but which many of us regard as a confusion of our Confessional witness which weakens the pure preaching of the gospel and the right administration of the sacraments.

"Consensus in the gospel" is an apt summary formulation of what all Christians already have as the gift of God's Spirit as well as the continuing goal of our ecumenical efforts. But the very point that "consensus in the gospel" can be thought of as both gift and task (*Gabe und Aufgabe*) illustrates the conceptual ambiguity that inevitably makes our discussion of such questions difficult and sometimes confusing. The key terms in this ongoing discussion, namely, "church," "gospel," and "unity," are all employed in the Lutheran Confessional tradition in narrow and broad senses, and we take little comfort in the fact that our sixteenth century Confessional forebears also had to labor at making proper distinctions and at explaining interrelationships. Close at hand are other considerations like the role of Holy Scripture and the meaning and extent of doctrinal agreement. To summarize basic aspects of these interrelationships from the standpoint of the Lutheran Confessions, I would like to propose six basic principles and then offer some observations and implications.

Basic Principles

1. *The church in the narrow or proper sense is the "assembly of believers"* (CA 7; BC 32). It is "mainly an association of faith and of the Holy Spirit" (Ap 7:5; BC 169) and not merely an "association of outward ties and rites." The great truth that the church is constituted by faith was articulated by Luther and his colleagues in the sixteenth century not only because of the polemical situation of that time, that is, to enable Luther to say in the Smalcald Articles, "We do not concede to the papists that they are the church, for they are not" (3:12:1; BC 315). Much more, this understanding of the church follows from the great apostolic and Reformation truth that we are justified by faith. Just as it is only through faith in Jesus Christ (or, the gospel in the narrow sense) that we become righteous in the sight of God, so the church is simply the totality of those who have such faith. The church is the body of Christ because it has a living relationship with him who is its head. Apart from a living relationship with the head there is no living relationship with other members of the body (Ap 7:5; BC 169). Apart from faith there is no church. What this means dare not be overlooked! It is not our membership in any congregation or denomination that makes us "church." The church properly speaking is the community of all those, and only those, in whom the Holy Spirit has created saving faith in Jesus Christ. It is therefore not coextensive with any denominational structure.

2. *The church is called and recognized by the use of the gospel and sacraments.* The church is GOD's creation. When the gospel is communicated or the sacraments are used, God does miraculous things! The Holy Spirit makes saints out of sinners by creating faith in Jesus Christ. When he creates faith, he places the faithful into a community called the church. The means through which the church is *called* is also

the means by which it is *recognized*. The church exists whenever his means are employed. Thus to find or recognize the church our Confessions urge us to look neither for imposing programs and structures, large and elaborate organizations, denominational labels, nor even for purity of life or excellency of love — important as all of these may be — but rather ask us to look for the pure and right use of the gospel and sacraments.

3. *The church is united spiritually; its unity is given with faith in the gospel.* We confess in the Nicene Creed: I believe in ONE, holy, Christian, and apostolic church. Properly speaking, there are not hundreds of churches in the world, but ONE church. We *are* one with every Christian who lives or has ever lived in this world's space and time. Christian unity is nothing other than the spiritual bond that unites all believers to their Lord Jesus Christ and thereby to each other. *Ubi ecclesia, ibi unitas:* "Where the church is, there is its unity." When the Augsburg Confession states in its Seventh Article: "For the true unity of the church it is enough to agree concerning the teaching of the Gospel and the administration of the sacraments," the Confession is not in the first instance making a programmatic statement about our modern ecumenical problem. (There have been widespread misunderstanding and misuse of this article. Its primary purpose was to state what is necessary for the true church to exist and by implication to affirm that the one, holy, catholic, and apostolic church was also present among Luther's followers.) To quote from the Apology, it is rather describing "true spiritual unity, without which there can be no faith in the heart nor righteousness in the heart before God" (Ap 7:31; BC 174). Unity is there correlated with faith and righteousness, *spiritual* realities rather than empirical objects. Such unity is found where the gospel and sacraments are used purely and rightly, a primarily *qualitative* concern — that is, where the gospel is preached and the sacraments are used without pollution and contamination by subjective additions or subtractions or by legalistic admixtures.

In this connection it may be helpful to distinguish between the unity *of* the church (which all believers *have* with each other) and unity *in* the church (which believers seek). Our Confessional tradition often used the term *concordia* (concord) when referring to the latter and *unitas* (unity) when speaking of the former.

4. *The church in the narrow sense is found only within the church in the broad sense.* The one church of believers and believers only exists within a larger assembly of people including hypocrites and unbelievers who for various reasons are gathered around the word and sacraments together with the true believers. The Confessions call this

assembly the "association of outward ties and rights" (Ap 7:5; BC 169) or the church in the broad sense. The hypocrites and unbelievers are only what the Apology calls "members of the church according to the outward associations of the church's marks" (Ap 7:3; BC 169) or "as far as outward ceremonies are concerned" (Ap 7:12; BC 170). The church in this broad sense, too, is identified by the use of gospel and sacraments carried on in its midst and which continue to retain their divine power and efficacy even when preached and administered by unbelievers. This is not a second church, for there is only one church. But it is the church in the broad sense that is in fact the ordinary identification of the word "church" today.

5. *The external unity of the church in the broad sense is to be based on agreement in the purely taught gospel and the rightly administered sacraments, that is, in "doctrine and in all its articles as well as in the right use of the holy sacraments"* (FC Ep 10:7; BC 493. Emphasis added). While unity is a "given" of the church in the proper sense, it is also a *goal* for the church in the broad sense. The Augsburg Confession was written not only to establish the fact that the one, holy, catholic, and apostolic church was present among Luther's followers, but to help restore an outward unity that had been lost. The Preface of the CA states this purpose very clearly, namely, "to have all of us embrace and adhere to a single, true religion and live together in unity and in one fellowship and church, even as we are all enlisted under one Christ" (CA Preface, 4; BC 25). Such outward unity is dependent on agreement in the gospel and use of the sacraments according to Christ's institution. We are here talking about agreement in the gospel in the broad sense, that is, about doctrine and all its articles. Why is such agreement necessary?

One can answer that question simply by observing that Christians want to be faithful and obedient to their Lord who commanded his church to "obey everything I have commanded you" (Matt 28:19, TEV).

But there is also a "gospel" reason for seeking agreement in doctrine and all its articles. And that is the fact that the gospel in the narrow sense (that is, the "good news" of the life, death, and resurrection of Jesus Christ for our salvation) is integrally related to *all* articles of faith. As our theologians have often said, all doctrines are either antecedent or consequent to the doctrine of justification by grace. The gospel in the narrow sense is central and primary within "doctrine and all its articles," and all articles of faith have a direct or indirect bearing on the gospel in the narrow sense. Because of this relationship the denial or falsification of any article of faith seriously injures the preaching of the gospel according to a pure understanding of it.

It should be noted that the Augsburg Confession in Article 7 calls for a gospel that is *purely* taught and for sacraments that are *rightly* administered (these adverbs were consciously inserted into the manuscript about three weeks before its presentation on June 25, 1530). They not only describe *qualitative* purity, but have *quantitative* significance as well; for the gospel through which the Holy Spirit calls, gathers, and enlightens his church ultimately embraces all articles of faith revealed in Holy Scripture. At Augsburg in 1530, for example, it was the Confession itself, not only its central fourth article on justification, that addressed consensus in the gospel.

In this connection it should be observed that agreement in the gospel in all its articles does *not* mean that "human traditions or rites and ceremonies, instituted by men, should be alike everywhere" (CA 7; BC 32). Uniformity in ceremonies (this word has broad connotations in sixteenth century usage, including matters of polity as well as ritual) may be useful, but ceremonies not ordained by God have no organic connection with the gospel and therefore cannot be criteria for the external unity of the church. But the antithesis in CA 7 is between the *divine* gospel and *human* ceremonies, and not between the gospel and "other" doctrines of Holy Scripture.

6. *Only such external unity as preserves and employs the means of grace in their essential purity serves the true unity, preservation, and extension of the church.* The Holy Spirit builds the church through the gospel and sacraments. Believing, teaching, and confessing the gospel according to Holy Scripture becomes the one essential task of the church and the one God-given means for seeking and finding true Christian unity. In other words, the primary mission of the church can be described as the faithful use of the means of grace. External unity in the church is not an end in itself but serves the primary task of the church. *Concordia* (that is, concord, external unity, or unity *in* the church) is intended to deepen and extend *unitas* (that is, true spiritual unity, or the unity *of* the church), and this is done only when the gospel and sacraments are faithfully preserved and consistently employed. Therefore we cannot automatically assume that the formation of denominations, organizational mergers, participation in church federations, or even ecclesiastical declarations of altar and pulpit fellowship in themselves advance the cause of true Christian unity, for the decisive criterion remains whether such actions advance and are faithful to the gospel. According to this criterion not every separation of Christians from other Christians is to be condemned (however much it is deplored), for God himself commands separation from all alliances that persistently falsify his gospel or tolerate such falsification.

To summarize: The church in the narrow sense, which consists of believers in Jesus Christ, is united spiritually by its common faith in the gospel in the narrow sense, but exists within the church in the broad sense so that external unity is to be based on agreement in the gospel in the broad sense. The gospel in the narrow sense is related to all aspects of the gospel in the broad sense and is the means by which the Holy Spirit creates and extends the church. The church is constituted by and committed to the pure teaching of the gospel and the right administration of the sacraments.

Some Implications and Observations

If we are to be instructed by the confessional understanding of the inter-relationship of gospel, church, and unity, it is imperative that we appropriate the Confessional understanding of the church as the assembly of believers rather than the all too common misunderstanding of the church that defines it primarily if not exclusively in sociological and empirical terms. When the latter happens, it is almost inevitable that denominational fellowship or organizational consolidation will be equated with Christian unity. Such thinking appears to have either forgotten or rejected the central importance of the spiritual unity of the church on the basis of its common faith in Jesus Christ.

The fact that the church consists of true believers, and believers only, has strong implications for our ecumenical efforts today. According to the Apology knowing that the church consists only of believers who enjoy the gifts promised by Christ is a great comfort against despair when we see "the infinite dangers that threaten the church with ruin" (Ap 7:9; BC 169). Moreover: "If we were to define the church as only an outward organization embracing both the good and the wicked, then men would not understand that the kingdom of Christ is the righteousness of the heart and the gift of the Holy Spirit but would think of it as only the outward observance of certain devotions and rituals" (Ap 7:13; BC 170). In other words, misunderstanding the church may involve a misunderstanding of the gospel itself. Likewise, because the real nature of the church's unity is spiritual, the merging or consolidation of ecclesiastical structures cannot in and of itself be regarded as the primary goal of ecumenical endeavor, however desirable it may be for other reasons.

By emphasizing that the church is the assembly of believers and that its reality is spiritual, the Augsburg Confession and its Apology link the church directly with the means that the Holy Spirit employs to create and sustain the church, namely, the gospel and the sacraments. The justification of the sinner takes place "only through the Word," for "one cannot deal with God or grasp Him except through the Word" (Ap 4:67; BC 116).

Because of the organic interrelationship between the Gospel and all of its articles, the "preaching of the Gospel according to a pure understanding of it" (CA 7; BC 32) is greatly impaired whenever any article of faith is either falsified or denied. This is underscored by the two important adverbs, *pure* and *recte*, as modifiers of our use of gospel and sacraments. There is no doubt in the minds of the Lutheran Confessors of the sixteenth century how the church determines what is pure and right in its use of the means of grace. That norm is Holy Scripture, described and employed throughout the Lutheran Confessional writings as the pure, truthful, and infallible word of God and the rule and norm for all teaching and teachers in the church. Any attempt to determine the content and extent of the gospel or the meaning and purpose of the sacraments apart from Holy Scripture merits Confessional rejection as "enthusiasm." Contemporary Lutherans guided by their Confessional norms can hardly talk about consensus in the gospel apart from the recognition of the unique authority of the Scriptures for the faith and life of the church under the gospel.

Although this is not the place to articulate a full-blown exposition of the Confessional understanding of the nature and authority of Holy Scripture, it is important to underscore the fact that the Confessional emphasis on the christological content and the soteriological purpose of Holy Scripture is closely linked to the understanding and acceptance of Holy Scripture as God's own authoritative and infallible speech not only to his people centuries ago but to his people today. The Scriptures are *Deus loquens* (God speaking) as well as *Deus locutus* (God has spoken).

An indissoluble connection exists between the *sola scriptura* and *solus Christus* principles. The former ultimately has meaning only in the unfolding of Scriptures christological content for its soteriological purpose, while the latter has its validity only from the Scriptures authored by God and used by him in various forms to bring people to faith in Jesus Christ. The church confesses the Christ of *Scripture* even as the church grounds its theology on the Scripture testifying to *Christ*. Biblical authority and infallibility are linked with theology and proclamation rather than directly with faith itself.

Some Christians argue for a very high view of Scripture and assert its infallibility and authority simply on the basis of the obedience and reverence man owes God as the author of Holy Scripture. Such an emphasis is surely true as far as it goes, and it can even serve to remind the church that every trifling with or departure from the word of God is an act of pride and rebellion against God himself. But this view of biblical authority often stops short and fails to capture the gospel understanding of biblical authority so keenly perceived and articulated in the Lutheran Confessional writings.

Lutherans do not regard the Scriptures merely as a storehouse of divine information, but rather see the preeminent function of the Scriptures as God's unique instrument for the work of the Holy Spirit in bringing people to salvation both by providing the content of the means of grace and by serving as the norm for the church's life-giving use of word and sacraments. As CA 7 reminds us, it is through the "pure" preaching of the gospel and the "right" administration of the sacraments that the Holy Spirit creates and sustains saving faith in Jesus Christ, the faith which is of the very essence of the church and its unity. An impure or erroneous preaching of the gospel and administration of the sacraments deprives the church of God's very life-giving power. In Confessional Lutheranism Holy Scripture is esteemed as God's way of helping to keep the church's proclamation pure and its sacramental administration right.

The determination of what is pure or right is made by Holy Scripture, not merely by individualistic or corporate decision. To be sure, recognition of the divine authority of Holy Scripture is a fruit of our faith in the gospel of Jesus Christ; but the *biblical* content of the gospel we preach and administer is in turn our assurance that our gospel message comes from *God* and therefore expresses *his* will and possesses *his* power. Whatever is faithful to the message of Holy Scripture serves the gospel, and whatever opposes Holy Scripture threatens the gospel. In this view advocates of a fallible Bible or a Bible over which the interpreter sits in critical judgment not only dishonor God as the author of Scripture, but call into question the very means he has given to keep our use of his life-giving instruments pure and right. Far from making Holy Scripture an object of saving faith (as some critics mistakenly charge), this Confessional position professes a high view of Holy Scripture simply in order to allow it to carry out its God-intended servant role on behalf of the gospel and the sacraments.

Let us understand, then, that the Confessional *locus* of biblical authority is to be found neither in the doctrine of the sovereignty of God nor in the doctrine of saving faith and its object, but in the recognition that our sovereign God has graciously given us the Scriptures in order to preserve his church from the subjectivism and enthusiasm which would destroy the purity and rectitude of our use of the gospel and sacraments, through which he creates and preserves saving faith in Jesus Christ.

Whenever the church substitutes its own ideas (even under the presumption that it is being guided by the Holy Spirit) or appeals to its own intuitive reading of the times or devises its "gospel" on the basis of its own understanding of a particular situation or time or treats the gospel of Jesus Christ as though it were a free-floating idea rather than what we learn it to be from the Scriptures or claims to find the meaning of the gospel above, beyond, or behind the clear text of Scripture, in *all* such cases the church has ceased to be *under* the Scriptures of God and has fallen victim to "enthusiasm." We need to be reminded that subjective human ideas, like human works, may well endanger the gospel itself.

From all that has been said about the proper relationship between Scripture, gospel, and church, it is readily apparent why the church under Scripture is concerned about "doctrine" and why our Confessions, hymns, prayers, and ecclesiastical literature are filled with references to "pure doctrine." Scripture itself exhorts us in many ways and throughout both Old and New Testaments to hold fast to good, sound, pure, and right doctrine, and, conversely, to oppose, resist, and avoid false doctrines and false teachers. "Doctrine" is not some third entity in addition to "gospel" and "Scripture" to which church is related; it is rather the scriptural articulation of the gospel in all its articles. "Doctrines" are organically related to the "doctrine" of the gospel. Indeed, one can find virtually all of Christian doctrine from creation to eschatology expressed or implied in such a "simple" expression of the gospel as John 3:16! In this view "consensus in the gospel" and "doctrinal agreement" are the same thing!

With this gospel understanding of "pure doctrine" it is not surprising that our Lutheran Confessions exhibit great concern for the intrusion of false doctrine into the church. Let us not forget that the Reformation itself was a struggle on behalf of the gospel of Jesus Christ in opposition to every perceived falsification of it, whether Roman Catholic, Reformed, Anabaptist, fanatical, or intra-Lutheran. The Lutheran Confessors are content not only to set forth the true doctrine, but to reject every kind of error, both ancient and modern. The antitheses and condemnations of our Lutheran Confessions are very much a part of the Confessional principle of Lutheranism. The authors of the Formula of Concord explain:

> We wanted to set forth and explain our faith and confession unequivocally, clearly, and distinctly in theses and antitheses, opposing the true doctrine to the false doctrine, so that the foundation of divine truth might be made apparent in every article and that every incorrect, dubious,

suspicious, and condemned doctrine might be exposed, no matter where or in what books it might be found or who may have said it or supported it. (FC SD, Rule and Norm, 19; BC 507).

The condemnation of error is not an act of ecclesiastical self-righteousness, but rather stems from the realization that error distorts the gospel, divides the church, and endangers God's people. Like impure milk, it neither gives nor sustains life. For that reason the Formula of Concord asserts that "the opinions of the erring party cannot be tolerated in the church of God, much less be excused and defended" (FC SD, Rule and Norm, 19; BC 507).

With this gospel approach to the understanding and condemnation of false doctrine, it goes without saying that our Lutheran Confessions oppose both a minimalistic and a pluralistic approach to relationships with erring Christians. Such approaches to doctrine and life in the church fail to take seriously the destructive potential of error and often reflect an indifferentism to revealed doctrine that dishonors God's word, weakens the gospel that sustains the church and its true unity, offends brethren, and ultimately promotes the external disunity of the churches. In spite of the fact that such approaches may well be a reaction against the intolerance and lovelessness that have all too often characterized us Christians in our relationship to each other, their end result is that no word of warning is sounded to those who may believe the error and jeopardize their relationship to God. How then can it be proper or helpful simply to drop the condemnations of the Reformation, as was done, for example, by the Leuenberg Agreement of 1973? Because Confessional theses and antitheses condition, support, and explain each other, it must be asked whether the elimination of the antitheses does not also lose the theses and thereby change the Confession itself.

Although the Confessional concern about false doctrine is clear and forthright, it should also be noted that our Confessional writings place limits on their condemnations and exhibit a great deal of pastoral concern for those who err. Our Confessions urge us to "make a sharp distinction between needless and unprofitable contentions (which, since they destroy rather than edify, should never be allowed to disturb the church) and necessary controversy (dissension concerning articles of the creed or the chief parts of our Christian doctrine, when the contrary error must be refuted in order to preserve the truth)" (FC SD, Rule and Norm, 15; BC 506-7). Nor should any church condemn another for the sake of "ceremonies not commanded by God" (FC Ep 10:7; BC 493). In the condemnations there are no names of persons and no titles of books. Nor are the condemnations directed against "those persons who err ingenuously and who do not blaspheme the truth of the divine Word" (Preface; BC 11). Nor do the Confessions direct their polemic against "entire churches inside or outside the Holy Empire of the German nation" in which one can find many pious and innocent people (Preface; BC 11). It is the responsibility of theologians and pastors, says the Preface to the *Book of Concord*, "Duly to remind even those who err ingenuously and ignorantly of the danger to their souls and to warn them against it, lest one blind person let himself be misled by another." Condemning errors is not to give occasion for any "persecution of poor, oppressed Christians" with whom "Christian charity causes us to have special sympathy" (Preface; BC 12). Clearly, our Confessions know the distinction between "heresy" and "error." All churches and individuals are subject to error, but not all errors amount to heresy, for the latter is the persistent insistence upon error in the doctrine of the gospel in spite of the instruction and admonition of the brethren.

The Confessional concentration on the gospel and sacraments, proclaimed and used on the basis of the Scriptures and for the sake of the church and its unity, is not only a priceless legacy, but an enduring contribution to our understanding of "consensus in the gospel" as both gift and task. This concept of "consensus in the gospel," far more than any worldwide ecclesial structure or *communio* of churches, remains the true heart and center of the Lutheran church.

Conclusion

In the New Testament the church not only learns who it is but hears the Lord of the church, exhorting it to proclaim and preserve his *truth*, that is, the pure doctrine of the gospel in all its parts; to maintain the *unity* of the Spirit and the bond of peace; and to show *love* toward all as we carry out the *mission* of Christ to disciple the nations. As we reflect on our ecumenical principles and practice in the pursuit of stronger and deeper relationships among all Christians, it may prove helpful for us to keep these principles firmly in mind: truth, unity, love, and mission. The manner in which Christian groups emphasize one or more of these principles and relate them to each other often provides the rationale for their ecumenical endeavors. Some Christian groups and perhaps we ourselves sometimes act as though there were no other principle involved than the truth principle. Others appear to emphasize that the only way to unity is through love, perhaps even suggesting that "love unites, doctrine divides." At times some Christians appear to be quite indifferent toward the great truth imperatives of the New Testament. For many others the unity principle, frequently understood in a superficial or purely sociological manner, is evidently regarded as the chief criterion for ecumenical practice, if not the primary concern of the church. Still others in their commendable zeal to carry out Christ's evangelistic mission for the church sometimes seem to pass quickly over all other principles. But how then do we relate truth, love, and unity to each other as we carry out Christ's mission?

Our Lutheran Confessional heritage makes it quite clear that none of these great principles is to be omitted in the ecumenical activity and concern of Christian brothers and sisters. But our biblical and Confessional heritage also reminds us that the truth principle is central, for it is through the proclamation and administration of God's gospel truth in word and sacraments that ecclesiastical unity is created and nurtured. Moreover, it is through the Holy Spirit's working through the same gospel truth of God in word and sacraments that Christians are enabled and empowered to manifest love toward God, toward each other, and toward the world for which he gave his Son. To be sure, true Christian love is never in conflict with the truth, for love rejoices in the truth. But Christian ecumenical action must recognize and express the priority and basic nature of the truth of the gospel, both in the bestowal of unity and in the activity of Christian love. To be sure, given the complexities of our modern day and the intricacies of ecclesiastical life, it goes without saying that the application of these broad New Testament principles to our situation is seldom easy, particularly when our concern for God's truth appears to be in conflict with our desire to express love and unity for sisters and brothers in Christ. Our ecumenical activities therefore require our mutual prayer, humility, and charity. Contention for the faith once delivered to the saints does not justify sin against either love or unity any more than the pursuit of unity justifies the disregard of either truth or love.

Let us then rejoice in everything that advances the cause of the gospel of Jesus Christ, while sorrowing over everything that shames his name or causes doubts about his truth that alone brings eternal salvation, wherever in Christendom this may occur. For our consensus in the gospel, no matter how inadequately or imperfectly we may understand, express, or pursue it, remains a precious gift from the Lord of the church, who daily forgives our failures to love one another, to manifest our unity in his Son, and to confess his truth before the nations without weakness or compromise.

John Travis

DR. RALPH BOHLMANN, president of The Lutheran Church — Missouri Synod, has presented a strong confessional statement of Lutheranism in his essay, "Consensus in the Gospel." If one is to appreciate such a 'defense of the faith,' one must understand also the context within which it is set. It would not be an exaggeration to claim that the speaker is reacting to a unionist effort within the Lutheran Confessional family in the United States whose new identity is founded less on dogmatic agreement and more on structural uniformity. His remarks that "our Confessions urge us to look neither for imposing programs and structures, large and elaborate organizations, denominational labels" or "legalistic admixtures" bears this claim out (p. 89).

If Dr. Bohlmann's concern for any deviation from the purity and rightness of faith is justified for reasons that he as a Lutheran is aware of, the Orthodox must also voice concern, as they speak within their own ecclesiological self-understanding, of what lies ahead for the new Evangelical Lutheran Church in America. I suspect that Dr. Bohlmann is intentionally signaling in his essay a negative reaction to structural representational models of the new church as patterned after the 'secular' forms of our American legislative processes which are a betrayal of the strong theological tradition of historical Lutheranism. Then who can blame the Orthodox for insisting on asking key questions of their Lutheran sisters and brothers which have a *direct* bearing on the unity/diversity principle of ecclesiological *koinonia:* namely, where does the authority within the principle of 'representational' democracy lie; what is the meaning of ordination; of commissioning; how are 'commissioned' ministers to be regarded in relation to 'ordained' ministers and the laity ("baptized ministers")? — to name only a few.[1]

If theological dialogue is to be something more than academic diatribe but instead intimately connected with the spirituality of the practicing faith community, then the way these ecclesiological questions are to be addressed in the life experience of the Evangelical Lutheran Church in America will have a direct bearing on the continuing North American dialogical efforts between Lutherans and Orthodox. We must be prayerfully vigilant and see.

Perhaps the strength of Dr. Bohlmann's paper, as a statement of the Lutheran Confessional heritage with its emphasis on proclamation and mission "through God's gospel truth in word and sacraments" (p. 98), lies in reminding U.S. Lutheranism on the eve of this new 'unionism' that it keep steadfast to its Confessional identity as its early history has experienced.

The question is whether such a statement, which at its best enthusiastically exhorts Confessional identity, excludes at the same time an ecumenical outreach: namely, finding ways to learn to grow together in the 'fulness' of the faith. Herein lies the fundamental weakness of Dr. Bohlmann's position: it does not give the partners in dialogue that leverage needed to grow in agreement, much less to work toward *koinonia*. Growth at this level produces possibilities which in turn have a "transfigured charismatic" potential, directed to the fulness of the apostolic faith embodied in a fully ecclesial life.[2]

I would like then to recast Dr. Bohlmann's concerns under two headings: revelation and human experience, and Scripture and the church, in order to suggest two 'ecumenical' possibilities.

1. Revelation and human experience. It is not Scripture which is being preached, but Christ himself who is *in* the world. Is not the gospel message to be understood as a relationship between divine revelation (the content of the gospel message) *within* the world (human experience)? If this relationship is granted, then human experience is not simply affirmation or denial of faith (functional theology), but something deeper and broader: it is human experience of divine revelation. For the Orthodox tradition with its emphasis on Logos theology, a participatory theology, this experience entails sharing the same experience with others and communicating *personally* (and not individually) with Christ.[3]

I cannot find this ecclesial character of experience of divine revelation in Dr. Bohlmann's paper and, of course, the work of the Holy Spirit which alerts against individualism and rational one-sidedness. Moreover, I see a bifurcation between revelation and human experience, as if the gospel is set against the world as another system of propositions *about* the world.

I suggest this ecumenical possibility: Can that ecclesial participatory element of the 'Logos theology,' which professes Christ not only as the head of the church but as the 'cosmic' Christ in the world, be connected to Luther's evangelical witness to the primacy of God's initiative in human development? In other words, can we begin to find common ground between a 'theology of facts,' namely a history of salvation which entails the personal, the ecclesial, and the cosmic *koinonia*, with a theology of redemptive experience, thus addressing both to lived religious experience?

This theological reorientation propels us, I think, out of Dr. Bohlmann's restrictive and 'Nestorianizing' Christology as confined only to scriptural evidence and acknowledges "the world-universal-catholic dimension of Christ's event as operating for the whole of humankind, intentionally and potentially saved, by virtue of the incarnation, cross, and resurrection."[4]

2. Scripture and the church. I am unable to follow Dr. Bohlmann's argument concerning the Confessional understanding of the inter-relationship of gospel, church, and unity (p. 88). If the lowercase letter 'c' in the word church indicates Dr. Bohlmann's understanding of the church as being derivative, his description of church unity in terms of 'narrow sense', 'broad sense', 'external unity' are alarmingly vague, as if unity is an afterthought on the nature of *ekklesia*. What is more perplexing is the description of the church as merely "an assembly of believers." Where is the 'whole' Christ in the midst of his 'whole' church? Can this entity which he describes have anything to do with the un-broken continuity, namely, a faithfulness to all that has been transmit-ted by Christ to the apostles and through the church to all of us through the ages? Without believing the church, no Confession of faith in the divine revelation is possible. Faith in the historical person of Jesus as the Christ of God is ecclesial in nature.

Dr. Bohlmann resurrects the issue of authority on the side of *sola scrip-tura* (p. 93). Such a conceptual structure of authority is inconceivable for the Orthodox. The criterion rests with tradition, not as something external but as the apostolic teaching, the *regula fidei* transmitted from Father to Father. The scheme which Saint Athanasius presented in his letter to Bishop Serapion is instructive: The Lord gave *(edoken)*; the Apostles preached *(ekeryxan)*; and the Fathers preserved *(ephylaxan)*. Tradition *(paradosis)*, teaching *(didaskalia)*, and faith *(pistis)*, then, are the constitutive elements of the unity and solidarity of tradition. It is the catholic interpretation of Scripture which the church offers.[5]

Let me suggest this 'ecumenical' possibility in the context of our pres-ent dialogical thinking. How can the church, whose responsibility is to proclaim the word of God, i.e., to make the teachings more explicit and relevant and to transmit in order to give witness, be one with the determinative of biblical exegesis, namely, the context of the living apostolic tradition? To state it in another way: How can the proclamation of the word, understood not as a fixed core of propositions but rather as insight into the meaning and impact of the revelatory events, reflect that living context, that comprehensive perspective called tradition, in which the only 'true' intention and total design of divine revelation itself can be grasped?[6]

This ecumenical possibility concerning Scripture and the church overcomes a historically unfortunate polarization of Scripture and tradition which had precluded any internal harmony or consistency between the two.[7]

It would be relevant here to highlight a few reorientations emerging within the North American Orthodox-Lutheran dialogue as they apply to the two ecumenical possibilities already suggested. I leave their assessment unanswered inasmuch as the dialogical process, still in its infancy, has not as yet produced any agreed statement.

There are two reorientations surfacing among the Lutherans which have to do with scriptural exegesis and the patristic inheritance. Concerning scriptural exegesis, Lutherans are beginning to realize that a straight exegetical process cannot solve all the problems. I make reference to *Mary in the New Testament: A Collaborative Assessment by Protestant and Roman Catholic Scholars*: "The task force agreed that the question of the historicity of the virginal conception could not be settled by historical-critical exegesis, and that one's attitude towards church tradition on the matter would probably be the decisive force in determining one's view whether the virginal conception is a *theologoumenon* or a literal fact."[8] Since Mariology has not yet been discussed in the Orthodox-Lutheran dialogue in North America, I cannot add to this statement. It will be interesting, though, to see whether the original understanding of justification by faith finds its application in Mariology. It will be even more timely to discover within this dialogue to what extent a denial of synergy derives from a defective anthropology, even more so from a monotheletite Christology.

As to the patristic inheritance, Lutherans are realizing that the limitations of historical criticism force a return to the *history* of interpretation. A patristic renewal has been noted to have taken place recently in Lutheran American seminaries, followed by an affirmation among Lutherans that the Fathers are an inheritance shared also by them, not only by the Orthodox.

If these reorientations appear to be fragile breakthroughs on the part of the Lutherans, they also are significant and must be regarded as important steps for the future of the dialogue. The same can be said about the Orthodox.

There is a heightened appreciation among the Orthodox that Lutheranism is not a rigid and fixed theology; it has receptivity, especially in liturgical renewal, less in the doctrinal context of tradition. The difficulty, however, rests within Lutheranism's own self-identity; liturgically the Lutherans are not Protestants, but historically they are Protestants. Where does the continuity lie? In the liturgy or in the Confessions or in both?

The difficulty is compounded by a historically conditioned methodology of doing theology. Built into the methodology of the Lutherans is a polemic which seeks to argue defensively and apologetically, namely, that they are not innovators seeking to establish a new church, but rather 'evangelical catholics' attempting to restore the church to its apostolic purity. For the Orthodox it is not a question of the restoration of that unity as much as a preservation of the oneness of the common faith. What cannot be abandoned is the substance of the existing truth or doctrine. But this also means that under the guidance of the Holy Spirit the Orthodox Church accepts new answers to emerging issues in the life of the church provided they express the same truths and are in continuity with the apostolic faith. Such a process is well known in its synodal history.[9]

I would like to end my response by thanking Dr. Bohlmann for his paper, which offered much food for thought in the emerging dialogue among us. As those reorientations in the North American Orthodox-Lutheran dialogue become more experientially rooted within those ecumenical possibilities, I should hope that our 'doing theology' will seek a methodology which becomes a discriminate witness to the church's lived experience and a conviction that one and the same Spirit guides our renewed and transfigured life.

Notes

JOHN TRAVIS
   1. See *Report and Recommendations of the Commission for a New Lutheran Church* (Minneapolis: ELCA, 1986).
   2. See *Report of a Consultation of Eastern and Oriental Theologians,*

Crete 1975 in *Orthodox Contributions to Nairobi,* WCC (Geneva: WCC, 1975) 25-33.

3. I am indebted here to N. Nissiotis, "An Orthodox Contribution to Consensus," *Consensus in Theology? A Dialogue with Hans Küng and Edward Schillebeeckx* (ed. L. Swidler; Philadelphia: Westminster, 1980), esp. 101-3.

4. Ibid., 103.

5. See G. Florovsky, "The Function of Tradition in the Ancient Church," *Collected Works of Georges Florovsky* (Belmont, MA: Nordland, 1972) 1:83.

6. Ibid., 79-80.

7. Refer to the 1574-82 correspondence between Patriarch Jeremias II and the Tübingen Lutherans.

8. R. Brown et al., (eds.), (Philadelphia: Fortress, 1978) 291-92.

9. Emilianos Timiadis, "Strengths and Weaknesses of Theological Dialogues," *Les Dialogues Oecuméniques Hier et Aujourd'hui* (Chambésy-Geneva: Éditions du Centre du Patriarcat Oecuménique, 1985) 396.

8

Fundamental Consensus and Church Fellowship

A Lutheran Perspective

Harding Meyer

The Problem

EVERY PERIOD has its typical keywords, its verbal symbols descriptive of its distinctiveness which it parades before it to demonstrate its dominant concerns. Other periods will have other verbal symbols.

Applying this to the ecumenical movement of recent decades, I would say that the main verbal symbol in the 1960s was undoubtedly the word "dialogue." This word was suddenly on everyone's lips, exercising a powerful fascination far beyond ecumenical circles. It was encountered as a key concept in countless church statements, was the theme of ecumenical pronouncements and theological consultations, and constituted the central focus of a whole library of publications.

Today in the 1980s another concept has become the ecumenical keyword: the term "reception." We find the same thing happening in the case of the term "reception" as we found in the case of the term "dialogue" in the sixties: ecumenical pronouncements, church statements, theological consultations, and a plethora of publications focused on this theme.

The question naturally arises: What came between these two themes? What was the key term in the 1970s? As might logically be expected and was in fact the case, the focus in the seventies was on the result of "dialogue" and the object of "reception," namely, on the "consensus" aimed at in the dialogue and due to be received in the reception process.

However, in spite of the fact that the consensus to be reached and formulated was the nub of all our endeavors at that time, the actual idea or notion of "consensus" did not itself receive anything like the attention and study given earlier to the notion of "dialogue" or at present to that of "reception." The general impression may have been that what constituted "consensus" was quite obvious and required no special attention, a mistaken impression in many respects and one with serious consequences. For this lack of a clear idea of the meaning of consensus in the context of ecumenical effort becomes painfully evident at the very latest when we come to the question of receiving the agreements reached. We then realize that the agreements or consensuses presented for reception do not at all match the generally accepted idea of "consensus" or "agreement."

This is why we are repeatedly confronted in the present reception process with such questions as the following: Are the dialogue results proposed for reception really "consensuses" in the true meaning of the term? Or are they not just immature forms of consensus still awaiting the transition to "genuine" consensus? Are we not dealing here with nothing more than "convergences" falling short of "full" consensus? Are we not still in the realm of provisional and even superficial agreements which leave still unfathomed and yet unsolved the real depths of Confessional differences and church divisions?

There are many reasons therefore why it is urgent for us to achieve clarity and agreement as to the real meaning of "ecumenical consensus" and as to the nature and extent of the consensus needed for unity. For from the standpoint of all of us here and not just of the Lutherans among us, it is presumably a creedal matter and not just a question of ecumenical method and convenience to affirm that church fellowship can be achieved and maintained only where consensus exists concerning the message of Christ attested by the apostles.

This is what is required by the Augsburg Confession in its seventh article, so cherished by Lutherans. It notes, so to speak, a "consensus about the consensus," affirming that there is an agreement among the churches of the Lutheran Reformation concerning the necessity of a consensus in the pure understanding of the gospel and its corresponding proclamation in word and sacrament as prerequisite for church fellowship. Therefore the interconfessional dialogues conducted by the Lutheran churches are regarded by them primarily as "doctrinal dialogues," i.e., as a means to arrive at this consensus in the Christian truth.

From this angle to say that "in ecumenical terminology, consensus in the sense of agreement in practical questions. . . has the final word" and that "the step towards doctrine. . . is hardly taken"[1] is either a fatal objection or else a crude distortion.

Focusing the Limits of Ecumenical Consensus

It has often been pointed out in Lutheranism that the Lutheran Confessional writings, while definitely demanding theological consensus as the condition and basis of unity, at the same time and no less definitely and explicitly reject the notion and ideal of a total or maximal consensus.

I refer, of course, to the well-known *"satis est"* clause of Article 7 of the *Confessio Augustana*, the full text of which reads as follows:

> It is sufficient for the true unity of the Christian Church that the Gospel be preached in conformity with a pure understanding of it and that the sacraments be administered in accordance with the divine Word. *(Et ad veram unitatem ecclesiae satis est consentire de doctrina evangelii et de administratione sacramentorum.)*

This is then underlined and given greater precision by the next statement:

> It is not necessary for the true unity of the Christian church that ceremonies instituted by men should be observed uniformly in all places. *(Nec necesse est ubique similes esse traditiones humanae seu ritus aut cerimonias ab hominibus institutas.)*

In spite of certain problems of interpretation we are agreed, I think, as to the twofold intention of the statement:

a) Reinforced and elucidated by the *"nec necesse est"* affirmation, the *"satis est"* statement is meant to emphasize, out of the total wealth of church life and church data, that which is central, fundamental, or essential for the church and to confine or, better still, to focus the consensus required for unity on these central, fundamental, or essential elements or aspects.

b) That which requires consensus is identical to that which, according to Reformation convictions, makes the church the church: namely, the divine gospel rightly understood and proclaimed in word and sacrament and not that which has come into existence in the church by human or historical developments.

I realize that a series of questions arise at this point which are not only put to but also discussed among Lutherans. However, these critical questions do not deal with (or at least very seldom) *whether* or not a focusing of the consensus required for unity is legitimate. They rather deal with the scope of what is included or excluded and whether this is correctly defined or not.[2] The fact *that* there can and must be a focusing of the consensus required for unity seems hardly challenged at all.[3]

When one examines Lutheran commentaries on these affirmations of the Augsburg Confession, one not infrequently gets the impression that the idea of defining the limits of or focusing the consensus required for unity and consequently the rejection of a total or maximal consensus is a distinctive Lutheran view and a specifically Lutheran contribution to ecumenical thinking. One of the important questions for our present consultation is whether other church traditions are not also quite familiar with an analogous view, so that the idea of a delimitation or focusing of the consensus required for unity and the hesitancy over the notion and ideal of a total or maximal consensus would be, as it were, a common heritage of our different churches, one which would need to be exploited in our ecumenical efforts far more deliberately than has been the case hitherto.

Without wishing in any way to preempt the findings of this consultation, I venture to doubt the existence of some sort of Lutheran copyright for this position,[4] although it seems to be given special emphasis in the Lutheran tradition.

This is true also of Luther himself, as can be seen, for example, from his preface to the Bohemian *"Confessio fidei,"* where he makes the distinction between, on the one hand, rites, ceremonies, and statutes which, by virtue of "human, geographical, historical differences," cannot be "uniform and the same" and, on the other hand, the "doctrine of faith and morals" which "should always and everywhere be the same."[5] Such a distinction also influences the structure of the doctrinal system, as is evident from the division of certain Lutheran Confessional documents into — putting it bluntly — important and less important articles.[6]

What are the reasons or motives for this differentiation and along with this the focusing of the consensus required for unity and the rejection of a total or maximal consensus?

The keywords "unity" and "peace" appear[7] and thus indicate an "ecumenical" concern in the sense that the unity of the church is protected and not sacrificed to the conflict over secondary matters and trivialities. But this ecumenical concern is very closely connected with the basic theological or soteriological concern of the Reformation and, in the final analysis, subordinated to it, i.e., the emphasis on the gospel of the gracious acceptance of the human being as articulated by the Reformation doctrine of justification. The message and doctrine of justification by faith must be maintained also in the realm of ecclesiology and not allowed to vanish there. In the final analysis this is the purpose of the *"satis est"* and the *"nec necesse est"* of the seventh article of the Augsburg Confession: The message of the gift of salvation free from all human conditions is not to be thwarted by a view of the church and its unity which makes human factors and statutes appear to be in the strict sense "necessary," i.e., constitutive, for the being and unity of the church.[8]

"Fundamental Consensus" in Lutheran Ecumenism

The rejection of the quest for total or maximal consensus and thus the acceptance of the idea of defining or focusing the consensus seems to have been part of the heritage of the modern ecumenical movement from the very beginning.[9] It has also informed Lutheran endeavors toward church unity.

The attempts to achieve Lutheran fellowship

Even in efforts to maintain or recover inner Lutheran unity a choice had again and again to be made between a maximal doctrinal consensus embracing all the Confessional writings of the Reformation and a doctrinal consensus which concentrated on the original and basic Lutheran Confessional documents, particularly on the Augsburg Confession.

It is safe to say that insistence on a maximal consensus would have made it impossible to achieve Lutheran unity even in Germany, let alone at the European or world level. As we know, the decision of the Lutheran World Federation, which honored the earlier decision of the Lutheran World Convention, was to relate its constitutional "doctrinal basis" to "the Confessions of the Lutheran Church" while concentrating "especially on the Unaltered Augsburg Confession and Luther's Small Catechism" as "a pure exposition of the Word of God."

In the course of Lutheran efforts toward unity as they were being pursued mainly under the auspices of the LWF, further decisions were taken. A *"cause célèbre"* was the admission of the Indonesian Batak Church for membership in 1952. Instead of accepting the Augsburg Confession, this church had formulated a Confession of its own which was recognized by the LWF "as a satisfactory proof of its Lutheran confessional position."[10] "The LWF has accepted this church as a member church because it was of the opinion that its confession was *substantially in agreement* with the Lutheran confessions."[11] This important decision was subsequently renewed when other Indonesian churches which had not accepted the Augsburg Confession either were admitted as members of the LWF.

I am unable to verify whether the concept of "substantial agreement" was employed in the LWF's 1952 decision. It is certainly found later in a resolution of the Evian Assembly of the LWF in 1970. The question then was whether united churches resulting from the union of an LWF member church with non-Lutheran churches could be accepted as members of the LWF. An affirmative answer was given to this question: "Becoming a part of a united church by a member church should not lead to a break in relationships with the LWF if the united church's confessional statement is in *substantial agreement* with the doctrinal basis of the LWF."[12]

The concept and notion of "substantial agreement" with the Lutheran Confessions as a sufficient prerequisite for fellowship among the Lutheran churches themselves were later reaffirmed and, in certain respects at least, clarified, in a preparatory paper for the Dar es Salaam Assembly of 1977.[13]

Once the admission of a united church which is not "Lutheran" in a formal Confessional sense to membership of the LWF is recognized as possible, providing that its doctrinal declaration is in "substantial agreement" with the Lutheran Confessions, the transition has already in principle been made from the area of inner-Lutheran unity to that of wider ecumenical fellowship.

Principles of Lutheran ecumenism

The already mentioned demand of the Augsburg Confession for a consensus concentrating on the understanding of the gospel and its proclamation in word and sacrament, the so-called *"satis est"* clause, is undoubtedly a basic principle of Lutheran ecumenism. There is hardly a single representative Lutheran statement on the question of church unity and the ecumenical problem which does not refer to this *"satis est"* statement. Here, it is often said with a certain solemnity, the ecumenical endeavor is focused on the "essentials," on what is "absolutely necessary and sufficient,"[14] and thereby "liberated"[15] from the pressure to concern itself with the wealth of secondary questions[16] in whose toils it would undoubtedly in the end suffer shipwreck.

We have already noted that Article 7 of the Augsburg Confession not only insists in principle on the limits of the consensus required for unity but also provides more concrete indications as to where consensus is needed and where it is not.

In this respect studies and developments in contemporary Lutheranism, which must be seen, of course, in the context of the development of ecumenical thinking in general, have brought about clarifications which are important for our inquiry. They resulted in the insight that the delimitation or focusing of the consensus as advocated by the Reformers does not mean an *external distinction* between the area of normative Christian doctrine *(doctrina fidei et morum; doctrina fidei)* on the one hand and the area of historically originating and humanly conditioned ceremonies, church orders, and patterns of church life on the other, but rather a *structural differentiation within the consensus itself.*

Let me explain. If we consider the difference between that which the consensus has to cover and that which it need not cover, as the *Confessio Augustana* defines it and as is also apparent from the structure of certain Lutheran Confessional writings, it seems at first glance as if the difference were made in a primarily "quantifying" or "external" manner. This appears to have been the traditional interpretation which dominated the scene for a long time and produced a view which can be described as follows in three points:

a) There are whole areas in the life of the church in which "uniformity" cannot and should not be required. These are the *"traditiones humanae seu ritus aut cerimoniae ab hominibus institutae"* (CA 7). For where it is a matter of what has been produced by men or is historical in origin, the governing factor is in fact the creaturely *"varietates hominum, regionum, temporum"* (Luther).

b) However, in the area of the *"doctrina evangelii et administratio sacramentorum"* the situation is quite different. Here, in respect to the understanding and proclamation of the gospel in word and sacrament, no diversity is admissible but uniformity has to be required; the *"doctrina fidei et morum"* must be the same at all times and in all places *(debet esse eadem;* Luther).

c) The reason why the demand for uniformity is rejected in the one area and insisted on in the other is to be found in the different nature of these areas: on the one hand, that which has been produced by men or is historical in origin, based essentially on the *"varietates hominum, regionum, temporum"*; on the other, that which has been established and instituted by God, essentially unaffected by the *"varietates hominum."*

But this reading of Article 7 of the Augsburg Confession and of similar statements by the Reformers cannot be the last word on the subject. It is imperative to interpret these statements about the unity of the church and about necessary consensus and permissible diversity more consistently in the light of the Reformation doctrine of justification, as the Apology of the Augsburg Confession suggests.[17]

What this means can once again be described in three points:

a) The "main question" (krinomenon),[18] as the Apology calls it more than once, is not whether or not there can be human and historical diversity in the church. The important point, rather, is that the gospel of the gracious and unconditional acceptance of the human being be maintained and not blurred anywhere in the life of the church, neither in the understanding and proclamation of the gospel in word and sacrament nor in the realm of ceremonies and church orders. It is in respect to this, the message of justification, and only in respect to this that "concord" or "consensus" is strictly indispensable for the life and unity of the church.

b) The problem therefore is not the "varietates hominum" nor the question whether these "varietates" are permissible or excluded in this or that area of the church's life, for by themselves these do not conflict with the message of the gracious acceptance of the human being. The problem is rather the "opera hominum." It is these "opera hominum," understood as a prerequisite for salvation, which have to be excluded not only from the understanding and proclamation of the gospel in word and sacrament but also from the area of ceremonies and church orders into which they seep and so falsify the gospel *once it is required that these human and historical ceremonies and church orders must necessarily be uniform for the sake of the true unity of the church.*

c) Once we recognize that our conceptualities and images in which the gospel of the gracious and unconditional acceptance of the sinner now as in the past finds its theological and doctrinal expression are likewise human and historical, then here too, i.e., in the area of the *doctrina evangelii"* or *doctrina fidei,"* we are forbidden to insist on uniformity unless we wish to elevate what has been produced by man or is historical in origin to the status of that which is necessary for salvation.

For our inquiry this means: The delimitation or focusing of the consensus required for unity, as advocated by the Reformers, does not mean any external or "quantitative" delimitation of certain areas of church life. It is instead a matter of the *inner structure* of the agreement required for unity, one which concerns in principle *all* areas of church life and all interchurch differences. The distinction between "variable" and "invariable" is likewise changed from an "external" distinction into an "internal" distinction. It becomes the distinction between, on the one hand, that which in respect to every single question is part of or related to the center or substance of faith and requires consensus and, on the other hand, that which pertains to the stratum of human and historical expressions, conceptualities, perspectives, and emphases, and as such need not necessarily be the object of consensus.

Thus the consensus required and sufficient for unity *(id quod requiritur et sufficit)*[19] adopts in principle a form which may be defined as "fundamental consensus." To the extent to which we recognize that no aspect or area of the church's life is totally exempt from being humanly and historically conditioned, not even the normative teaching of our churches, the consensus necessary and sufficient for unity cannot be but such a "fundamental consensus."

The question of what the *content* of the "fundamental consensus" in a given question must embrace and what in detail forms part of the area of permissible diversity cannot be answered *a priori* and in abstraction, except for what has already been said. Here different Confessional presuppositions play an important part as well as the process of rapprochement taking place in dialogue, so that what the "fundamental consensus" for a specific question is and what it must embrace has to be ascertained together in the process of dialogue. The test as to whether this "fundamental consensus" has been achieved is its ability to "render tolerable" the remaining differences and to relieve them of their divisive character.

In the last thirty years the Lutheran view of the consensus required for church fellowship has developed with growing clarity in the direction of this concept of consensus, even if the term "fundamental consensus" has only emerged very recently. This is clear from a series of official Lutheran statements on the question of unity: for example, in the "Guidelines on Church Fellowship" of the United Lutheran Church in Germany (VELKD; 1968), the LWF Study Document "More than Church Unity" (1970), the statement on "Models of Unity" by the Dar es Salaam LWF Assembly (1977), and the statement of the LWF Assembly in Budapest on "The Unity We Seek" (1984).[20]

There is a repeated and explicit emphasis in all of these statements to the effect that even differences in the area of church Confession and church doctrine (different conceptualities, forms of expression, images, perspectives, or emphases) do not hinder church fellowship provided there is a consensus "in the right proclamation of the gospel," in "fundamentals," "in the basic view of the gospel," in the "heart of the message of salvation." Agreement in "one and the same apostolic faith," it is said, can also find expression in "a multiform confession." It can even be affirmed that, given this fundamental consensus, the "confessional expressions of the Christian faith in all their distinctiveness possess an abiding value" and represent the "vitally needed diversity within the one body of Christ."[21]

These declarations of the last two Assemblies of the LWF on the unity of the church center around the concept of "reconciled diversity" and demonstrate that there is a close and intimate correspondence between this concept of unity and the concept of "fundamental consensus." Indeed, the only possible basis for a unity which is conceived and sought as unity in diversity and not as uniformity is a consensus corresponding in its form or structure to this unity.

"Fundamental Consensus": The Idea and the Term in the Catholic-Lutheran Dialogue

How do things stand at the level of the interconfessional dialogues conducted by the Lutheran churches? Are the principles and concepts described in this paper so far, in particular the concept of the "fundamental consensus" as the logical development of the idea of a delimitation or focusing of the consensus required for unity, being applied on this level?

The answer in general cannot but be positive. In the course of the dialogues the concept of the "fundamental consensus" begins to emerge already at a very early stage and subsequently develops an ever clearer profile. Although each of the dialogues conducted by the Lutheran churches lends itself to analysis, I shall concentrate here on the international Catholic-Lutheran dialogue.

Reflections on the consensus

Early in this essay I already made the point that the dialogues of the last two decades were almost exclusively concerned with the achievement of consensus and seemed hardly to consider at all the question of the nature of the consensus required and sufficient for unity. On the whole that also applies to the Catholic-Lutheran dialogue. There are nevertheless some passages in the published dialogue documents which do consider this question indirectly and on occasion even directly.

a) This is the case in the recent volume *Facing Unity* where it reflects on the nature of unity. Even the term "fundamental consensus" can crop up in this context. It is stated there:

> The unity we seek will be a unity in diversity. Particularities developed within the two traditions will not merely be fused, nor their differences completely given up. . . . What is really at stake is that a theologically based agreement of the type that already exists in the Catholic-Lutheran dialogue should work through divergences to the point where they lose their church divisive character. At the same time it should both clarify and

make certain that remaining differences are based on a fundamental consensus in understanding the apostolic faith and therefore are legitimate.[22]

b) Another common conviction arrived at quite early in the dialogue is at least close to the idea of a "fundamental consensus." I refer to the passage in the "Malta Report" (1972) which relates the Reformation notion of the "center of the Gospel" to the Catholic idea of "a hierarchy of truths."[23] In that both ideas affirm that there are Christian truths which are closer to the "center" or higher up in the theological "hierarchy" than others, both ideas are closely related to the idea of a necessary focusing of the consensus required for unity and aimed at in ecumenical dialogue.

c) The most detailed and most important reflections on the nature and structure of the ecumenical consensus are to be found in the volume *Facing Unity*, particularly in its section on "Unity of Faith in the Diversity of its Forms of Expression."[24] It should be read in its entirety as an explanation of the concept of "fundamental consensus" used earlier in the document. It is all the more important as it appeals to the teaching of the Reformation churches (e.g., the Augsburg Confession) as well as to official Roman Catholic statements (e.g., Paul VI) and also exemplifies with reference to certain Lutheran-Catholic agreements (Eucharist; ministry) what is meant by "unity of faith in the diversity of its forms of expression." (Since the text speaks for itself, it need not be quoted and commented upon here.)

The idea of consensus in the process of consensus building

When we turn to consensus building itself as it is taking place in the dialogue, we are struck by the fact that the term "consensus" is almost never applied to the agreements reached without the use of additional qualifications. It is said, for example, that in the interpretation of justification a "far-reaching consensus" is emerging[25] or that there is a "consensus on the reality" in respect to the doctrine of the *"character indelebilis,"*[26] a "far-reaching agreement" that fidelity to the apostolic preaching and doctrine is the primary element in the understanding of the apostolic succession,[27] a "basic accord" in the understanding of the church,[28] or "fundamental mutual understanding" in respect to the sacramental nature of ordination.[29]

This is also where the term "convergence" comes in. There is talk of a "significant convergence" in respect to the understanding and praxis of *episkope*,[30] of a "substantial convergence" in respect to ordination and its sacramental character,[31] to a "growing convergence" in the questions of the understanding of the Eucharist as a sacrificial Mass and the doctrine of the *"opus operatum."*[32]

What is the reason for this usage? It can have two meanings: Either there lies behind these qualifications of the achieved consensus the view that the agreement required for the unity of the church has not yet been achieved and that the effort to achieve consensus must therefore be continued; or, what is expressed in this usage is that, while the required agreement has been reached in the individual questions discussed, the term "consensus" as such is inadequate to describe the nature and structure of this agreement and is therefore in need of further verbal precision. The deficit lies therefore either in the agreement reached or in the term "consensus" as currently used.

It cannot be denied, of course, that the dialogue still faces questions in which the agreement required for unity has not yet been reached, even though it is possible to point to certain convergences and common views. In these cases the qualified use of the term "consensus" or the use of the term "convergence" can indeed indicate a deficit in agreement.

But that in no way applies in all cases. Mostly the situation is rather that the dialogue, in affirming a "far-reaching consensus," a "consensus on the reality," a "basis accord," or a "convergence" does indeed mean to point to an agreement sufficient for unity and not at all defective. It nevertheless refrains from speaking simply of a "consensus" but feels obliged to make the term "consensus" more precise by the qualifications mentioned or by similar qualifications. In these cases, therefore, the deficit is not in the extent of the agreement reached but in the inadequacy of the term "consensus" used in isolation, which describes the agreement reached either inadequately or else in a misleading way.

In these cases the qualifications employed indicate the *inner structure* of the agreement reached in precisely the same sense as the statements of the *Confessio Augustana* (Article 7) and the document *Facing Unity* describe it[33] and which can be designated by the term "fundamental consensus." Those qualifications of the term "consensus" are then, one would wish to say as a Lutheran, nothing other than an equivalent for the *"statis est"* and *"nec necesse est"* of CA 7; *they indicate the boundary line which runs within an agreement reached between the consensus required for unity and the remaining differences agreed upon as permissible.* An agreement or "consensus" of this kind has for example been reached, according to the Dialogue Commission, in respect to the doctrine of justification, the ecclesiological significance and basic structure of the church's ministry, the sacramental character of ordination, the doctrine of *"character indelebilis,"* the eucharistic presence of Christ, the sacrificial nature of the Eucharist, the understanding of sacrament, the *"opus operatum"* doctrine, to mention only a few. In each of these and in many other cases we have an agreement which is differentiated in, on the one hand, fundamental agreements reached, and remaining differences, on the other, agreed upon as permissible. That the "far reaching," "substantial," or "growing consensus," or the "convergence" noted in these and other questions, really represents an agreement sufficient for unity (that is, a real "fundamental consensus") is shown by the fact that the remaining differences have no church divisive character. They are no longer subject to earlier doctrinal condemnations nor do they call for any doctrinal condemnations.[34]

"Fundamental Consensuses" and "The Fundamental Consensus"

As discussed and described in this essay so far, the term "fundamental consensus" has a clear tendency toward the plural. It primarily describes the agreement striven for and reached in individual controversial questions, so that we speak correspondingly of a "fundamental consensus" in respect to Christ's eucharistic presence, of a "fundamental consensus" in respect to the sacramental character of ordination, and so on. In other words, we have to speak first of all of "fundamental consens*uses*" in the plural. However, there is also the singular use of this term. In the setting of the Roman Catholic-Lutheran dialogue, indeed, the singular usage comes first chronologically. We encounter it as a kind of key concept for the first time in connection with the discussion of Roman Catholic "recognition" of the *Confessio Augustana* (1977-1981).[35]

In the statement on the Augsburg Confession of the international dialogue commission "All Under One Christ" (1980), based on the findings of the Roman Catholic-Lutheran study on the Augsburg Confession, "Confessing One Faith,"[36] the term "fundamental consensus" is introduced and indeed used quite programmatically:

> Reflecting on the Augsburg Confession. . .Catholics and Lutherans have discovered that they have a common mind on basic doctrinal truths which points to Jesus Christ, the living center of our faith. This basic consensus *(Grundkonsens)* also comes out in and is confirmed by the documents of the official Roman Catholic/Lutheran dialogue today.[37]

The conclusion of the statement states:

> Our newly discovered agreement in central Christian truths gives good ground for the hope that in the light of this basic consensus *(Grundkonsens)* answers will also be forthcoming to the still unsettled questions and problems, answers which will achieve the degree of unanimity

required if our churches are to make a decisive advance from their present state of division to that of sister churches.[38]

These statements of the dialogue commission should be grouped with official church declarations on the *Confessio Augustana* from the same period:

The Pastoral Letter of the German Catholic Bishops, "Thy Kingdom Come!" (January 1980), says with reference to the *Confessio Augustana* and its jubilee: "We are happy to discover not simply a partial consensus on some truths but rather a consensus on central truths."[39]

In the same year Cardinal Willebrands described the *Confessio Augustana* as "a basis for the common confession of central doctrinal truths." It reconfirms "the conviction that the division which then took place (namely in the sixteenth century) did not strike to the heart of the common root and that our common belief goes essentially deeper and reaches further than what divides us."[40]

In his address on the Anniversary of the Augsburg Confession, Pope John Paul II used the image of a bridge and spoke of "important piers of that bridge" and the "common foundations of our Christian faith" which remained "great and solid" in "the storms of that age."[41] Later, in his address to the Council of the Evangelical Church in Germany, Pope John Paul II endorsed the statement of the German bishops about "a consensus on central truths" which is not simply "a partial consensus on some truths."[42]

The statement of the Executive Committee of the Lutheran World Federation in 1981, gathering all this together, speaks repeatedly of the *"basic consensus* in faith" affirmed in the "joint discussions on the Augsburg Confession."[43]

In the later document, *Facing Unity*, by the international dialogue commission, the notion of "fundamental consensus" maintains, as we have seen, its central significance and also there is used in the singular.[44]

What is the meaning of this use of the term "fundamental consensus" in the singular? Obviously it does not mean an all-inclusive consensus formula or statement of faith which, so to speak, describes in one fell swoop the common basis of faith, in light of which the remaining differences can be endured and lose their divisive character. What is meant, rather, is the following:

The agreements reached, which in most cases have the structure of "fundamental consensuses" in the sense described earlier, are no longer just a series of scattered individual and partial agreements. Rather, as a whole they begin to acquire a new quality. Like the individual stones which together constitute a foundation, the individual agreements together gain such a solidity that they can be seen to constitute a whole which increasingly embraces the essential, central, fundamental aspects and elements of Christian faith. In this sense "the fundamental consensus" is the necessary and sufficient basis for church fellowship which is growing out of plural "fundamental consensuses" and is constituted by them.

It is true that the dialogue commission uses the term "fundamental consensus" in the singular still with a somewhat restrictive meaning. Whereas in respect to individual questions such as the Eucharist and ministry it is certainly able to affirm already that "fundamental consensuses" have here been reached which cover everything essential in these areas, it does not yet say this in respect to *the* fundamental consensus."

Nevertheless, the individual "fundamental consensuses" are beginning to unite and consolidate in their totality into "the fundamental consensus." The measure of what has been achieved up to now confers on us the confidence that the questions still left open will find answers, and thus "the fundamental consensus" will be reached as the necessary and at the same time sufficient condition for the realization of church fellowship.

Notes

1. G. Sauter, "Consensus" *Theologische Realenzyklopädie* (Berlin: de Gruyter, 1981) 8:187.

2. Cf. U. Duchrow, "Confessio Augustana VII und die Entwicklung zur Ein-Mann-Pastoren-Kirche," *Kooperation im Aktionsraum Kirchenbezirk* (Geneva: LWF, 1972) 39-48; L. Vischer, ". . . satis est?" *Christliche Freiheit im Dienst am Menschen* (ed. K. Herbert; Frankfurt: Lembeck, 1972) 243-54.

3. Even the authors of the "Confutatio" (Diet of Augsburg, 1530) had reacted in this way. They did not criticize the *"satis est"* or the *"nec necesse est"* as such and even praised them. But they asked for a distinction to be made between, on the one hand, "specific," i.e., stronger locally and regionally conditioned rites and customs, and, on the other hand, "universal rites" and ceremonies, valid for the whole of Christendom and probably of apostolic origin. In the former instance variety was necessary and alterations possible, whereas in the case of the latter this was not so. *(Die Confutatio der Confessio Augustana vom 3. August 1530* [ed. H. Immenkötter; Munster: Aschendorffsche Verlagsbuchhandlung, 1979] 97.)

4. At least in the Reformed, the Anglican, and the Methodist traditions, it is relatively easy to find affirmations which make a very similar differentiation between that which is necessary for unity in the church as far as agreement is

concerned and that which is not necessary, and which thereby advocate a delimitation of the consensus required for unity. For example, the affirmations of the Confessio Helvetica Posterior (Art. 17), of the Thirty-Nine-Articles (Art. 19), and of the Historic Articles of the North American Methodists (Art. 13 and 22), all of which are very similar to Article 7 of the *Confessio Augustana*. With regard to Roman Catholic theology, see Yves Congar, *Diversity and Communion* (Mystic, CT: Twenty-third Publications, 1984).

5. *Prefatio Doctoris Martini Lutheri,* WA 50:380: *"Quod si quae differentiae in hac eorum Confessione occurrent, de ritibus et ceremoniis vel de coelibatu, meminerimus nunquam fuisse neque potuisse omnium Ecclesiarum omnes ritus et observationes esse aequales vel easdem. Id enim non permittunt hominum, regionum, temporum rationes et varietates, modo salva sit doctrina fidei et morum. Haec enim debet esse eadem."*

6. The Augsburg Confession accordingly has two parts, one part about the "Articles of Faith and Doctrine" *(Articuli fidei praecipui;* Art. 1-21) and a second part about the areas in which abuses have been corrected *(Articuli in quibus recensentur abusus mutati;* Art. 22-28). The Smalcald Articles, with their tripartite structure, likewise make such distinctions.

7. For example: Ap 7:30-34; BC 173-75.

8. The Apology sets it out clearly, when with regard to the *"satis est"* and the *"nec necesse est"* of CA 7 it says: "Now we are not discussing whether it is profitable to observe them (namely, useful and ancient ordinances) for the sake of tranquillity or bodily profit. Another issue is involved. The question is whether the observance of human traditions is an act of worship necessary for righteousness before God. This must be settled in this controversy. . ." (7:34; cf. 37; BC 175).

9. The Lausanne Faith and Order Conference already in 1927 affirmed: "The Unity of the Church. . .does not mean uniformity." This directly implied the idea of "legitimate variation" as well as the question of the "limits" of such legitimate variation and thus of the limits of the consensus required for unity *(Reports of the World Conference on Faith and Order,* Lausanne, August 1927 [Boston: The Secretariat, 1928], 20). Similarly, the Third World Conference on Faith and Order (Lund 1952), in its section on "Continuity and Unity: Unity and Difference," stated: "It is agreed that there are *necessaria* (necessary articles) in the Christian faith. . .but we are not unanimous about their number and nature," *(A Documentary History of the Faith and Order Movement, 1927-1963* [ed. L. Vischer; St. Louis: Bethany Press, 1963], No. 47).

10. H. Meyer, "Das missionarische Zeugnis der Kirche als Grund und Gegenstand echter Theologie. Gedanken zur Arbeit der Sektion II Äussere Mission auf der Tagung des Lutherischen Weltbundes in Hannover," *Lutherische Rundschau* 3 (1953) 374.

11. H. Weissgerber, *The Church and the Confessions. The Role of the Confessions in the Life and Doctrine of the Lutheran Churches* (ed. V. Vajta and H. Weissgerber; Philadelphia: Fortress Press, 1963) 21. Emphasis added.

12. "Statement concerning the Attitude of the LWF to Churches in Union Negotiations" in: *Sent into the World.* The Proceedings of the Fifth Assembly of the Lutheran World Federation, Evian, France, 1970 (Minneapolis: Augsburg Publishing House, 1971) 142f. Emphasis added.

13. *Ecumenical Relations of the Lutheran World Federation.* Report of the working group on the interrelations between the various bilateral dialogues (Geneva: LWF, 1977) No. 140-41; cf. 142.

14. "More than Church Unity," *Lutheran World* 17 (1970) 46.

15. "Theses of the LWF-Plenary Assembly in Minneapolis," The Proceedings of the *Third Assembly of the Lutheran World Federation* (Geneva: LWF, 1958) 86; "More than Church Unity" (n. 14 above) 46.

16. "Lutherans and Ecumenical Movements," *The Lutheran World Almanac for 1937,* 36.

17. Ap 7:34; cf. 37; BC 175.

18. Ibid.

19. See here the paper of J. M. R. Tillard, "Towards a Common Profession of Faith," presented at the Bangalore Faith and Order meeting (1978), which centers around this maxim so closely related to the "*satis est*" and "*nec necesse est*" of the Augsburg Confession and to our inquiry about fundamental consensus, *Bangalore 1978, Sharing in One Hope,* Report and Documents from the meeting of the Faith and Order Commission, World Council of Churches (Geneva: WCC, 1978) 223-32.

20. "Leitsätze der Vereinigten Evangelisch-Lutherischen Kirche Deutschlands (VELKD) zur Kirchengemeinschaft" of October 1968, *Lutherische Monatshefte* 8 (1969) 525; "More than Church Unity" (see n. 14), 46-47; "Statement on Models of Unity," *"In Christ—A New Community."* The Proceedings of the Sixth Assembly of the Lutheran World Federation, Dar es Salaam, Tanzania (Geneva: LWF, 1977) 173ff; "Statement on The Unity We Seek," *"In Christ—Hope for the World,"* Official Proceedings of the Seventh Assembly of the Lutheran World Federation, Budapest 1984 (Geneva: LWF, 1985) 175.

21. All quotations in this paragraph are taken from the texts referred to in note 20.

22. *Facing Unity.* Models, Forms and Phases of Catholic-Lutheran Church Fellowship. The Lutheran World Federation (Geneva: LWF, 1985), No. 47.

23. Malta Report, No. 25: GiA, 174. This is taken up again in *Facing Unity,* No. 53.

24. *Facing Unity,* No. 61-66.

25. Malta Report, No. 26 and 28: GiA 174-75; The Ministry in the Church, No. 9: GiA 250; "All Under One Christ," No. 14: GiA 243.

26. The Ministry in the Church, No. 39: GiA 261.

27. Ibid., No. 60: GiA 267.

28. "All Under One Christ," No. 16: GiA 244.

29. The Ministry in the Church, No. 34: GiA 259.

30. Ibid., No. 44: GiA 263.

31. Malta Report, No. 59: GiA 182; The Ministry in the Church, No. 32: GiA. 258.

32. The Eucharist, No. 61: GiA 207.

33. *Facing Unity,* No. 47.

34. This is where the recent study of the Ecumenical Working Group *(Ökumenischer Arbeitskreis)* of Protestant and Catholic theologians in the Federal Republic of Germany on the mutual doctrinal condemnations comes in *(Lehrverurteilungen — kirchentrennend? Rechtfertigung, Sakramente und Amt im Zeitalter der Reformation und heute* (ed. K. Lehmann and W. Pannenberg; Freiburg: Herder; Göttingen: Vandenhoeck & Ruprecht, 1986). This study, which

demonstrates that the mutual doctrinal condemnations of the sixteenty century no longer apply to the partners today, answers a question which the dialogues again and again refer to without being themselves able to come to terms with; cf. *Facing Unity,* No. 67-69; cf. also No. 123.

35. With regard to this, see H. Meyer, (ed.), *Lutheran/Catholic Discussion on the Augsburg Confession.* Documents 1977-1981 (LWF, Report 10; Geneva: LWF 1982).

36. This study of the Augsburg Confession *(Confessing One Faith.* A Joint Commentary on the Augsburg Confession by Lutheran and Catholic Theologians [ed. G. W. Forell and J. F. McCue; Minneapolis: Augsburg Publishing House, 1982]) does not yet use the concept of "fundamental consensus" as such. However, it comes close to it when it speaks in its summary of "a common understanding of the center of the Christian faith," of a "deep consensus," or of the fact that "we have found the CA (Augsburg Confession) to be 'confessing one faith', even if open questions still remain. . ." (337-38).

37. "All Under One Christ," No. 17 and 18: GiA 244.

38. Ibid., No. 25: GiA 245.

39. *Lutheran/Catholic Discussion on the Augsburg Confession.* Documents 1977-1981 (see n. 35), 55.

40. Ibid., 57.

41. Ibid., 60.

42. Ibid., 64.

43. Ibid., 76; cf. 78. Emphasis added.

44. *Facing Unity,* No. 123, *passim.*

9

Fundamental Consensus and Church Fellowship

An Orthodox Perspective

Archbishop Methodios

IF ONE IS to speak on this subject from an Orthodox point of view, one needs, first of all, to make clear that both terms, "consensus" and "fellowship," do not express in the context of Orthodox ecclesiology what followers of the contemporary ecumenical movement would have wished to express with them.

Again from an Orthodox point of view, the designation "fundamental" is relative, as opposed to being absolute, because, on the premise that "consensus" means agreement or consent, we cannot divide Christian truths into "fundamental" and "non-fundamental" ones. This is also the case because Orthodox ecclesiology presupposes the sum total of Christian truths in order to allow "consensus" to lead to "fellowship," if by the latter we mean Christian "*koinonia*."

Whenever we speak about "church fellowship," we always presuppose a "consensus on the constitutive elements of the church." On the indisputable premise that all the constitutive elements of the church, i.e., "faith," "Bible," "tradition," "sacraments," "apostolic succession," and "pastoral powers," are inside the church, we shall conclude that no one who stays outside the church has the key for coming inside the church. This means that whenever "fellowship" is granted, it is granted *by* the church to be realized only *within* the church and not just *with* the church.

"Fellowship" is the visible unity of the members of the church, which exists concretely where eucharistic communion is practiced. Eucharistic communion presupposes valid sacraments and valid sacraments presuppose consensus on the true or right (orthodox) faith. The true or right faith, expressed in terms or articulated formulas, constitutes a dogma, i.e., an authoritative and undisputed statement of faith. A dogma, explained or expanded, is a theological doctrine. For everyone who accepts all the true or right faith of the (Orthodox) church, in other words, for everyone who accepts the dogmatic consensus of the church, participation in the fellowship of the church is natural, legitimate, and salutary. In all this the basic principle which regulates the dogmatic consensus on the true (or right) faith is best expressed by St. Vincent of Lerins: *"Quod semper, quod ubique, quod ab omnibus creditum est."*

Another notion which helps us to clarify the consensus which leads to the fellowship of the church is that of "apostolic succession." Apostolic succession stands for the three basic principles underlying Christ's commandments: truth, life, and way, which stand for dogma, canon, and discipline respectively. These are derived from Christ's Gospel claim, "I am the *way*, the *truth*, and the *life*" and imply: a) the historical humanity of Christ, b) Christ's eschatological operation in the sacraments, and c) the unity of the church of Christ. The first represents the deposit of the faith, the second the deposit of the sacraments, and the third the deposit of the apostolic powers. The first two create communion in the sacraments, and the third communion under the authority of the shepherds, though analyzed in this way they all create one consensus and lead to one church fellowship of communion.

In view of the above, if one is to express an opinion on the subject of "Fundamental Consensus and Church Fellowship" from an Orthodox point of view, one runs the risk of speaking in a paradoxical manner. To be more specific, though at this moment I am able to engage in dialogue with heterodox Christians and perhaps even to pray with them, in other words, to do something which is natural and Christian, I do not have the right to do so from the perspective of purely Orthodox teaching. Neither am I allowed, as a Hierarch, to give permission, if I am asked to do so, to anyone among the priests who serve under me to participate in common prayer with heterodox Christians. If, then, neither I, nor indeed any other Orthodox Hierarch, is allowed such a simple and harmless action, how could we possibly agree that there is a consensus on "fundamentals" which may leave out "non-fundamentals"? How can such a view be entertained if everything in Orthodox teaching is fundamental?

On the other hand, one can point to a number of practical facts connected with inter-church relations which occur almost in defiance of the theory. We observe, in other words, that within the Orthodox Church action (practice) does not always fall in line with the teaching, or, rather, that action sometimes assumes a teaching role. For a proper evaluation and appreciation of this seeming paradox or contradiction, we need to bear in mind that in the Orthodox Church the teaching is defined by the decisions of the ecumenical synods and the practice is defined by the life of the church and that the latter, even though it offers examples of infringement of church canons, *never attempts to abolish* these canons. The importance of this can be better understood if one compares the practice of the Orthodox Church with that of the heterodox churches in the same context of inter-church relations.

This great facility which enables the Orthodox to act appropriately in inter-church matters, infringing but not abolishing the canons, is called "ecclesiastical economy."[1]

Only on the basis of economy, i.e., *Kat' oikonomian*, to use the exact Orthodox terminology, and only in certain circumstances could the notion of "consensus on fundamentals," which leaves out "nonfundamentals," be allowed.

If we take into consideration that the Orthodox Church regards the decisions of the ecumenical and many local synods as belonging to the "fundamentals" of the one undivided church and that the Protestant churches have rejected many of the basic principles and decisions of the synods, we cannot but draw the inevitable conclusion that there is a great difference between those two. The Orthodox Church remains faithful to the apostolic teaching, which it regards as "fundamental" for church fellowship. Furthermore, the Orthodox Church knows that when its decisions are taken in the Holy Spirit, they are all infallible and therefore it cannot deny or alter any of them by means of newer decisions without the guidance of the Holy Spirit. If it were to accept later "confessions" and "statements" which purportedly emend her previous decisions, then the church ceases to be an infallible establishment and the presence of the Holy Spirit in it becomes a mere pretence.

The Orthodox Church believes in its infallibility and is in no way prepared to assail it. We believe that the church as a totality never errs. Protestants, however, are always ready to declare the opposite. How, then, can infallibility be reconciled with deception?

The Orthodox Church believes in the personal presence of Christ in the church. It does not believe only in Christ's teachings. It regards Christ as being present in its life, walking along with it, the Christ "who offers and is offered." It does not seek to find proofs of Christ's existence because it lives in the assured faith that the Lord was born, taught, was crucified and buried, rose again, and after his resurrection appeared to many. He remains present, alive, and true in the life of the Orthodox. Consequently the Orthodox Church cannot possibly embrace the theology of doubt. This is why it refuses to engage in dialogue with theologians who seek to find the faith in nature or in the so-called "natural" or "scientific" theologies. It is exactly for the same reason that it vehemently rejects as blasphemous the syllogisms of the Bishop of Durham and his tactics, which recall the pseudonymous teachings of the innumerable heretics which the church was able to overrule through the wisdom of the Fathers. It should be stressed at this point that the Orthodox Church does not persecute nor impose any capital punishment upon heretics. It simply condemns them and cuts them off from its body, waiting for their repentance and salvation. Neither is the Orthodox Church terrified or terrorized by the modern so-called scientific/academic criticism of Christ since it is not in a state of confusion, because it makes sure to discover and confidently live according to the will of God.

The case of "consensus," then, presupposes the certainty of the church that it stands upon the right faith and life. It is through these two presuppositions that it is already given to enjoy the state of concordance and fellowship which are expressed but not created by the "fundamental consensus." Certainly we do come across cases of deviations from this concurrence of faith and life, but these cases do not constitute an abolition of the rule but a sort of condescension. This occurs only rarely and provided that the essence of the faith is not abandoned. When the character of the "consensus" is regulated in this way, then we know that it is the result of the operation of the Holy Spirit who safeguards the infallibility of the church.

I understand that it is a shameful scandal that those who proclaim their allegiance to Jesus Christ, the Son of the living God and Savior of the world, the only sure hope in ages past and to come, are still unable to join together at his Table. But it is an ever greater scandal that a large part of these people emphatically refuses to do so and still far worse that some of them continue to demonstrate an unchristian attitude toward their fellow Christians. This indicates that the quest for consensus cannot be only a theological point, but also an ecclesiological and a psychological one. Thus Christian division cannot be overcome by any sort of agreed consensus. Getting together in common gatherings or demonstrations does not impress the Orthodox. Services of intercommunion, I am afraid, do not move the Orthodox, who simply do not believe that the Holy Spirit operates outside the church or without the church's declared intention. The ecclesiological teaching of St. Cyprian on this point continues to be applicable and powerful among the Orthodox. Both St. Cyprian's and St. Augustine's views on this issue have never been disproved.[2]

But you may well ask, "What is the difference between the practice of the Orthodox Church and that of various Protestant Confessions?" In the Orthodox Church practice never stands in opposition to or in antithesis with the history of the one undivided church, while the "Confessions" represent a negation of it since they reject essential elements of its teaching. "Confessions" are allegedly designed in order to maintain the apostolic faith and its creedal doctrinal formulations. In fact, however, they are crippled because they are deprived of the catholicity of the faith as it was specified by St. Vincent of Lerins. Besides, the Protestants who produce these "Confessions" were cut from the church and created other bodies without having any right to do so, since Christ founded one church, whose leader he himself is. Having cut themselves off from the church, Protestants rejected the church's infallibility and then engaged in an endless search for the "*consensus fidei*," which in my view is none other than the teaching of the Orthodox Church. It is the very nature of the church that makes it recognize only its members, the members, that is, of its own body, and not just followers of Christ. The followers of Christ should become its members so that they may be able to live the life of the Holy Spirit which exists only in it.

Honesty demands that we should make the right diagnosis concerning "fundamental differences" in our search for "fundamental consensus," however unpleasant or even painful this may prove. I believe that to oversimplify the case of "consensus" not only will be counterproductive for the effort to reach rapprochement among the divided Christian churches, but also lead to a serious dilution of the Christian faith itself. This is unfortunately the case of many contemporary Anglicans. In the light of what I have said thus far, you may guess that I do not agree with those who contend that "in essence doctrinal differences justifying the separation of the Roman and Protestant Churches no longer exist."[3]

We can acknowledge that there are, indeed, common fundamental elements among the divided Christian churches, but we must also insist that these elements are not sufficient for establishing any adequate consensus, let alone "fundamental consensus."

When we Christians often venture to say that as Christians we have the same faith and consequently we also have "the fundamental consensus in faith," in fact we delude ourselves because it is not our faith which measures the faith of the church (the "*consensus fidei ecclesiae*"), but the other way around, even if both of them refer to the same God. What emerges here as the basic factor in the articulation of the faith is the apostolic teaching. No church fellowship makes sense without the genuine apostolic tradition. In other words, the faith and the church are mutually intertwined and can never be separated from each other. We cannot claim that we obey God without obeying him through his church because faith in God and the church coexist. The separation of faith in Christ from the church makes the church superfluous. If, however, the church is superfluous, Christ would not have established it, nor would St. Paul have insisted so much on its well-being. The truth is that Christ founded the church that it may teach and baptize. How, then, can we assert that we believe in the one, holy, catholic, and apostolic church when we have not been baptized by it on the basis of accepting its faith, but by followers of vague and often ambiguous biblical Confessions? It is obvious to me that the desired Christian consensus is coextensive with the Orthodox Church which remains firmly established on the Orthodox life (*lex orandi*) and the Orthodox faith (*lex credendi*).

It is only "by convention" and not properly or literally (*katachrēstikōs* but not *kuriolektikōs*) that we Orthodox speak of divided Christians. We know that it is not true to say that the church is divided because the church is always one. Consequently those Christians who are found outside the church can be regarded as followers of Christ and be designated as Christians, but they are not incorporated into the church and therefore lack the assurance of salvation. The following statement of a great Russian theologian, Alexis Khomiakoff, concerning the soteriological significance of the unity of the church and the necessity of the incorporation of Christians into it, will clarify what I have been saying at this point. "We know that when any one of us falls, he falls alone: but no one is saved alone. He who is saved is saved in the Church, as a member of her, and in unity with all her other members. If any one believes, he is in the communion of faith; if he loves, he is in the communion of love; if he prays, he is in the communion of prayer. Wherefore no one can rest his hope on his own prayers, and every one who prays asks the whole Church for intercession, not as if he had doubts of the intercession of Christ the Advocate, but in the assurance that the whole Church ever prays for all her members. . . ."[4]

Obviously Khomiakoff stresses here the significance of the unity of the church, which cannot be seen merely as Christian charity or Christian virtue, but as an institution established by God which draws everyone out of loneliness, isolation, and enmity with others and introduces everyone into the *fellowship* of his universal family, which is concretely realized and expressed by the church. Thus acceptance of the symbol of the faith (the creed) becomes effective only for those who are members of the church.

The idea of the mystical body of Christ can truly be regarded as the culminating point of the whole Bible. The announcement of the New Testament is that all has been fulfilled and that the church is the true heir of the Old Testament and of the New Testament. The phrase of

St. Cyprian *extra ecclesiam nulla salus* exactly represents the New Testament teaching because the church is the sphere of the salvation which has been accomplished through Christ. The church is described in the New Testament in terms of a family, or household, or the bride of the Messiah, or the body of Christ, or the temple of God, or the city of God, the heavenly Jerusalem. Particularly pertinent is here the notion of the body which is presented as though it has many members; the hand, the foot, and the eye are all necessary to one another: "There are diversities of gifts, but only one Spirit. . . . " (1 Cor 12; Rom 12:1-8; Eph 4:1-16)

The Christian churches which exist outside the Orthodox and Roman Catholic Churches present very deep differences when compared to one another. The Orthodox, in spite of all their difficulties, lean upon the tradition of the one church in order to carry out their mission. Protestants think that the only problem they have to face is how to find church unity in some way or another by focusing on the solution to contemporary problems in human society and the international community through the cooperation of members of the churches. The Orthodox Church firmly believes that without the church there can be no real reconciliation of the world with Christ. The Orthodox attach paramount significance to the preservation of the Christian truth and are determined not to yield to the temptation to proclaim a Christian message which is conformed to the passing images of the present age.

If therefore we are to be specific about the "fundamental consensus," we need to take into account not only baptism, Eucharist, and ministry but also the rest of the holy sacraments and above all *The Church,* to whom these sacraments are essential by nature. How can we regard these three sacraments as the basis of the sought "consensus" without special reference to the Holy Spirit? Or without assiduous definition of apostolic succession? Or without explicit acceptance of the decisions of the ecumenical synods? Or without believing that ecclesiastical administration is of absolute necessity for the existence of the church? "Consensus" is tantamount to unanimity in the total mind of the church. Thus for the Orthodox Church the fundamental consensus for church fellowship is "the whole faith of the Orthodox Church." In the case, however, of the union with it of Christians who exist outside it, it is possible "for a certain time" (*pros kairon*) and only in order to facilitate this union that the "fundamentals" may be restricted to a minimum. It should be understood here that this could happen only *by deviating* from the dogmatic teaching of the church as an accommodation to this specific case and for the benefit of the church and never as a purposeless or useless compromise. The Orthodox Church has at its disposal in such cases the flexibility to take appropriate action in order to facilitate the salvation of believers through their union with it. This means that from the Orthodox point of view the efforts of the World Council of Churches and especially of the Faith and Order Commission to offer compromises cannot be accepted by the Orthodox Church although it praises these efforts because they express the agony of the divided Christians. The Orthodox Church does not accept compromises. It does know, however, how to condescend toward any one of its members as well as toward any Christians who wish to become members of its body.

Here I am bound to point out that the various texts which are signed by inter-church committees and which are composed by theologians from various traditions have a merely academic character, even though they are submitted to the local Orthodox Autocephalous Churches. This is because it belongs to the very nature of our church not to issue partial licenses to certain individuals alone for making official church pronouncements on its essential dogmatic truths. Such texts, as, for example, *Baptism, Eucharist and Ministry*, contribute, perhaps, to theological academic cooperation and to the promotion of mutual acquaintance, but not, unfortunately, to the discovery or achievement of "consensus." This is because the schisms which have torn themselves from the church do not merely represent misunderstandings but self-willed and carefully calculated divisions, which have taken place as revolts against the church on account of or with the pretext of opposing a purported corruption of the clergy, or, even, an allegedly deceptive fall of the church from true teaching into error. It remains a matter of fact then that Christians are united in sharing or claiming the name of the same Lord. But it also remains a matter of fact that the Lord does not consist only of his name, but of his real dimension "yesterday, today, and tomorrow." His "yesterday" relates to his eternity since the foundation of the world and to his incarnation by the Virgin Mary. His "today" relates to his church as he wanted it and his "tomorrow" to the implications of the sacraments. These, then, are the elements that constitute the "fundamental consensus": Christ, the church, and the sacraments.

I would have liked to analyze extensively the Lima text on *Baptism, Eucharist and Ministry*, but time does not permit. Thus I shall simply restrict myself to making a number of brief but pertinent observations:

1. I am of the opinion that agreement on the church ought to have preceded an agreement on the sacraments.
2. The text of the BEM cannot possibly be accepted by the Orthodox Church not only because it has an academic character, but also

because baptism, Eucharist, and priesthood cannot be separated from the rest of the sacraments.

3. The term "ministry" is unacceptable from an Orthodox point of view because it implies a sort of dilution of the true character of priesthood.

4. As a theological composition BEM contains, indeed, many useful elements, but this makes it insufficient to be adopted by the Orthodox Church because it needs to be totally Orthodox.

5. The BEM text contains expressions which are unacceptable from an Orthodox point of view. For this reason I do not share the views of those who assert that a possible agreement on it will lead to important prospects for the realization of the church's visible unity.

6. I particularly regard as unacceptable the following expressions and statements:

a) that "the Churches develop these doctrinal *convergences* step by step, until they are fully able to declare together that they are living in communion with one another in continuity with the apostles and the teachings of the universal Church." (p. ix; emphasis added)

b) that "within a fellowship of witness and service, Christians discover the full significance of the one baptism as the gift of God to all God's people." (B 10)

c) that "Insofar as Christians cannot unite in full fellowship around the same table to eat. . . ." (E 26)

d) that "The best way towards unity in eucharistic celebration and communion is the renewal of the eucharist itself in the different churches in regard to teaching and liturgy. The churches should test their liturgies in the light of the eucharistic agreement now in the process of attainment." (E 28)

e) that "Regarding the practice of reserving the elements, each church should respect the practices and piety of the others," etc. (E 32)

f) that "Churches which have preserved the episcopal succession are asked to recognize both the apostolic content of the ordained ministry which exists in churches which have not maintained such succession and also the existence in these churches of a ministry of *episkopé* in various forms." (M 53)

I regard the above as unacceptable: a) because they bear a syncretistic character and equate the Orthodox Church with the various Christian Confessions which lack the sacramental life of the church; b) because they present the Orthodox Church as seeking to find out the full meaning of the one baptism; c) because the Orthodox Christians are presented along with the heterodox as not being united around the Holy Table;

d) because the Orthodox Church is also being asked to "renew" her divine liturgy as if it were insufficient, not to say misguided!; e) because the unchangeable condition of the consecrated body and blood of Christ in the holy Eucharist is questioned; and f) because the Orthodox Church is being asked to recognize the "apostolic content" and the "episcopal office" in the various types of ministry of the other churches without demanding their restoration in the body of the church through the accredited canonical ecclesiastical procedure.

7. The Prologue to BEM in its entirety is not acceptable to the Orthodox Church. In saying this, I am not just putting forward my own ideas, but what I believe that the Orthodox Church would have said if it were asked to offer an official response. I think that the collaborators of Faith and Order and of the WCC in general have been carried away by utopian enthusiasm on account of the wide circulation of the BEM text. They should not confuse the circulation of the text with its acceptance (in any official sense) by the Orthodox Churches because such a confusion could never be adopted by the Orthodox.

8. As regards the appended instructions concerning the use of this text in worship, witness, and theological pursuits, I find them very poor.

9. The most important deficiency of the BEM text is that it lacks a patristic foundation. Patristic teaching should have been the basis for the texts on the Eucharist and apostolic succession.

Beyond, however, my personal views, which, as I said, are the views of the Orthodox Church from which I have no right to deviate, there are also certain expressed views on the BEM text which, in spite of their daring evaluations, do similarly express severe reservations about the seriousness of this text.[5]

These latter views do not constitute answers which are binding for the Orthodox Catholic Church since they do not represent the consensus of the Orthodox hierarchy and of the Orthodox people who bear authentic witness to the continuation of the true Christian manner of faith and life.

It is obvious then that the Orthodox Church does not understand the notion of "fundamental consensus" in terms of "good disposition" or "goodwill," but in terms of the total dogmatic teaching of the one, holy, catholic, and apostolic church. As for the notion of "church fellowship," the Orthodox Church does not understand it in terms of the fellowship which is incarnated in the WCC, i.e., "a fellowship of Churches which confess the Lord Jesus Christ as God and Saviour according to the Scriptures and who, therefore, seek to fulfil together their common calling to the glory of the One God, Father, Son and Holy Spirit" (Constitution). The elements which unite the churches in the World Council of Churches are so few and insufficient that they degrade the term "fellowship," reducing its meaning to a mere "superficial bond." Consequently we cannot adequately specify the meaning of the notion of "fundamental consensus" before we accurately interpret the notion of "fellowship."

William G. Rusch

A WORD OF appreciation and thanks must be expressed to the Archbishop for the essay he has written on church fellowship. He has brought to our attention several important points.

First, Archbishop Methodios reminds us that ecumenism is neither easy nor simple. Such a view of the ecumenical movement is a temptation for many. They think that a few individuals sit down for a few years of discussion and the divisions of the past are settled. Full unity has arrived for all the churches. The Archbishop's essay recalls for us all that full communion between divided churches is a gift and a task, (*Gabe und Aufgabe*).

Second, the Archbishop reminds us that we all belong to historical traditions. At times there is a danger of losing this sense of history. The essay brings to our attention either implicitly or explicitly the limitations of all historical traditions when an Orthodox archbishop moves beyond his own tradition to quote Cyprian, Augustine, or even Vincent of Lerins.

Third, the Archbishop reminds us that life in the church is a life of prayer and proclamation that transcends theological reflection, as important as such thinking is, especially for Lutherans.

Thus this essay of Archbishop Methodios has given us much. The presence of the Archbishop here is not accidental. It is the result of conversations at the Ecumenical Patriarchate. I would suggest that the Archbishop's participation in this conference indicates that many of his concerns about a wider context than the Western church were in the thinking of the planning group for this consultation.

Many of the points in the Archbishop's lecture were not new to most of us. This observation is, of course, a compliment. In my book on ecumenism in 1985 I spent some pages describing the statement of the

Orthodox Church in America on ecumenism.[1] This document in my opinion reflects an accurate picture of how the Orthodox view the ecumenical movement. I urge a reading both of that statement and Archbishop Methodios' essay.

Now I must move from my sincere appreciation of the essay to some aspects of it that I find troubling. In making these remarks I am trying, as someone committed to the ecumenical movement and with some knowledge of the tradition, to identify some further difficulties that must be addressed if we are to make further progress together. "To speak the truth in love" requires such comments.

The Archbishop observes that there is a problem of vocabulary. I think that he is correct, but not totally. The problems between Eastern and Western Christians are deeper than terminology.

For me at least one problem lies at a deeper level. It is the problem of history and the time-conditionedness of all aspects of the Christian faith. The gospel and indeed the Orthodox faith are not bound by a set of timeless propositions. The Archbishop's appeal to Vincent of Lerins is illustrative. As we now know from biblical and patristic scholarship, the issues are not as simple as Vincent once thought.[2]

The essay often speaks of faith as expressed in specific terms or in articulated formulas. As a Lutheran I can understand this. But surely the Christian faith is never wholly this. There is the doxological element. The Orthodox often remind us of it; I wish that we had heard it more strongly in the essay.

Several times the presentation of Archbishop Methodios refers to the fundamentals of Orthodox teaching. For him everything in the Orthodox teaching assumes this character. Yet certainly the Fathers of the church would have found such a view strange. They made important distinctions between what was fundamental and what was not. One clear example is Athanasius of Alexandria at the beginning of his *Contra Arianos*.[3]

A similar case could be made in regard to the councils and synods of the early church. As we all know, not all these councils agreed and not all were seen as having the same authority in the light of history. The Council of Nicea of 325 had a long struggle for acceptance. The Council of Ephesus of 431 and the Council of Ephesus of 449 must be distinguished. Orthodoxy itself has participated in this process.

The essay states rather clearly that the Orthodox Church could not accept "Confessions" or "statements" that purportedly emend previous decisions. Yet there is evidence in the history of the church that this is precisely what has been done. For example, in the second century and later the economic concept of the Trinity was widely held. During the fourth century controversy with Arianism the champions of the Nicene position completely denied an economic Trinity. This shift was accepted by the church in order to remain Orthodox.

At several points the presentation speaks of "Protestants" and various "Protestant Confessions." There may be persons and texts of the kind described in the essay, but these views are not accurate for the major traditions that arose in the Western church in the sixteenth century. Thus the descriptions are caricatures that do not aid ecumenical advance.

Jaroslav Pelikan has made a distinction that I have often found useful.[4] He speaks of traditionalism as the dead faith of the living. This is what Orthodoxy is not. Yet I fear at times this is the conclusion that could be drawn from Archbishop Methodios' paper. On the other hand, Professor Pelikan also mentions Tradition as the living faith of the dead, those who went before and yet live. That is Orthodoxy. It is the faith of the Orthodox Churches, the church of Archbishop Methodios. These are churches with which Lutherans internationally and in the United States are in serious ecumenical dialogue. It is why Archbishop Methodios is so warmly welcome at this consultation.

Notes

ARCHBISHOP METHODIOS

1. Cf. Archbishop Methodios, "On the Ecclesiastical Economy. A Reply to the Professors of Theology," *Theological and Historical Studies* 4 (1983) 153-310. As in the above work, so here, in this essay, I write with Orthodox "liberality," which represents Orthodox realism, rather than a particular view of my own.

2. G. Florovsky, "The Limits of the Church," *Church Quarterly Review* 117 (1933) 117-31.

3. Cf. H. Meyer, "Fundamental Difference — Fundamental Consensus. The Impact of Bilateral Dialogues on the Ecumenical Movement," *Mid-Stream* 25 (1986) 247.

4. W. J. Birkbeck, *Russia and the English Church* (London: SPCK, 1895) 216.

5. "Reply to the W.C.C. on the Text Baptism, Eucharist and Ministry" by the Ecumenical Patriarchate, *Episkepsis* 367 (1986) 8-12 (in Greek). "Inter-Orthodox Symposium on Baptism, Eucharist and Ministry," *Churches respond to B.E.M. Official responses to "Baptism, Eucharist and Ministry"* (ed. M. Thurian; Faith and Order Paper 129; Geneva: W.C.C., 1986) 1:122-29. The response of this Symposium to BEM is *very elastic*. "An Agreed Statement on

the Lima Document Baptism, Eucharist and Ministry," the Eastern Orthodox/
Roman Catholic Consultation, USA, *Diakonia* 19 (1984-85) 152-57. This consultation too makes allowances in order to facilitate the rapprochement of the
churches.

WILLIAM G. RUSCH

1. William G. Rusch, *Ecumenism — A Movement toward Church Unity*
(Philadelphia: Fortress Press, 1985) 106-109.

2. See for example, Jaroslav Pelikan, *Development of Christian Doctrine:
Some Historical Prolegomena* (New Haven: Yale University Press, 1969).

3. See William G. Rusch, "Some Comments on Athanasius' *Contra Arianos*
I, 3," in *Arianism: Historical and Theological Reassessments* (Philadelphia: The
Philadelphia Patristic Foundation, Ltd., 1985) 223-32.

4. Jaroslav Pelikan, *The Vindication of Tradition* (New Haven: Yale University Press, 1984) esp. 65.

10

Fundamental Consensus and Church Fellowship

A Roman Catholic Perspective

Pierre Duprey

FIRST OF ALL, I am glad to be concentrating here on the more positive side of the overall study project, "Fundamental Consensus." I have run through the already abundant literature about fundamental differences, real or possible. The fairly considerable variety of possible fundamental differences, it can be said in passing, hardly indicates that they are very fundamental. In any case, I am happy to be dealing with the positive side of it. But, second, I am glad that the question has been set in the framework of the church as communion. This at least is how I interpret the second part of the theme, "Church Fellowship." The theme of the church as communion has deep significance for me, as I will explain.

What I intend to do first in this presentation is to speak of an ecclesiology of communion as a framework for discussing basic consensus. Then I wish to comment from the perspective of Catholic experience on the ecumenical way in which we have been seeking consensus thus far. Third, in relationship to the question of how much consensus is necessary for unity, I will speak of a criterion for discerning consensus. I will then end with some concluding observations. But first let me say a brief word about approaching the notion of fundamental consensus.

In doing our task, it is possible to approach the notion of fundamental consensus in different ways. One could sketch what might be a fundamental agreement, a central point of agreement, which would remove supposed ambiguities from partial agreements and allow the progressive recovery between us of the organic unity found in the "faith which was once for all delivered to the saints" (Jude 3).

But the task required of me is more formal: To what sort of "basic consensus" should the search for unity be directed? This is by no means easier, nor do I believe it can be separated from the former alternative.

Ecclesial Communion as a Framework for Basic Consensus

I am more and more convinced that for Catholics the possibility of a genuine ecumenical commitment comes from the opening created by the Second Vatican Council for an ecclesiology of communion. Already in 1975 in a speech given at Vienna, Cardinal Johannes Willebrands saw the future of ecumenism in an ecclesiology of communion in all its dimensions.[1] Moreover, it is this standpoint which allows an authentic interpretation of a good many important passages in the conciliar texts.[2] The search for unity and the search for reestablishing full communion between our churches are for Catholics two synonymous expressions. I do not have to develop this notion of communion here. It has been done elsewhere.[3] I would simply like to note here that since *koinonia* is the relationship existing between persons or communities that participate in the same gifts of God, the understanding of *koinonia* and the depth of meaning that one will acknowledge it to have will depend directly on the depth of meaning that one attributes to these gifts themselves. I believe that this is particularly important for Catholics with regard to their sacramental conception of ministry in apostolic succession and the way in which it structures universal communion around the Bishop of Rome who, while existing within the communion, also presides over it. I mention it in order to place the notion of consensus, of agreement in faith, within the perspective of ecclesial communion. Still, agreement or consensus in faith is only one element of communion—fundamental, to be sure, but inseparable from other elements such as a common sacramental life in a community preserved in charity, faith, and hope by its pastors. These elements are inseparable just as Christ is inseparably the way, the truth, and the life.

They are inseparable, but, once dissociated, how can they be reintegrated? How can one have a common sacramental life, that is to say, a practical profession of a common faith in the shared mystery, while one is divided, and divided on the subject of the confession of that faith? Moreover, how does one rediscover that agreement in faith without common experience of the mystery in a community animated by fraternal charity? Is this a vicious circle, i.e., to search for the agreement which will allow us to establish communion without these conditions of communion necessary for agreement?

What this points to, I believe, is the organic, wholistic character of Christian unity, that is, of the communion of the life of members of one and the same body at all levels of that life.

First, *at the level of the life of faith.* Organic unity of Christian truth, as Vatican II wished to affirm it in the famous no. 11 of *Unitatis*

Redintegratio, is: "In confronting doctrines, they shall remember that there exists an order or hierarchy of the truths of Catholic doctrine by reason of their different link with the foundation of the Christian faith."

Christian truths are not simply juxtaposed to one another. They are not like a catalogue of propositions. They are organically articulated about a center or foundation. When the Council speaks of *foundation,* it is not thinking of fundamental notions of revelation, but of Christ the truth, the way, and the life. It is thinking of the only Son in whom and through whom humanity, renewed and recapitulated, can, in the Holy Spirit, be offered to the Father, to whom it returns to be consumed in an eternal unity of giving and of love.[4] The center or foundation is not just the truths revealed by Christ. It is the person himself who is given in word and sacraments, who through the Spirit makes us children and makes us share the mysterious life in the unity of the three divine persons, the origin and end of all being, the ultimate and whole foundation of all reality, which, insofar as it exists, reflects him. The truths are only glimpses of this mystery of being and of love.

But how precious are these glimpses, however partial, since it is God himself who has revealed them to us! Every effort of the church's faith through the ages, of the faith of believers throughout their lives, is to contemplate them, to scrutinize them, to discover the mysterious bonds which unite them to each other and make them illustrate each other. In this way we discover that certain truths are "explanations" or "protections" of the central mystery, the mystery of God one and three and God's plan of salvation.

The hierarchy of truths of which the Council speaks is not therefore a distinction between the objective content of the faith and the theological explanation, between a dogmatic truth and its theological explanation. It concerns an order among revealed truths. It concerns the organic links which provide the hierarchical unity of these truths, all of which are directed toward the ultimate and global truth of the God who is love, just as they are all illuminated by and reflect that ultimate truth. Obviously, to see how these truths are organized and ordered in relation to the foundation of the Christian faith, we must enter sufficiently into these truths. This is why I said earlier that this perception is the result of lifelong contemplation by the believer and by the church throughout the whole of its tradition. We shall return to this.

We cannot but recall here the decree of the Council of Trent on the Nicene-Constantinopolitan Creed, expressing the heart of the Christian faith in a short and powerful resumé of the history of salvation: ". . . this creed in which all who profess the faith of Christ necessarily join, since it is this principle and this *firm and unique foundation* against which the gates of hell shall never prevail. . . ."[5] Certain theologians have recently suggested that we should use as a profession of faith verses 3-13 of chapter 1 of the Epistle to the Ephesians where there is "a remarkable fusion of the biblical perspective of the people of God and the new idea of the Church as body of Christ"[6] which is at the heart of that organic synthesis of the divine plan of salvation.

Before trying to draw from these statements some consequences which I think can be useful for our purpose, I should like to emphasize another level of the church's life where this wholistic unity is manifested, the sacramental level.

The Catholic tradition, of which St. Thomas Aquinas is here also a notable witness, does regard the sacraments as an organic unity. The view of the sacraments offered by the Council of Trent, which here closely follows St. Thomas, forbids putting all the sacraments on the same plane and rather demands that a real hierarchy be maintained among them, with the Eucharist at the center, even though they are all equally sacraments, numbered one to seven.

An Ecumenical Way of Seeking Consensus

What consequences has this for our subject? What does it say about our way of seeking consensus? At first glance it might suggest that the first effort at restoring unity of faith ought to be to look for an agreement on the most fundamental principle of that faith and then to deduce its consequences by following the objective organic links so discovered. This deductive method is a possibility attractive in the highest degree to every truly theological mind. But would it be realistic and effective in the present state of division? I do not think so, and I shall explain why later.

I believe, on the contrary, that the organic character of Christian faith fully justifies the inductive method followed in the various dialogues. Moreover, I think it is the method indicated by Vatican II in the decree *Unitatis Redintegratio*[7] and that this was the standpoint from which it felt the need to affirm the existence of a hierarchy of truths.

In fact, by starting from the points on which divergence has brought about divisions, we do not separate those points from the organic whole to which they belong. By going into them deeply we bring out their connecting links and perhaps discover other difficulties to go into and overcome. Let me give some examples which do not directly involve Lutherans and hence may be less familiar to you.

In the Anglican-Catholic dialogue (ARCIC I), which began in 1970, we started with the Eucharist, convinced that without agreement on that there could be no real agreement on ministry and especially on the sacerdotal character of the ordained ministry, a nerve center of Anglican-Catholic controversy. It then became clear that an agreement on ministry and its structure was a necessary preliminary to any consideration of authority in the church. All this made up the final report of ARCIC I. It aroused among other things two kinds of reaction. Evangelicals said: Very well, you talk to us about sacraments and authority, but where is the fundamental principle of the Reformation, justification by faith alone? Catholics said: You speak of the Eucharist, of ordination, of authority, but nothing about the church as sacrament except in a very brief and over-condensed way in your introduction. These reactions were the point of departure for the work of ARCIC II, which has issued a document entitled "Salvation and the Church."

An altogether different type of dialogue is that between Catholics and Pentecostals. Here the starting point was the life of prayer. Our first concern in the first phase was to clarify together the primacy of the theological over experience, over the "happening." But very empirically our partners discovered with us that one cannot talk of prayer without talking of liturgy, nor talk of liturgy without talking of the Eucharist, nor talk of the Eucharist without talking of the church, nor talk of the church without talking of Christ and his relation to the Holy Spirit. And so on.

In "Faith and Order" I still believe that the Nairobi declaration on the unity we seek was and is very important. I say this without any provocative intention in the presence of certain friends who are promoters of an apparently opposing formula. I say this because I believe that what the Nairobi description of the unity looked for is also important methodologically, which is our concern here. It is a description which had been preceded, both before and after the colloquium at Salamanca, by many refinements aimed at avoiding confusion between "consilium" and "concilium" and at making clear the pre-conciliar nature of what we currently intend by councils of churches. It supposed also that the phrase "conciliar fellowship" be invested with the rich significations of *koinonia*. Patient though it may still be of differing interpretations, the formula "conciliar fellowship of local churches truly united" is not only objectively capable of a Catholic interpretation, but as a goal it can provide a unifying framework for other tasks of Faith and Order which aim to pinpoint the elements constituting a local church truly united and to outline precisely the elements which go to build a conciliar fellowship of local churches.

Baptism, Eucharist and Ministry is the most celebrated result of this work, but it is not the only one. Here too it is the organic hierarchy of Christian reality which prompts the development of research as long as there is care to maintain the direction and continuity of the research, for membership of the commission frequently changes and is not always fully aware of earlier work and its intentions.

The inductive method may seem scattered to those who do not see the need to involve wider and wider circles of the faithful in dialogue, so that conceptual difficulties may develop. The method may seem of little effect to those not sufficiently acquainted with the whole range of dialogues and their often converging development. It may seem too slow to those who see the urgency of common witness by Christians in the contemporary world and realize that such witness can never be fully common until there is agreement on its whole content and on all its conditions, which are not merely intellectual.

Partial agreements, both because of their subject and because of their limited character on any particular subject, bring out the need for global agreement. It is perhaps not cynical to say that in some cases the very progress of partial agreements frightens people, so that they take refuge in looking for fundamental differences, which will not be the root from which fundamental healing comes but rather an excuse for telling ourselves that such healing is impossible. I can only reject with all the force of my Christian convictions this form of defeatism.

The progress of partial agreements provokes the desire for a global agreement or (why not admit it) the fear of such agreement, a fear which is connected with that question of identity fashionable today when so many personalities do not reach maturity. In fact, I believe immaturity is the reason for the fashion, since problems of identity are typically problems of adolescence, and adolescence is not just a question of age.

Progress in partial agreements allows us to raise the question of full agreement and to begin trying to define what it might be. Here lies the usefulness, I would even say necessity, of the work we are undertaking. There can be more and more interaction between these two aspects of ecumenical work. We can see a kind of outline of this interaction in the work of Faith and Order trying to describe the goal and then going on to define its elements and conditions.

We can think also here of the recent Lutheran-Catholic document *Facing Unity*. Yet I think we must avoid suspending inductive and progressive enquiry and concentrating our study only on fundamental divergences or fundamental agreement.

There is still a lot of work to do on the first of these levels. Nothing causes delay so much as being overly hasty. The latter would mean forgetting that slow and profound work on particular points enables us to discern more exactly the conditions of full agreement and to progress toward it. We come back again to the organic and hierarchically ordered unity of revealed truth.

Consensus and Diversity?

Obviously this leaves untouched the question: How far is agreement required? How far can and should diversity remain? I believe it is difficult to determine this precisely and concretely *a priori*. We know that agreement on what belongs to faith should be complete. But then comes the question of discerning what belongs to faith and what is simply its expression, its organization. Given the unfathomable richness of the mystery[8] and the innate limits of all intelligence even when enlivened by the greatest gifts of the Spirit, the hierarchy of truths will be perceived differently, and we shall always be faced with many hierarchies of truths partly differing from each other. How far are these differences compatible and not opposed to full agreement?

During the centuries when East and West, in spite of tensions, acknowledged each other more or less explicitly as living and professing the same apostolic faith, comparison of the two traditions was a sure means of distinguishing between what belongs to faith and what is a matter of legitimate diversity. In order to do that, it was necessary for each party to trust in the good faith, in the *"intentio fidei,"* of the other. This attitude is still evident at the Council of Trent, which expressly avoided letting certain texts be interpreted as condemning some Eastern traditions.

We find this conviction to be even deeper today when John Paul II says that the church must learn again to breathe with both its lungs, the Eastern and the Western.

In the dialogues, too, we discover through better knowledge of each other and deeper study that some of what appears to be opposing positions are more "complementary than conflicting,"[9] and, when better situated within the whole and thereby better illuminated, they can cease to be a cause of division and be seen as matters of legitimate diversity.

What is the Criterion for Discernment?

What is the criterion for discernment? How do we apply it with precision? There comes to mind here something which surprised me at the time but which I now realize expressed profound truth. It was more than ten years ago, I think, during a meeting in London of representatives of united and uniting churches with secretaries of what were then called "World Confessional Families." The representative of the United Church of Christ in Zaire said: "You Catholics are a collection of confessional families. You place alongside an episcopal structure the powerful presbyteral structures of your religious orders, each of which has its own way of accentuating and organizing its conception of the Christian life. You keep all that in unity, even though not always without tensions, because you all acknowledge the authority and the magisterium of discernment found in the bishop of Rome."

I was surprised, and I have often reflected on it since. Now I would like to complete the statement by explaining it. The full meaning of this insight could be seen if he had added: "You all admit the faith of the church in all its dimensions."

I believe that here we reach an important point to which I have already alluded twice. For Catholics the whole effort of the church's faith through the ages has been to discover, preserve, illuminate, and to locate every aspect and every requirement of that faith given once for all to the saints. It is in the life of the church, with all its limitations and infidelities but with the Spirit keeping it indefectibly in the truth, that that truth is guarded and transmitted in its wholeness. The diversities which our Zairian friend pointed to were maintained in unity because they were located in the life of the church, which they enriched by their very diversity. Do we not go back here to the profound significance of a rite of the ancient church, the *traditio symboli?* It is the faith of the church that we receive, it is the faith of the church that we assimilate, it is the faith of the church that we profess and, during the whole course of our lives as believers, we strive to be docile before the Spirit who imbues us with that faith and by doing so, makes us steadily discover its organic unity and the wonderful coherence of the divine plan of salvation, the manifestation of the mystery of God who is love.

Only the church can maintain in unity the various attempts, always approximate, to express and live the hierarchy of truths. That hierarchy will never be fully disclosed to us except in the encounter "face to face," and then our wonder and adoration will go, as St. Gregory of Nyssa said, "from beginnings to beginnings through beginnings which never end."[10]

I think that our Zairian friend saw intuitively that we can never have fundamental agreement unless it totally accepts what is beyond us, where our subjectivity, our personal and community limits, are overcome by the acceptance, beyond any exclusive choice, of the whole faith entrusted to and passed on by the church. Is that not its mission and *raison d'être?* It is in the organic unity of the ecclesial communion that agreement continues and rises above diversities and tensions, onesidedness and exclusiveness. Think of the quarrels about grace between the Dominicans and the Jesuits, or the one about "pure love" in the days of Bossuet and Fénelon. In these cases and in many more today "it was as though the whole faith, the whole truth of the gospel, the whole church was at stake." The more we are rooted in the communion of the church and in its faith, the more open we are to legitimate diversity, the freer from onesidedness, exclusiveness, and intolerance.

Is not this the criterion suggested by the BEM document when it asks whether we find therein "the faith of the Church throughout the ages"?

Clearly this demands of each and every one of us in the ecclesial community and of the community itself that continual effort at conversion of heart and at renewal which is bound up with genuine Christian living, a continual effort to penetrate the faith, to purify its expressions, and to protect it against innumerable occasions that enfeeble and alter it. Pius XII once said that tradition was a continuing struggle with innovation in order both to remain faithful to one and the same Spirit in ever new circumstances and to deal with the problems new circumstances raise in cultural environments that the gospel must encounter.

The way to finding full agreement again surely requires us to recall the axiom: We are united by what we affirm, we oppose each other by what we deny. This has a lot to teach us, even in ecumenism. Every time we reject agreement, we arrest progress. Every time we try to affirm together positively what the rejection was intended to express superficially and in a facile way, we open the way to agreement or at least to an understanding of each other.

Suggestions for Moving Toward Fundamental Agreement

I said at the beginning that it was difficult to separate two aspects of "basic consensus": What type of fundamental consensus is required, or, on what points should agreement be reached to ensure the coherence of the whole, i.e., to eliminate ambiguity. I am conscious that I have perhaps not been strict enough and not distinguished sufficiently between these two aspects.

But I would like to conclude by describing some key issues, the deeper exploration of which could lead to a fundamental agreement which would overcome any fundamental divergences.

1. Do we think of the transcendence of God in too human a fashion? Do we project onto him our notions of transcendence by affirming

146

the fullness of God in such a way as to exclude real participation by man in that fullness, when, since St. Ireneus, we know that the glory of God is the living man and the life of man is the contemplation of God? This deepening of the notion of transcendence demands also reflection on the following issues.

2. Must we not deepen our theology of creation, which holds that the created being is brought into existence at the beginning with all his own dynamism, for we seem to forget that existence and that dynamism are only there because they are totally and here and now dependent on God's creative power? At stake is the question of time and its relation to the eternity of God.

3. Must we not examine further the efficacy of the word of God and consequently the reality and consistency of the transformation that it works in human beings through the Spirit and the reality of the new dynamism with which it charges them? Must we not examine the reality too of the gifts which God gives to justified man in justifying him, gifts which more and more help man on the way to his sanctification in total and actual dependence on the Spirit, both in his being and in his activity as a new human being?

4. Does not our conception of the church have to be enriched and deepened in view of the considerations I have put forward here so as to free that conception from being punctiliar and discontinuous, the more or less conscious result of a forensic and outdated notion of justification?

It is the totality of God which is in question; it is the *soli Deo gloria* we are concerned about, and that is what is thrilling, that only is truly thrilling.

A LUTHERAN RESPONSE

Eric W. Gritsch

FATHER DUPREY'S essay views the problem of "fundamental consensus" in the context of "the church as communion," a view that is grounded in Vatican II's "ecclesiology of communion." According to Father Duprey such a view "points to the organic, wholistic character of Christian unity, that is, of the communion of life of the members of one and the same body at all levels of that life. Life and faith are anchored in a "foundation" namely "Christ the truth, the way, and the life"; and Christian truths "are not like a catalogue of propositions," but "are organically articulated about. . . [this] foundation." In this sense doctrines are rooted in a hierarchy of truths "by reason of their different link with the foundation of the Christian faith." (pp. 139–40)

Father Duprey views the task of an ecclesiology of communion as the theological explication and ecclesial application of this view of the church as a body, with Christ as foundation (or head). All members of that body are to live in organic union with each other, participate in the same gifts in *koinonia,* and view the search for unity and the search for full communion with each other as two synonymous expressions. (p. 139) Father Duprey detects a strong convergence between such an ecclesiology and that of the Lima Document (BEM), which also focuses on "the organic hierarchy of Christian reality" as the basis of ecumenical research. (p. 143) If such a view were abandoned, the ecumenical enterprise, especially ecumenical dialogue, would end up in a search for fundamental difference rather than for fundamental consensus. (p. 143) But a dialogue based on the affirmation of the organic unity of the church can move, without fear, from partial toward global agreement. Father Duprey tries to show how such dialogue can catch glimpses of Christian unity by showing the connecting links between divergences and divisions and the organic unity of the Church, whose full expression is hidden in the future.

What is at issue in such an ecclesiology of communion is "the criterion for discernment." (p.144) Father Duprey is aware of the complexity of this issue because he knows that it involves discernment of the manifestations of the divine mystery of love in the plurality of Christian traditions. He contends that "Only the church can maintain in unity the various attempts, always approximate, to express and live the hierarchy of truths. . . [which] will never be fully disclosed to us except in the encounter 'face to face' " in wonder and adoration. (p.145) Father Duprey uses such eschatological and doxological language to describe the criterion of discernment. In this regard "we can never have fundamental agreement unless it totally accepts what is beyond us. . . beyond any exclusive choice, of the whole faith entrusted to and passed on by the church." (p.145)

Father Duprey's sketch of the foundation of an ecclesiology of communion is both attractive and provocative. It is attractive because it presents Roman Catholic juridical assertions about the church in the context of nonpropositional, imaginative language, using the images of body and organic relationships. It is also provocative because it places the notion of consensus within the perspective of ecclesial communion, the basic components of which are a sacramental conception of ministry in apostolic succession structured around the bishop of Rome. (p.139)

The question arises, "What and where is the church?" On the one hand, Father Duprey speaks of the church as the place where Christ, its foundation, is reflected and where Christian truths are only glimpses of the mystery of divine being and love. On the other hand, he speaks about the church whose foundation, Christ, is definitely linked to an apostolic succession of witnesses headed by the bishop of Rome. It seems as if eschatological and somewhat mystical theological reflections are combined with juridical and canon law assertions. The question is how the "hierarchy of truths" (*Unitatis Redintegratio,* no. 11) is related to the eschatologically perceived unity of the church and to the historical expression of this unity in the Roman Catholic Church as described in *Lumen Gentium* 8, namely "this Church, constituted and organized in the world as a society *(in hoc mundo ut societas constituta et ordinata)* subsists in the Catholic Church *(in Ecclesia catholica)* which is governed by the successor of Peter and by the bishops in union with him *(a successore Petri et Episcopis in eius communione gubernator).*" If *"subsists"* means that the Roman Catholic expression of the unity of the church is partial rather than full, then any global agreement among churches would have to be based on a fundamental consensus that all churches are partners in the search for unity. If, however, *"subsists"* means that the Roman Catholic Church is the only historical expression of the fullness of the church still hidden in time, then all other such expressions would be only a reflection of not yet recognized and accepted ways of being Roman Catholic.

The relationship between the church's foundation, Christ, and the historical expressions of the faith grounded in the center is to be defined by dialogue. Dialogue with the Roman Catholic Church has begun to deal with the tension between the affirmation of the organic unity of the church and the historical expression of such unity. The Lutheran-Catholic dialogue, both in North America and on the international level, has begun to clear the ground for long-range work on doctrinal and non doctrinal issues and their significance on what is and is not church divisive. In view of the partial results of this dialogue, Father Duprey's theological sketch of the rationale for a fundamental consensus as it relates to church fellowship needs to be amplified by further explorations of existing basic differences. These differences are rooted in the formation of traditions necessitated by the move from the affirmation of Christ as the foundation of the church to doctrinal and magisterial assertions based on specific structures of thought and practice.

It has become evident that the basic differences are related to the question of ministry, particularly the teaching ministry of the church, and any ecclesiology of communion must deal with this question. I would like to mention two aspects of the question and add them to the "key points" which Father Duprey listed for deeper exploration on the way to "fundamental agreement." (pp.146-47)

> The nature, function, and development of dogma, which could be called a "hermeneutics of dogma" (*Dogmenhermeneutik*); and

> the nature, function, and development of the ministerial office (*magisterium*), which could be called "a hermeneutics of the office" (*Amtshermeneutik*).

Much progress has been made in understanding the historical development of dogma, particularly when dogmas are viewed as historical expressions of the one truth, Christ, in a variety of thought structures. In this respect the notion of a "hierarchy of truths" has been quite helpful. But much less progress has been made in understanding the historical development of the ministerial office as a divinely instituted, indeed sacramental means to nurture and protect the gospel as it is disclosed in Scripture and in the apostolic tradition. If there is an inseparable link between Christ and the ministry through which he is mediated, as ecumenical research has shown, then the question arises about the legitimacy of the plurality of expressions of such a ministry.

Is there only *one* magisterium that is indefectible, indeed infallible? Or could there be a pluriform sharing of magisterial authority, a "magisterial mutuality" (L-RC 6:36,55) between churches, by which the nurture and protection of the gospel is assured? The answer to these questions may determine what constitutes "fundamental consensus," "basic difference," and "church fellowship," at least in the dialogue between Roman Catholics and non-Roman Catholics.

Father Duprey cited Pope Pius XII as saying, "that tradition was a continuing struggle with innovation in order both to remain faithful to one and the same Spirit in ever new circumstances. . . ." (p.146) Such a view of tradition recognizes the possibility of a negative development of dogma, an underdevelopment, and of an unfaithful exercise of magisterial authority. Thus it would be quite appropriate to include, in an ecclesiology of communion, the task of moving toward a fundamental consensus on the need for penance and renewal.

Notes

DUPREY
1. "L'avenir de l'oecuménisme," *Proche Orient Chrétien* 21 (1975) 3-15.
2. For example, UR 11; LG 8. Without this perspective the interpretation of these passages and of many others becomes distorted.
3. Cf. Pierre Duprey, "A Catholic Perspective on Ecclesial Communion," *Christian Authority* (Chadwick Festschrift; ed. G. R. Evans; Oxford: Oxford University Press, 1988) 7-19; also, Jean Tillard, "Ecclésiologie de communion et exigence oecuménique," *Irenikon* 59 (1986) 201-203; and *Eglise d'Eglises. L'ecclésiologie de communion* (Paris: du Cerf, 1987).
4. Cf. 1 Cor 15:20-28; Eph 1:3-4.
5. DS 1500. Emphasis added.
6. *Traduction oecuménique de la Bible*, 569.
7. UR 11, 19-23.
8. Cf. Eph 3:16-19.
9. UR 17.
10. PG 44:941A.

11

Fundamental Consensus and Church Fellowship

A Reformed Perspective

Paul R. Fries

THE FOLLOWING ESSAY essay will explore what might constitute a "fundamental consensus" leading to "church fellowship" from the perspective of the Reformed tradition. What do Reformed churches look for before agreeing to make a covenant of mutual recognition? What do they hold to be necessary for "altar and pulpit fellowship"? The answers to such simply stated questions are far from obvious; indeed, their pursuit thrusts us directly into a snarl of methodological issues. A response to the problem of fundamental consensus in Reformed perspective is possible only after an examination of such difficulties and the establishment of a credible method.

An imposing difficulty is immediately encountered when the question of a Reformed perspective on "fundamental consensus" is addressed. Who speaks for the Reformed tradition? Even a superficial reading of church history reveals the polysemous character of the Reformed family. There are over seventy million Christians who identify themselves as Reformed at the present time, most of whom are affiliated with the World Alliance of Reformed Churches. Of the 161 member churches, two-thirds are in the so-called Third World. Can any one person hope to articulate for so great a diversity the meaning of fundamental consensus? Where shall we seek the Reformed "position"? A survey of reports produced by bilateral and trilateral consultations on the national and international levels proves instructive, but hardly solves the problems of fundamental consensus. Who such documents speak for and their authority, if any, remains uncertain. Moreover, the interests and emphases of the several reports vary, each document reflecting concerns raised by dialogue partners and the theological inclinations of the Reformed participants. For example, as Andre Birmelé points out, in the Reformed-Baptist dialogue the little said about the Reformed view of ministry has a congregationalist ring; in the Reformed-Roman Catholic conversations, ministry is presented in a classically Reformed manner; and in the Reformed-Anglican bilateral an almost catholic view of ministry is offered.[1] Can such statements be harmonized to yield a Reformed doctrine of ministry?

The statements of particular Reformed churches on fellowship would carry us no further in our search for an authoritative Reformed voice. Certainly no one familiar with the Reformed tradition would suggest that any given church could represent others. No inclusive Reformed ecumenical council has been held since Dort in the seventeenth century, and its pronouncements are certainly not universally accepted by Reformed churches. Surveying a number of documents on ecumenical issues produced by the churches of the Reformed tradition in our day and cataloging their pronouncements on fundamental consensus might prove interesting, but the result would be an artificial construct which would represent no actual Reformed body and thus carry no formal authority.

The polyphonous character of the Reformed tradition does not represent the only difficulty encountered when addressing the question of fundamental consensus. Reformed voices not only vary, but have often spoken in opposition to one another. This has been especially evident in debates over issues of ecumenical significance. From its earliest days Reformed theology has been represented by both narrow and broad "constructionists," and Reformed churches have exhibited both centrifugal and centripetal impulses. These become evident in the ecumenical stance exhibited by churches of the Reformed family.

The frequently made observation that the Reformed tradition has been committed to church unity from its inception is not without historical evidence. Calvin's efforts to bring unity to the churches of the Swiss cantons is well known, while his eagerness for fellowship with Lutherans was so strong that McNeill and Nichols describe it as an "almost pathetic craving."[2] Those guided by Calvin's theology also affirmed the oneness of the church, as is indicated by at least some of the Confessional statements produced during the Reformation. Under Beza's leadership the *Harmonia confessionum fidei* appeared as an elegant but vain attempt to bridge the fault separating Lutherans and the Reformed by showing the fundamental agreement of Reformation Confessional statements.[3] In the Netherlands Calvin's solicitousness for the unity of the church was reflected in the efforts of distinguished theologians such as Junius, Arminius, Grotius, and Oldenbarnevelt.[4]

Similar Reformed concern for the unity of the church is evidenced during the following centuries. In our own time Reformed participation in the ecumenical movement has been noteworthy. Ecumenical leadership has frequently come from the Reformed family, ecumenical theologies from its scholars and teachers, designs for fellowship from its administrators. Strong affirmations of ecumenical commitment have come both from national churches as well as from the World Alliance of Reformed Churches. A statement of the Princeton General Council of WARC illustrates twentieth century Reformed ecumenical commitment:

> We believe that the deep stirring among the churches and Christian groups to surmount the barriers and to express the unity of the community of believers in accordance with the mind and will of Jesus Christ, the Head of the Church. . . is of God, not of men, a sign of the Holy Spirit.[5]

Such a statement expresses an understanding of the church consonant with the unitive spirit expressed in Calvin's theology and ministry. It testifies to a broad and centripetal understanding of Reformed theology modest in its definition of what is "fundamental" for fundamental consensus.

As notable as such evidences of Reformed commitment to the task of church unity may be, self-congratulation is hardly warranted. Every instance of centripetal Reformed action appears to be countered by scores of examples of centrifugal tendencies. Not only have Reformed churches frequently erected dikes to keep out the eroding influences of other Protestant churches, but the Reformed family itself has again and again been torn by fractious action. The cause of the great Dutch advocates of unity mentioned above was defeated by an assertive Calvinism which recognized fellowship only on the basis of the so-called five points of Calvinism, thus forcing the formation of the Remonstrance church in the Netherlands. This split was a harbinger of things to come. Through the eighteenth and nineteenth centuries Reformed Christianity was ravaged by division after division, on the continent, in Scotland, and eventually in America. There is a Dutch adage which holds that one Calvinist makes a theologian, two a theological dispute, and three Calvinists a split into two churches. Unfortunately the extolled Reformed principle *ecclesia reformata quia reformanda est* often served not to preserve the unity of the church through continuing reform, but like the formula spoken by the sorcerer's apprentice, to initiate seemingly endless and unstoppable multiplication.

Happily, the twentieth century has seen the slowing of this historic fractioning of the Reformed family and even, in some instances, its reversal. But it is sobering to note that mergers even within a Confessional family are infrequent and difficult while those uniting Reformed churches with other traditions even rarer and more difficult. As encouraging as was the formation of the Presbyterian Church (U.S.A.) through the joining of the Presbyterian Church in the United States and the United Presbyterian Church in the U.S.A., this remarkable accomplishment was overshadowed by the absence of the smaller Presbyterian churches and the formation of a new dissenting church. And even in our century of heady ecumenism, a number of Reformed bodies continue to resist the call to unity, articulating the conditions for fellowship in accordance with those established by the Calvinistic orthodoxy of a prior age.

The plurality and division evident in the Reformed tradition must to a significant degree be attributed to its understanding of church order. A long established principle of Reformed ecclesiology holds that no authority is superior to the highest judicatory of a particular church.[6] This means that for most churches of the Reformed tradition, representatives of presbyteries or classes in regular synodical gathering exercise ultimate authority. No church may speak for another. The acts of the Synod of Dort, for example, carried no formal authority for the non-Dutch churches represented at the Synod.[7] Only through ratification in its own assembly does a particular church give authority to the action of another body, whether that body be a local church or council of churches. While one may be sympathetic with the purposes prompting the 1982 Assembly of the World Alliance of Reformed Churches to declare a *status confessionus* in response to the indefensible position of the white Reformed churches of South Africa on apartheid, its authority to do so is questionable. Similarly, as noted above, the conclusions of bilateral or trilateral consultations involving Reformed participants have no official status until adopted by a local church, and then speak only for that body. These reflections carry us to the heart of the methodological problem before us.

Reformed theology makes no provision for pronouncements on behalf of its tradition. One may rightly speak of a Reformed *magisterium,* but only in reference to its churches, not to the tradition itself. When someone talks of "the Reformed position," such a statement represents a generalization and not an accurate statement of Reformed theology. Thus to ask the question in such a way that it implies a unified Reformed view of fundamental consensus must be ruled out of court on *a priori* theological grounds.

Still, to refuse to engage the issue of fundamental consensus would result in the withdrawal of Reformed participation from significant arenas of ecumenical conversation. We believe that there is a method which would allow the identification of a Reformed perspective, but caution that its results will be neither definitive nor normative. The method we propose will take into account the decentralized understanding of authority characteristic of Reformed churches. The Reformed tradition may be imaged as a musical composition in which each section of an orchestra renders common themes according to a particular vision of music and performance. The unity of tradition would be sought not in the themes themselves, for Reformed churches have never claimed to represent anything but the Christian faith, but in the manner of their interpretation and rendering. When we speak of the Reformed tradition, we refer to fundamental evangelical teachings of the catholic church as interpreted and rendered by the churches of the Reformed Reformation. Our method, then, will attempt to formulate a Reformed perspective on fundamental consensus by analyzing the faith and practice of the churches of the Reformed family, much as a musicologist might attempt to generalize about the works of a composer by examining the way the material is symphonically developed.

We have already spoken of the diversity of the Reformed family. The pluriformity of the tradition is seen also in the practices of its churches. For example, most Reformed churches are Confessional, but not all. Congregationalists subscribe to no Confessions, although faith is confessed through covenants written by the congregation. Moreover, Confessions do not provide the basis for unity even among those churches which employ them. Confessional standards used by the various Reformed churches differ, and their role in the life of a denomination varies. The Presbyterian Church (U.S.A.), for example, has added a large number of Confessional statements to the historical Westminster Catechism, while the Reformed Church of America subscribes only to three reformational standards, *viz.,* The Heidelberg Catechism, The Belgic Confession, and the Canons of the Synod of Dort. Some Reformed churches continue to write Confessions (the most recent one, to my knowledge, being the so-called Belhar Confession of the colored Zendings Kerk of South Africa), while others have refused to do so.

The same pluriformity is evidenced in Reformed church order. The presbyterian form of government, so closely associated with the Reformed tradition, is not found among British Congregationalists or in the American United Church of Christ. Thus the Reformed elder, rightly regarded as one of the unique contributions of the Reformed Reformation to the world church, does not exist in all Reformed churches! Some Reformed bodies acknowledge two offices in the church, the minister of the word, and elder; others three, minister, elder, and deacon; and at least one retains Calvin's office of doctor of the church. The office of bishop, not regarded as a feature of Reformed order, has been long established in the Hungarian Reformed Church.

Other examples of diversity in the Reformed tradition might be given. Since, as has already been seen, such pluriformity is to a certain degree an expression of Reformed theology, it should not be regarded as an accident of history but rather an essential feature of the Reformed tradition. Thus any understanding of Reformed Christianity must build on it. At the same time the question of what unifies the Reformed family remains. Articulation of a Reformed consensus on fundamental perspective must develop out of this tension between unity and diversity. How shall we proceed? The constitution of the World Alliance of Reformed Churches suggests a fruitful approach. It acknowledges the pluriformity of the tradition it represents when refusing to establish any *conditio sine qua non* for Reformed identity, speaking rather of a "biblical, evangelical, and doctrinal ethos." We take ethos to mean those theological values, norms, and objectives implicit in the total life of a church: its liturgy, order, administration, education, hymns, mission, style, mores, and the like. Generally these are assumed and may not be recognized until made explicit through preaching and teaching. Our question becomes, then: What elements constitute the unifying ethos of the Reformed family?

Lukas Vischer identifies a number of characteristic elements of the Reformed ethos. Its cornerstone is Christ as testified to in Scripture as the sole Lord and Savior of the world. Jesus is a gift of God's free and pure love which will not abandon us to the death and destruction occasioned by sin. The Reformed Confession (and confessing) is an acknowledgement in thanksgiving of our absolute dependence on God and Jesus Christ. Since Jesus is the Lord of the church, it must be one; the Reformed tradition did not begin as an effort to create a new church but to reform the existing one, "to assemble this one Church once again around its Head." Reformed churches see themselves as a movement in the church and thus know their dependence on other churches.[8]

As eloquent as this presentation is, one searches without success to discover what Vischer believes to be characteristic Reformed tonalities of the ethos. Few traditions would be reluctant to make such affirmations. Vischer's grasp of the christological center of the Reformed ethos is on target; what is missed is the way in which other doctrines combine with it to produce those qualities identified with the faith, order, and practice of the churches of the Reformed tradition. Vischer, for example, ignores the important Calvinistic doctrine of *unio mystica cum Christi,* which teaches that Christ and his benefits are present in the church through the action of the Spirit who links the Lord to his people. We believe this to be a critical omission. The Reformed ethos

157

is to be explained not through its Christology alone, but through its unique conjoining of the doctrines of Christ and Spirit.

The importance of the Holy Spirit in the Reformed tradition has often been slighted. One may search the reports of the WARC-sponsored dialogues, for example, and discover little substantive discussion of the role of pneumatology in the Reformed tradition. This is a serious oversight. It would be no overstatement to assert that no Protestant tradition, including the Pentecostal, has been more profoundly influenced by a theology of the Holy Spirit. Since in our view the Reformed ethos can hardly be understood apart from the doctrine of the Holy Spirit, nor can a response to the question of fundamental consensus be given without taking this doctrine into consideration, the balance of our discussion will focus on Reformed pneumatology.

John Calvin, seminal theologian of the Reformed tradition, has been called the theologian of the Spirit *par excellence*. Throughout the *Institutes,* but especially in Book 4 where he discusses the church, Calvin highlights the work of the Spirit in the historic mediation of salvation. The Spirit is the divine intermediary between the ascended Christ and the Christian community, working not only in the hearts of the faithful, but also through the offices and order of the church. The real presence of the flesh and blood of Christ in the Lord's Supper is a work of the Spirit, but so is the discipline exercised by the elder. A number of Reformed theologians subsequently undertook investigation of the work of the Spirit; one thinks of a number of Puritan authors, but also of contemporary Dutch theology where A. Kuyper, G. Hoenderdaal, O. Noordmans, A. A. Van Ruler, and H. Berkhof have given prominence to this doctrine in their theological works.

The paradigmatic significance of the work of the Spirit for the Reformed ethos depends on the clear separation made by Calvin and the early Reformed Confessions between the work of the earthly and heavenly Christ.[9] Salvation comes only through communion with the living Christ. But since Jesus no longer shares our earthly life, the Spirit links us to the ascended Lord and the ascended Lord to us. The ascension thus assumes an important formative role in Reformed faith and practice. With the ascension God is yet in human flesh, but is no longer God-with-us-in-human-flesh. We are linked to the Jesus of history, now ascended, by the Spirit, and the *beneficia Christi* (benefits of Christ) are spiritually mediated through the church (the pneumatological body of Christ) to history.

A Dutch theologian, A. A. Van Ruler, has called attention to some of the implications of this distinction between the work of the Messiah and the Spirit.[10] Borrowing terms from Reformed Scholasticism,

Van Ruler contrasts the manner in which the Logos relates to humanity with how the Spirit relates to humanity. The messianic *assumptio carnis* (assumption of the flesh) is singular; God the son is present in a single divine-human life, and once and for all; there are no further incarnations. Moreover, the impeccability of Christ is affirmed through the *assumptio carnis*. We may not speak of an incarnation of the Spirit, Van Ruler contends. The Spirit is indeed linked to humanity, but not in the mode of the *assumptio carnis*. The appropriate notion is indwelling, or *inhabitio*. The Spirit indwells the heart of the believer and the church, the body of Christ. At this point we may no longer speak in the singular, for the Spirit indwells congregations and churches throughout the world. Nor does the doctrine of the *eph hapax* (once for all) apply, for the *inhabitio* continues generation by generation until the return of the Lord. Such a pneumatological understanding of the church also forbids any doctrine of infallibility, for there is no doctrine of impeccability which derives from the *inhabitio*. Finally, all uniformity is also excluded since the Spirit indwells churches composed by human beings shaped by various cultural, historical, and personal factors.

Van Ruler's theology, rising as it does out of a profound understanding of the genius of the Reformed tradition, helps us grasp the implications of the doctrine of the Spirit for the Reformed ethos. But we must underscore that Spirit and Christ always belong together in Reformed faith and practice. Necessary are both the salvation once and for all accomplished by God incarnate — which the believer receives in faith through actual union with the ascended Christ, and the action of the Spirit which accomplishes this union, not "spiritually" with a small "s" (that is, through inwardness) but through the Spirit's use of historical, earthly instruments, such as preaching, sacraments, liturgy, confession, teaching, theology, office, discipline, and tradition. Every activity of the Holy Spirit has one norm, content, and object: Jesus Christ. In him sin and death are overcome, a new humanity received, and signs of God's kingdom established in the world. Jesus as the norm, content, and object provides to the Reformed ethos its fixed point; here is its singular center, its unchanging foundation; here is its unity. The instrumentalities by which the believer is drawn into a relationship with Jesus, as noted above, are the plural, changing, and pluriform actions of the indwelling Spirit. As the Spirit engages women and men from various cultures, through the various periods of history, the instrumentalities of grace appear in a number of forms and experience myriad transformations. Variety and change do not contradict the Reformed ethos; as a work of the Spirit they confirm it. But the purpose of the plural and changing work of the Spirit is Christ and his salvation. *The plural works of the Spirit bring the unity of Christ to the Reformed ethos.*

This is not to suggest that there is no continuity in the Reformed tradition. An analysis of Reformed heritage will reveal recurring practices and values. Reformed churches do not all require Confessional subscription, but all are confessing. Reformed churches underscore, along with word and sacraments as means of grace, the importance of discipline; they insist on the authority of the Bible, the centrality of preaching, the prevenience of grace, and justification by faith alone. There are attitudes toward theology, worship, the Christian life, and mission which appear to be constants of the Reformed tradition. But these too have appeared in plural and changing ways. They continue in Reformed churches because in one form or another they uniquely serve the union pneumatically effected with Christ. Finally, it is Christ, mediated by the Spirit, who provides the guarantee of continuity in the church.

Does such an ethos empty the "forms" (they are called instrumentalities above) of substance, rendering them arbitrary? Reformed theology and practice often skates on thin ice here. When a Dutch theologian, O. Noordmans, asserts that every time we go to church the Holy Spirit does not necessarily do so, he is dangerously close to a docetic ecclesiology. Noordmans wishes to safeguard the freedom of God. But in doing so he jeopardizes God's faithfulness. We can be sure God goes to church when we do because of God's promise to use preaching and the sacraments to bring us grace. The forms are not indifferent; the signs carry the reality they signify by the working of the Spirit. In the Reformed view, the church is neither a sacred nor secular entity: it is spiritual, inhabited by the Holy Spirit who is also very God of very God and who brings the real presence of Christ to it.

We may now return to the question: What do Reformed churches look for in other churches before agreeing to make a covenant of mutual recognition? Simply this: that in the varied forms of faith and practice which prevail in other communions Christ is communicated as content, norm, and object of the church. This may seem ecumenical minimalism to some. If so, it is born out of Reformed evangelical conviction and not theological indifference. Eccesiologies which understand the church as an extension of the incarnation can find little room for plurality and mutability; a pneumatological ecclesiology is confirmed by plurality and mutability.

Reformed pneumatology, then, predicating as it does diversity and change, allows Reformed churches to expect and accept forms of church life and theological articulations which differ from their own. As long as the christological and soteriological norms and values which it confesses as evangelical are recognized in another body, fundamental consensus is possible. For example, the understanding of the ministerium in most Reformed churches includes the office of elder, an office which has no counterpart in the Lutheran tradition. Nonetheless, Reformed churches have recognized Lutheran order to be evangelical.[11] And while, with the exception of the Reformed Church of Hungary, no Reformed church has an episcopal office, Reformed theologians have recognized this office in Lutheran churches as a biblically warranted form of oversight.

There are times when Reformed churches are unable to discern an evangelical content in the forms of another tradition. Care must be taken when this seems to be the case for the problem may lie in the difficulty one tradition finds in grasping the meaning of the practice of another. But the case may be that substantive differences do separate Reformed churches from those of other traditions. The ministry section of *Baptism, Eucharist and Ministry*, for example, was attacked by many Reformed theologians because its understanding of office seemed to compromise the sufficiency of Christ alone. Further study and discussion may reveal that Reformed criticism is unjust. Or it could reveal that the historic Reformed understanding of the *ministerium* requires "reformation." But a fundamental consensus with churches subscribing to an understanding of office in the spirit of BEM could not be reached until Reformed churches were satisfied that the gospel stood in no danger of compromise.

Our observations on a fundamental consensus in Reformed perspective turn on our conviction that pneumatology has played a much greater role in the ethos of the Reformed family of churches than is sometimes recognized, even by theologians of our tradition. We are also convinced that a deeper ecumenical inquiry into the doctrine of the Holy Spirit promises to shed new light on the meaning of unity in plurality. Perhaps this will become an important item on the ecumenical agenda for the twenty-first century.

A LUTHERAN RESPONSE

John F. Johnson

ROSEMARY RUETHER has extended the label "post-ecumenism" to the way in which the conclusion of formal ecumenical dialogue and church unity can be anticipated today.[1] In large measure the consultation for which the essays in this volume were prepared reflects such "post-ecumenical" thinking, not in the sense that the ecumenical movement is deemed to have achieved its task entirely or that continued dialogue between traditions is irrelevant, but in the sense that, having isolated some of the presuppositions for accomplishing unity in the churches, those involved in the ecumenical movement must now attend to a much more basic question. How does the claim expressed in certain ecumenical dialogues that a "fundamental consensus" has been reached relate to the equally voiced contention that "fundamental differences" between churches remain unrecognized or unexplored? Paul R. Fries offers a Reformed perspective on this issue in his helpful essay.

Fries treats the notion of a fundamental consensus from the perspective of Reformed thought by pursuing two lines of analysis. In the first he brings to the surface a plethora of methodological difficulties; in the second he suggests that the Reformed ethos (those theological norms and values made explicit in the preaching and teaching of the church) is to be explained through "its unique conjoining of the doctrines of Christ and Spirit."

No doubt Lutherans will resonate strongly to the methodological concerns identified in the Fries presentation. Parallels abound in Lutheran experience. He notes, for example, how the polyphonous character of the Reformed tradition affects the question of fundamental consensus. There exist differing judgments within the Reformed community concerning a common basis for "church fellowship." Indeed, he asserts, Reformed churches have acted on both "centrifugal and centripetal" impulses in their ecumenical stance.

One would be forced to acknowledge that the record of Lutheran ecumenical commitment is similarly checkered. Some within the Lutheran family maintain that agreement in the gospel as the basis for fellowship means the gospel in its broadest sense, the entire body of Christian teaching (named gospel *a parte maiore*). Other Lutherans prefer the model of "reconciled diversity": that while certain elements of common Christian understanding are indispensable, external unity can be based on agreement in the gospel in a narrower sense which allows for disagreement in other aspects of faith and order. Lutheranism, like the Reformed tradition, has not always been single-minded on the matter of unitive Christianity.

Other examples of Reformed pluriformity cited by Professor Fries find echoes in contemporary Lutheranism and frequently constitute a similar difficulty in identifying the conditions for a fundamental consensus (e.g., varied understandings of the extent of Confessional subscription and differences in polity). In other words, the methodological impact of Fries' question "To which Reformed voice do we listen?" has affinities for the Lutheran context as well.

Despite these methodological concerns, Fries appears to argue for two foci central to the Reformed ethos: "the salvation once and for all accomplished by God incarnate which the believer receives in faith through actual union with the ascended Christ, and the action of the Spirit which accomplishes this union. . . ." That is to say, the question of fundamental consensus from the Reformed perspective hinges on Christology and the doctrine of the Holy Spirit. Consequently, Fries turns from the problem of method in his essay to a discussion of Reformed pneumatology.

On this point, it seems to me, the Lutheran response must be a mixed one. The observation that the topic of the Holy Spirit is among the *lacunae* in recent ecumenical dialogue is a significant one. The importance of the Holy Spirit in the churches of the Reformation has not always been appreciated. As Alasdair Heron, one of the participants in this consultation, notes: "Most Protestants today, if asked what the Reformation was primarily about, would not immediately think of the Holy Spirit."[2] However, the way in which Reformed theology has historically articulated its doctrine of the Spirit, especially in connection with Christology, is at variance with historic Lutheran understanding. It may just be that in identifying the work of the Spirit and the *unio mystica cum Christi* doctrine as that which serves as a "fundamental consensus" *within* the Reformed tradition, Professor Fries has identified a "fundamental difference" *between* Lutherans and the Reformed.

Fries' statement that John Calvin was "the theologian of the Spirit *par excellence*" is most apt. Among all of the sixteenth century Reformers

Calvin undertook the most systematic study of the Spirit.[3] He did this, of course, because the work of the Spirit links us to the ascended Christ. Christ is the repository of all grace. To receive those benefits which the Father bestowed on the Son we must be joined to Christ; a spiritual union must be effected. To be sure, in Reformed theology there cannot be an ontological identification between Christ and us, but there must be a living union. While Professor Fries' mention of the *unio mystica cum Christi* is appropriate, the union of which Calvin spoke is technically not a *unio mystica* but an *insitio in Christum*. At any rate, this union is effected by the Spirit:

> . . . so long as we are without Christ and separated from him, nothing which he suffered and did for the salvation of the human race is of the least benefit to us. To communicate to us the blessings which he received from the Father, he must become ours and dwell in us . . . the very nature of the case teaches us to ascend higher, and inquire into the secret efficacy of the Spirit, to which it is owing that we enjoy Christ and all his blessings.[4]

Fries is correct; Calvin highlights the work of the Spirit in the mediation of salvation.

While Calvin and other theologians in the classical Reformed tradition tend to analyze more closely the activity of the Spirit in regeneration and sanctification, it is certainly the case that for Luther the Spirit mediates the living and resurrected Christ to the believer. The particular task of the Spirit is to convert the abstract narrative about Christ into personal and present gospel. It is by the Spirit that we can hear in faith God's word. But for Luther especially the work of the Holy Spirit always means a relationship to the living and present Christ; the task of the Holy Spirit is to conform us to Christ. As Regin Prenter suggests, the Spirit takes Christ out of the remoteness of history and heavenly glory and places him in the very midst of our own life with its suffering, conflict, and death. The work of the Holy Spirit is to mediate the "real presence" of Christ.[5]

Insofar as this leads us into the area of Christology, the "fundamental difference" between the Reformed and the Lutheran traditions becomes more pronounced. There has always been substantial agreement ("fundamental consensus") between Lutherans and the Reformed on many aspects of christological doctrine. There is, for example, agreement that in Christ there is only one person but two natures; that these two natures comprise a personal union; that by the power of this personal union the properties of both natures have become common to the person of Christ; and that to the mediatorial acts of Christ each nature contributed its own part.[6] But the two traditions have disagreed on the omnipresence of the humanity of Christ. The Reformed position has been that the body of the exalted Christ is locally confined to a place at the right hand of God: "The Gospel story teaches very clearly that Christ's human nature was conceived in the womb of the blessed Virgin, formed in it, born of it, and so came into a light in which it was not, and that the man Christ moved from place to place both before and after the resurrection and ascended from earth to heaven — The presence of a visible, local body is nothing but a visible, local, circumscribed one. . . ."[7]

The ramification of this teaching which has proved to be the most divisive over the years has to do with the Holy Eucharist. Professor Fries speaks in his paper of "the real presence of the flesh and blood of Christ in the Lord's Supper" as a work of the Spirit. This must be interpreted, consistent with Reformed thought, as a spiritual presence. Calvin denied the real presence of the body and blood of Christ. This is clear from the *Consensus Tigurinus,* composed in 1549 as a statement of agreement between Calvin and Bullinger, Zwingli's successor in Zurich. According to the *Consensus* it is "absurd to place Christ under, and to unite him with, the bread." The basis for this statement is that "insofar as Christ is a man, he is to be sought nowhere else than in heaven and in no other manner than with the mind and the understanding of faith." Concerning the words of institution, the document states, "Beyond controversy, they are to be taken figuratively."[8] If the body of Christ is confined to heaven, then he is obviously present in the Sacrament only "spiritually."

On the other hand, Lutheran christological teaching sets forth the doctrine that in the personal union the divine nature has communicated its full majesty and glory to the human nature. "Because the human nature in Christ is personally united with the divine nature in Christ," says the *Formula of Concord,* "the former (when it was glorified and exalted to the right hand of the majesty and power of God, after the form of the servant had been laid aside and after the humiliation) received, in addition to its natural, essential, and abiding properties, special, high, great, supernatural, unsearchable, ineffable, heavenly prerogatives and privileges in majesty, glory, power, and might above every name that is named."[9] The sentence is admittedly awkward but the thrust is clear: Christ, by virtue of his divine omnipotence, can make himself present in various ways.

For the most part Lutheran-Reformed dialogues have respected this disagreement concerning the *mode* of Christ's presence in the Lord's Supper (which involves the further question of whether Christ's body and blood are received orally and its implications for the Lutheran concept of the *manducatio indignorum*). They have claimed a fundamental consensus concerning the sacramental character of the Supper.

To be sure, there are other dimensions of Fries' pneumatological understanding of the church which deserve response. He makes the point that Reformed pneumatology "forbids any doctrine of infallibility." The implication is that this does not comport with the idea that the church is *"semper reformanda."* However, Lutherans are agreed on a doctrine of the church's infallibility (or rather indefectibility). The promise that the gates of hell will not prevail against the church means that doctrinal error will not prevail against it. The indefectibility of the church is compatible with its continued openness to reform rather than contradicted by it as long, at least, as the identity of the church is not exclusively vested in its institutional character *per se* but in the gospel. Profitable as this discussion might be, it is the twin notions of pneumatology and Christology, so emphatically presented by Professor Fries as integral to the Reformed ethos, that has occupied my attention. They persist, as they have for centuries, to be fundamental differences for our traditions.

Still, Fries concludes his essay on a note on which Lutherans can heartily concur. He expresses the hope that the doctrine of the Holy Spirit might become an important item for future ecumenical dialogue. If it is indeed the case that for both Lutherans and the Reformed there is the confidence that the Spirit guides the church's continuing history, then giving prominence to the study of that Spirit can only serve our search for fundamental consensuses.

Notes

FRIES

1. Unpublished study prepared for the Lutheran-Reformed International Dialogue.

2. James T. McNeill and James Hasting Nichols, *Ecumenical Testimony* (Philadelphia: Westminster Press, 1974) 23.

3. Ibid., 36-37.

4. Ibid., 63-70.

5. Lukas Vischer, "The Ecumenical Commitment of WARC," *The Reformed World* 38:5 (1985) 262.

6. See, for example, The French Confession of Faith, 1559, Article 30, which states "no church shall claim any authority or dominion over any other."

7. See Maurice G. Hansen, *The Reformed Church in the Netherlands* (New York: Board of Publication of the Reformed Church in America, 1884), for a detailed discussion of the Synod of Dort and the responses of foreign representatives.

8. Vischer, 265-66.

9. Question 49 of the Heidelberg Catechism provides a particularly eloquent testimony to the importance of the ascension, describing its benefits. The final benefit is the gift of the Spirit who, according to Question 53, "makes me share in Christ and all his blessings." See also the Scottish Confession of Faith, 1560, Chapter 11.

10. Van Ruler's pneumatology is most accessible in the essays "Structuurverschillen tussen het christologische en pneumatologische gezichtspunt," *Theologisch Werk* (Nijkerk: Uitgeverij G. F. Callenbach N.V., 1969) 1:175-90, and "Hoofdlijnen van een pneumatologie," *Theologisch Werk* (Nijkerk: Uitgeverij G. F. Callenbach, N.V., 1973) 6:9-40. See also my "Spirit, Theocracy and the True Humanity: Salavation in the Theology of A. A. Van Ruler," *The Reformed Review* 39 (1986) 206-13.

11. James E. Andrews and Joseph A. Burgess (eds.), *An Invitation to Action* (Philadelphia: Fortress Press, 1984) 24-31.

JOHNSON

1. Rosemary Ruether, "Post-Ecumenical Christianity," *Ecumenical Theology No. 2* (ed. Gregory Baum; New York: Paulist Press, 1967) 74-82.

2. Alasdair I. C. Heron, *The Holy Spirit* (Philadelphia: Westminster Press, 1983) 100.

3. Especially in Books III-IV of the *Institutes*; see also W. Krusche, *Das Wirken des heiligen Geistes nach Calvin* (Göttingen: Vandenhoek and Ruprecht, 1957).

4. *Institutes,* III, 1, 1; quoted in Heron, 103.

5. Regin Prenter, *Spiritus Creator* (Philadelphia: Muhlenberg Press, 1953) 27-28.

6. T. Tappert, "Christology and Lord's Supper in the Perspective of History," *A Reexamination of Lutheran and Reformed Traditions* (New York: World Alliance of Reformed Churches and USA National Committee of the LWF, 1964) 2:30.

7. Quoted in Heinrich Heppe, *Reformed Dogmatics* (Grand Rapids: Baker, 1978) 447.

8. For the Latin text see J. C. L. Gieseler, *Lehrbuch der Kirchengeschichte* (Bonn: Adolf Marcus, 1853) 5, 2: 176.

9. FC SD 8:51; BC 600-1.

12

Fundamental Consensus

An Anglican Perspective

J. Robert Wright

I

MY TASK is to explore from an Anglican point of view the term and the concept of "fundamental consensus" as it may be known in my tradition, its origin, meaning, use, and ecumenical relevance, as well as its implications for levels of church fellowship.

The term itself, "fundamental consensus," I have to say at the outset, is not well known in the longer history of Anglicanism, and it is only within the last decade or two that anything like it has begun to emerge, not without its problems, in the context of materials emanating from our bilateral dialogues, especially with Roman Catholics and to a more limited extent with Lutherans. I shall devote the later and longer part of this essay to its analysis as it appears in these ecumenical endeavors.

First, however, I shall offer some few remarks about the presence of this concept within the Anglican understanding of levels of church fellowship, or *koinonia,* as it refers to the unity of the church. The reason that here my remarks will be rather brief is that any explication of the *concept* necessarily involves the *content* of fundamental consensus, and about such content one could write entire papers and even books. For this presentation, though, suffice it to say that the *concept* of fundamental consensus may be examined as its *content* is understood, first, for full church fellowship or *koinonia within* the Anglican Communion, and then, second, as it relates to the Anglican understanding of what is necessary for full church fellowship or *koinonia* in ecumenical reunion *with other churches.* In either case it should be noted that the Anglican expression more common than "full church fellowship" is "full communion" and that there is a long Anglican history of the use of this expression, how it has been somewhat differently defined at no less than three Lambeth Conferences as well as by some national synods and other authoritative bodies, its relationship to terms such as inter-communion, partial communion, and just plain communion, what kind of conditions and obligations are carried with each situation, how it has functioned in our relationships with the Old Catholic Churches under the Bonn Concordat of 1931, how it has been understood in our longstanding, warm, and amicable relationships with the Eastern Orthodox Churches, the study project on "Full Communion" undertaken recently by the Anglican Consultative Council, and so on. All these possible topics can only be entered here by title, though, and I now return to the concept of fundamental consensus as it relates to full church fellowship.

Within the fellowship of the Anglican Communion the content of fundamental consensus is generally defined by the Book of Common Prayer, which of course includes the Ordinal and the Thirty-Nine Articles as well as the Apostles' and Nicene Creeds. Virtually every one of the twenty-eight national or regional churches constitutive of the Anglican Communion has had and does have a Book of Common Prayer that is more or less recognizably "Anglican" on the basis of the English Book of 1662 or other related Books (such as the Scottish), which is recognizably traceable through previous Books back to 1549, which Book in turn was an English distillation of the later medieval service books under the influence of the patristic, biblical, and humanistic revivals that flourished in the period of the Western Renaissance and Reformation. Challenged recently though this fundamental consensus has been from the modern liturgical movement which has continually widened the scope and content of Anglican unity by producing in the middle and later twentieth century many new Books of Common Prayer for different countries and regions that are increasingly different from one another, it nevertheless still exists and still defines our fellowship within the Anglican Communion and still provides the major source of our doctrine as well as our principal statement of the church's purpose. The church exists primarily for the worship of God, for doxology, we would tend to say, from which everything else in the church's mission is derived, and for this purpose we have a Book of Common Prayer, from which our basic doctrine is derived. *Legem credendi lex statuat supplicandi,* or *lex orandi lex credendi* ("the law of prayer determines the law of belief," or, "the law of prayer is the law of faith"), we would tend to say with St. Prosper of Aquitaine from the fifth century. Deviations from the Book of Common Prayer are occasionally tolerated in local situations for a limited period of time, but generally we would say that Anglican worship is to be conducted from it, Anglican doctrine to be derived from it, Anglican life to be lived by it, and Anglican clergy must be prepared to use its contents and to say and lead its words in public worship, with a consenting mind. The limits of our doctrine are determined by the interpretation of its contents.

All this is summarized in the Lambeth 1978 Report on the Basis of Anglican Unity. After speaking of Lambeth Conference resolutions and reports, synodical resolutions, constitutional documents, canon law, and so on, this Report devoted its major attention to the Book of Common Prayer and concluded: "Accordingly, in order to find out what characterizes Anglican doctrine, the simplest way is to look at Anglican worship and deduce Anglican doctrine from it."[1]

Fundamental consensus among and within the churches of the Anglican Communion is defined therefore by the Book of Common Prayer, and although we generally expect other *churches* who wish to *become Anglican* (and some have) to adopt it in some form, we certainly do *not* expect *adoption* of it by other churches who become our partners in ecumenical fellowship. We do not expect them to become just like us. For full church fellowship of other churches *with* the churches of the Anglican Communion, the standard we generally use is what we call the Lambeth Quadrilateral, or the Chicago-Lambeth Quadrilateral, which was endorsed in its earliest form by the American Episcopal House of Bishops meeting at Chicago in 1886 and then, slightly revised, in its abiding form by the Lambeth Conference of Bishops at London in 1888. This year we observe, even celebrate, its one hundredth anniversary; it is now printed at the back of the latest American edition of the Book of Common Prayer. The Quadrilateral enumerates four points or articles or elements of the faith upon which all Anglican churches believe agreement is necessary for a basis of an approach to the ecumenical reunion of the Anglican Communion with other churches: the Holy Scriptures of the Old and New Testaments, the Apostles' and Nicene Creeds, the gospel sacraments of baptism and Eucharist, and the historic episcopate "locally adapted in the methods of its administration."[2] Historians will here recognize immediately in these four points a similarity to the developments that are sometimes called the institutional marks of early catholicism, as the church of the patristic period sought by these institutional means to spread the gospel in the Roman Empire as well as to define itself over against the Gnostic heretics. There is no proof that the compilers of the Quadrilateral had all this in mind, but it is true that the bishops as they endorsed these four points at Chicago in 1886 did affirm what they called "the principles of unity exemplified by the undivided Catholic Church during the first ages of its existence."[3] Since that time there have been many official and unofficial expositions and explications of the Quadrilateral, especially of the fourth point on the historic episcopate (which is of course the most controversial). Generally the Lambeth Conferences (meetings of all Anglican bishops about every ten years), as well as the (triennial) General Conventions of the Episcopal Church in the USA, have continued to affirm, and have refused to replace or even significantly alter, this Quadrilateral as the fundamental Anglican consensus for full *koinonia* or fellowship with other churches. It is for us the basis, for example, for our official relationships of full communion with the Old Catholic Churches and for the Episcopal Church's new and partial relationship of Interim Sharing of the Eucharist with the Evangelical Lutheran Church in America. Its four points are only a beginning, not an ending; they are a basis for an approach; and they do imply much more than they specify. Space unfortunately precludes a fuller treatment of the Quadrilateral here.[4]

II

I turn now from the *concept* of fundamental consensus as it may be present in or derived from the traditional way that Anglicans understand church fellowship or *koinonia* or full communion to an analysis of the *term itself* or, rather, of terms like it, as they have appeared on the Anglican scene in the last two decades largely as a by-product of some of our ecumenical dialogues. My major focus will be upon the Anglican-Roman Catholic dialogue, where the term (with variations of wording) has had the most extensive use, discussion, and problems. Since this is primarily a Lutheran forum, though, I shall first analyze the variations of this term as they have functioned in our dialogues with Lutherans.

"Agreement" in several "fundamental areas" was claimed by the first round of Lutheran-Episcopal Dialogue in the USA (1969-1972), which added in particular that it had reached "fundamental agreement on the Holy Eucharist, though with some differences of emphasis."[5]

The second series of Lutheran-Episcopal Dialogue (1976-1980) asserted that "substantial areas of agreement"[6] has been found in the first round of the dialogue and went on to claim that "consensus" had been "achieved in the discussions of LED I and II on the chief doctrines of the Christian faith."[7] Of the five brief joint statements of these doctrines published with LED II, however (on Justification, the Gospel, the Eucharistic Presence, the Authority of Scripture, and Apostolicity), only one of them, Apostolicity, used any variant of the term now under consideration. It referred to the "substantial agreement which we share with regard to the Church's apostolicity," which it also called a "convergence"[8] and "basic and extensive elements of agreement."[9] In addition, LED II admitted "serious *divergence* in the actual ordering of the Pastoral Office in the two Communions as well as in the importance generally accorded to the historic episcopate"[10] and in a related footnote it listed four additional "weighty matters" which it believed to "require further discussion": "1) the relationship between presbyteral succession and episcopal succession, including a discussion of the role and office of the bishop; 2) the relation of the pastoral office to the priesthood of all believers; 3) the possibility of a mutually recognized ministry of Word and Sacrament; and 4) the question of the ordination of women."[11] Hence for LED II there were five joint statements including one "substantial agreement" or "convergence" on apostolicity, which was not however complete and which was juxtaposed to one "serious divergence" with four additional "weighty matters" requiring further discussion.

From the International Anglican-Lutheran Conversations, authorized by the Lambeth Conference and the Lutheran World Federation, we have the extensive Pullach Report, released in 1972, which does not use any such terminology, and also the 1982 Report of the Anglican-Lutheran European Regional Commission, which similarly avoids such terms apart from a section called "Agreements and Convergences."[12]

In the fall of 1982 the General Convention of the Episcopal Church as well as the conventions of the LCA, ALC, and AELC all passed the historic Lutheran-Episcopal Agreement, which has generally been received quite positively and about which very much more could be said were it the only subject of this essay. The text of this agreement is relatively free of the "fundamental consensus" terminology except at two points. It welcomes and rejoices in the "substantial progress"[13] of the national and international Lutheran-Anglican dialogues, and it affirms on the basis of their studies that "the basic teaching of each church is consonant with the Gospel and sufficiently compatible with the teaching of each other church that a new relationship of Interim Sharing of the Eucharist is hereby established" under limited guidelines which are carefully set forth.[14] The fact that this is only a partial agreement, not yet complete (as, we recall, LED II anticipated when it found one serious divergence and four additional weighty matters for further discussion), is indicated by the fact that the Lutheran-Episcopal Agreement is "looking forward"[15] to the day when full communion may be established and that it authorizes a third round of the dialogue,[16] which is now fruitfully under way. Already there is the possibility of a fundamental consensus on the Implications of the Gospel as well as on an Anglican recognition of the Augsburg Confession and Lutheran recognition of the Book of Common Prayer.

To summarize: The terminology of "fundamental consensus — fundamental difference" and variant terms has been employed only to a very limited extent in the statements of the Lutheran-Anglican dialogues and is fairly clear in its meaning and application.

III

Next I turn to the major locus of such terminology for Anglicans, the place where such terms have entered the Anglican ecumenical vocabulary with great significance but not without problems in the last two decades: our international bilateral dialogue with the Roman Catholic Church (ARCIC), the ecumenical "front line" that has most captured and puzzled Anglican attention over the last several years.

I shall concentrate upon the Final Report of the ARCIC because it is for Anglicans the single most important locus for the appearance of terms that claim to announce anything like a fundamental consensus. A very careful verbal analysis of this document is especially appropriate even though it will be somewhat tedious, since it is claimed in the foreword to the American edition of this Report that "each word was agreed to by all members of the Consultation." I was not a member of ARCIC I, for which this claim is made, but I do know this is *not* true for ARCIC II, of which I am a member, because the steering committee from Lambeth and the Vatican has in fact changed some words in the final text of the latest statement, *Salvation and the Church*. (I do not here object to such procedure; I merely record the fact because the same claim cannot be made of ARCIC II.)

It is in the foreword to the American edition of the ARCIC Final Report that the term "consensus" first strikes the reader's eye, and in this same context: "It must be remembered that the Statements are consensus statements: each word in them was agreed to by all members of the Consultation."[17] Thus it is here claimed, and this will be repeated later in the text of the Report itself (in the elucidation to the Windsor statement), that "consensus" implies unanimous verbal agreement. This maximal definition of "consensus" is a bold claim but, once made, it calls for us to evaluate their work on the same strict basis, on the precise words they have used or not used, rather than upon some more lenient standard that could easily be applied if the Commission had not made its claim so absolute. For this reason any "consensus"

173

terminology found in ARCIC II can and must be subject to careful scrutiny, for the Commission is willing to be held accountable not merely for its ideas and intentions but also for its specific choice of words. Now I proceed to the Final Report itself, released in 1982. I shall scrutinize its contents chronologically, in five layers or strata, since I think this analysis will best enable us to see what the Commission was saying about "fundamental consensus." My method will thus be analytical, reflective, and chronological. These are the five strata: 1) 1971; 2) 1973; 3) 1976; 4) 1979; and 5) 1981.

We now turn first to the Windsor Statement on Eucharistic Doctrine, finalized in September of 1971: the earliest stratum. In the Preface to this Statement, which as Preface carries the authority only of the two co-chairmen, it is stated that the Commission has "reached agreement on essential points of eucharistic doctrine," that "nothing essential has been omitted," and that the intention of the Commission was "to reach a consensus at the level of faith."[18] And these claims are echoed in the statement itself where in the Introduction, paragraph 1, we find that the Commission claims to be expressing "the consensus" it has reached. Earlier in the same first paragraph the Commission observes that "An important stage in progress towards organic unity is a substantial consensus on the purpose and meaning of the eucharist."[19] They do not say that they have *reached* "substantial consensus," but only "consensus"; yet they allow it to be inferred that they have reached *"substantial* consensus." I would not even bother to record this difference of terminology were it not for their earlier bold (perhaps even excessive) claim to have achieved unanimous verbal agreement.

The problem expands at the end of the same document, only eleven paragraphs later, when the Commission concludes (still presumably weighing its words with precision) that it has reached "substantial *agreement* on the doctrine of the eucharist."[20] Why did they vote to use the word "agreement" at this point rather than "consensus"? Whether there is a difference between consensus and agreement we are not told, and thus we do not know whether some theological refinement led the Commission to progress from consensus in paragraph 1 to agreement in paragraph 12 or whether the different word is introduced only for the sake of English language variety. Whatever the case may be, and the opinions of those I have asked who were members of the Commission do vary, here in the earliest chronological stratum of the ARCIC Final Report we encounter the term, really two terms, that come the closest in Anglican ecumenical usage to the term fundamental consensus: "substantial consensus" and "substantial agreement."

Next we turn to the second chronological stratum of the Commission's Final Report, the Canterbury Statement on Ministry and Ordination, finalized two years later in September of 1973, and we find that, perhaps under criticism of its earlier terminology, the Commission now does not use either term, "substantial agreement" and "substantial consensus," but rather simply "consensus" and now also *"basic* agreement." [21] The Commission does not explain why it chose in its second document to claim a *basic* agreement rather than a *substantial* one, or a substantial consensus, but some definition seems indicated in its concluding claim that "What we have to say represents the consensus of the Commission on essential matters where it considers that doctrine admits no divergence." More on this claim later. One related point to note in the conclusion to the Canterbury Statement, however, is a reference to "our consensus, on questions where agreement is indispensable for unity."[22] Would it have made any difference, though, to say "our *agreement,* on questions where *consensus* is indispensable for unity"? I doubt it, given the Commission's use of terms up to this point, and thus I reach and now record my preliminary conclusion that for ARCIC I "consensus" and "agreement" are interchangeable terms, just as are "basic" and "substantial." There does seem to be a preference for "agreement" over "consensus," since in its most direct language the Commission calls the Windsor Statement a "substantial agreement" and the Canterbury Statement a "basic agreement."

Now we turn to the first statement on Authority in the Church, finalized at Venice in September of 1976 (this is stratum 3) and here, three years after the last statement, we find an interesting development. Gone are two of the four previous terms: "basic" and "substantial," and now we have an altogether new term, "significant convergence."[23] Whether by this the Commission means to convey the same idea only with intentional verbal variety, we shall see, but I do note that the Commission near the end of its Venice Statement claims that its convergence is "theological" or "doctrinal," but then goes on to say that it has "experienced" this doctrinal convergence[24] — not written it, or revealed it, or cogitated it, but "experienced" it! What now led the Commission to "experience" a convergence rather than to "reach" a consensus or agreement, we are not told, but since it chose its words with precise verbal agreement, there may well be some significant difference that eludes the outside reader.

In its same text the Commission does also refer to this as a "consensus" or "agreement,"[25] and in the Preface to Venice the co-chairmen refer to it as a "consensus."[26] Thus we are now left with an ever expanding question, since the Commission does not call its Venice

Statement on Authority in the Church either a "substantial" or "basic" consensus or agreement, but rather a "significant convergence," yet also a consensus and agreement. It seems *not* to intend the term "significant convergence" to indicate a substantial or basic consensus or agreement, but only a consensus or agreement that is not basic or substantial. Perhaps the key is to be found in the co-chairmen's Preface to this Statement, when they remark that "Our consensus covers a very wide area; though we have not been able to resolve some of the difficulties."[27] Clearly for the co-chairmen it is possible to have a "consensus" that is not complete, and it may be for this reason that neither they nor the Commission call the Venice Authority Statement a *substantial* or *basic* consensus or agreement. It *is* a significant convergence, it *is* an agreement, it *is* a consensus, but not basic or substantial or complete, the reason obviously being the four difficult papal claims that are cited in its paragraph 24.[28] These "four outstanding problems," as the Commission calls them (Petrine texts, *jus divinum,* jurisdiction, and infallibility), which in turn are later largely reconciled (except for certain aspects of infallibility) in the fifth stratum of the Commission's work, are the nearest points to anything like an identification of fundamental differences in the ARCIC documents. Hence "outstanding problems" (perhaps fundamental differences?) seem to have prevented the Commission at this third stage of its work from claiming substantial or basic consensus or agreement.

Next we consider the fourth stratum of the ARCIC Final Report, the material dated from 1979, and in this layer we find the Commission's first two "elucidations," as it called them. These elucidations, the Commission asserts, expand and explain the Commission's previous work. The elucidation to the Canterbury Statement on Ministry and Ordination yields no terminology useful for our present study, but the elucidation to the Windsor Statement on the Eucharist does, for here there is an entire paragraph (# 2) about "substantial agreement." It is appropriately placed here, in elucidation of Windsor, because it was only Windsor (the Commission's very *first* statement) that *claimed* to have reached "substantial agreement." The word "substantial" is generally not used in the major ARCIC statements after Windsor, that is, after stratum 1, and even though the term *"basic* agreement" in the Canterbury Statement (stratum 2) seems to function in exactly the same way as "substantial agreement" in Windsor, the Commission's elucidation to Windsor avoids any such admission or equation of "substantial" with "basic," but rather does offer a definition, in response to questions, of what "substantial agreement" is supposed to mean. "It means that the document represents not only the judgement of all its members —

i.e., it is an agreement," the Commission begins, and then rephrases: a substantial agreement is "their unanimous agreement."[29] This is very similar to the point made by the foreword to the American edition, namely, that "consensus" for ARCIC implies the unanimous agreement of those who have reached it.

The other half of ARCIC I's definition of the term "substantial," the "but also" that follows, is the Commission's assertion that a substantial agreement is a unanimous agreement "on essential matters where it considers that doctrine admits no divergence." Here of course the Commission is quoting, as it acknowledges, from its Canterbury Statement on Ministry and Ordination, the second stratum of its work, in which it did not use the term "substantial agreement" at all, but rather "basic agreement"(# 17). And therefore for the Commission I think we must conclude that "substantial" clearly means "basic," although it does not say so directly. Thus my preliminary conclusion is now affirmed, that for ARCIC I "consensus" and "agreement" are interchangeable, as are also "basic" and "substantial."

The second half of the Commission's definition raises another question. For substantial agreement, for basic agreement, even for fundamental consensus, must there be agreement only on *some* essentials or on *all* essentials? In the phrase "essential matters *where* it considers that doctrine admits no divergence," the word "where" is ambivalent. Does "where" mean "i.e.," thus defining "essential matters" as those that admit no divergence of doctrine? Or is it possible that there are *other* essential matters, omitted here, upon which the Commission *does not* consider that doctrine admits no divergence? The co-chairmen in their Preface to Windsor on the Eucharist back on 1971 (the earliest stratum) did state that "nothing essential has been omitted," but it seems significant that the Commission itself was never moved to say that "nothing essential has been omitted" from *any* of its agreed statements in *any* of the five strata. The Commission's example of a "substantial agreement," given in the same elucidation (# 9), is interesting but not really helpful in solving these queries: "That there can be a divergence in matters of practice and in theological judgements relating to them, without destroying a common eucharistic faith, illustrates what we mean by a *substantial* agreement."[30] Can there, though, be any disagreement in "essential doctrine"? Who decides what is essential?

This is the appropriate point to introduce two of the critical observations that have been made about the Commission's choice of words, since by the time of stratum 4 it had publicly acknowledged that such questions had been raised. The first observation is that of the official Anglican-Roman Catholic Consultation (ARC) in the USA, which in its 1974 response to the Canterbury Statement noted that ARCIC I had claimed to reach agreement on essential matters about Ministry and Ordination where doctrine admits no divergence and yet did not mention at all the ordination of women.[31] Here, then, we have a test case: Was ARCIC I recording its substantial agreement on *all* essential matters where doctrine admits no divergence, or did it choose to omit one such (admittedly very controversial) essential matter? The ordination of women is not mentioned in the Canterbury Statement, but every ARCIC I member whom I have asked admits that it was a major subject of many of the informal conversations over tea and sherry at the Commission's meetings around that time. Clearly so eminent and knowledgeable a commission knew the ordination of women was a problem; yet it claimed, unanimously, both Roman Catholic and Anglican members, to have reached agreement, precise verbal agreement, on "essential matters" about Ministry and Ordination "where doctrine admits no divergence." This basic, substantial agreement was completed in 1973, and I can certainly say that the non-mention of the ordination of women by ARCIC I in its Canterbury Statement was one of the positive factors that had an eventual influence upon the 1976 General Convention of the Episcopal Church to believe that something like "fundamental consensus" would be possible, sooner or later, with Roman Catholics on this question because it was apparently *not* for ARCIC an essential matter about Ministry and Ordination where doctrine admits no divergence. The Commission itself even seemed to concur in this estimate when in its 1979 elucidation to the Canterbury Statement (stratum 4) it recorded its belief that "the principles upon which its doctrinal agreement rests are not affected by such ordinations" (of women).[32] Especially the Roman Catholics who were members of ARCIC I will need to defend these claims, as it is sometimes now suggested by Roman Catholic authorities that doctrinal objections that admit no divergence do exist against the ordination of women.

Interestingly, the International Commission went on to say in the same 1979 elucidation to the Canterbury Statement (stratum 4) that "Objections, however substantial, to the ordination of women are of a different kind from objections raised in the past against the validity of Anglican Orders in general."[33] Here we have another related term, a new one, that seems to be raised for the first time in stratum 4, that of "substantial objections," or in the Commission's language "objections, however substantial," with the possibility that there can even be degrees of substantiality. But given the Commission's claim that the Canterbury Statement is a basic or substantial agreement on ministry and ordination, given its subsequent definition of substantial agreement, and given its self-proclaimed care in the choice of words, we now may ask whether there can really be "substantial objections" to a "substantial agreement." I believe it is just possible that the Commission is now speaking equivocally rather than univocally and that its two uses of "substantial" both in stratum 4 are not the same, "substantial" in "substantial agreement" meaning "essential" and "substantial" in "substantial objection" meaning "considerable." The word does have problems even when the Commission claims to be trying to use it precisely.

All this may be what lies behind the second critical objection that has been raised about the terminology of ARCIC I, namely, the assertion voiced by the Vatican that the phrase "substantial agreement" in the ARCIC Final Report is "ambiguous." As the 1982 Observations of the Congregation for the Doctrine of the Faith put it (and here if not elsewhere I think they have a point), the English adjective "substantial" can mean "real" or "genuine," or it can mean "fundamental . . . about points which are truly essential,"[34] The CDF also observed, as I have already noted, that at times ARCIC I does not by its terminology indicate whether it believes that its agreements are complete, and if not complete whether the differences that remain are only secondary. Thus, from both these critical observations, of ARC-USA and of the CDF, from a lack of clarity about the meaning of substantial or basic consensus or agreement, a lack of clarity that was presumably not intended by the authors but has certainly been perceived later by their various constituencies, I think we can see one way in which the ARCIC reception process has been impeded.

We turn now, finally for ARCIC I, to the fifth and final stratum of the Commission's material, coming from 1981 and consisting of the Preface, the Elucidation to Authority I, and the second statement on Authority, all of which say nothing for the purpose of this present essay; the Introduction, which, in spite of all the earlier criticism, reintroduces the controverted term by asserting that "substantial agreement on these divisive issues (treated in the Report) is now possible,"[35] and the Conclusion, which interestingly remarks that "It is our hope to carry with us in the *substance* of our *agreement* not only Roman Catholics and Anglicans but all Christians."[36] What, we must finally wonder, is the "substance" of a "substantial agreement"?

IV

The foregoing detailed analysis has been necessary in order to see what ARCIC I actually said, but it has also been somewhat tedious, as I warned; therefore I now summarize up to this point. Terminology very

179

much like "fundamental consensus" has been extensively employed in the most significant way for Anglican international ecumenical dialogue in ARCIC I, although not without problems needing clarification. Generally the terms used are "substantial" or "basic" rather than "fundamental," and "agreement" seems interchangeable with "consensus." As to why the term "fundamental" was not used by ARCIC I, the Commission collectively did not say and different members have expressed different opinions. Unless the choice of this term simply did not occur at the time, I think there are two possible reasons why it was not used: 1) It seems that for ARCIC I there can be *several* substantial or basic agreements on points that have divided us in the past, for example, on Eucharist, on ministry, and so on, and thus it is just possible that for the Commission, although it never says this, between Anglican and Roman Catholics a *fundamental* consensus may already exist, unbroken, needing only to be healed by various substantial agreements and their subsequent reception; 2) or it may be that for the Commission the fundamental consensus still lies ahead in the future, as being the sum total of all the individual substantial agreements, with no substantial difference remaining, and that the Commission did not use the term "fundamental" because it never reached that point. Moreover, still in summary, it would seem that for the terminology of ARCIC I a "consensus" has to be unanimous, but does not have to be complete; an incomplete consensus may be called a "significant convergence." A *substantial* consensus, on the other hand, has to be a unanimous agreement on some, or on all, essential matters where doctrine admits no divergence; it is normally complete, but it may not be. Insofar as all these terms are unclear, though, and it is the contention of this essay that they are somewhat unclear, the *reception* process of the ARCIC Final Report has been made more difficult, as we shall soon see.

Lest my analysis be taken as to imply that I am basically or even "substantially" in *dis*agreement with the conclusions of ARCIC I, let me at this point emphasize that I am not. To scrutinize the terminology does not mean that one is unsympathic with the intention, or with the process, or with the results, and members of the former ARCIC I should be cautioned not to draw such inferences from those who analyze their work. I do have some doubt whether the Commission always chose its words as carefully and consistently as has been claimed, but it was obviously searching for terminology adequate to the remarkable agreement it was reaching on matters of high significance, and it no doubt recognized that provisional labeling was necessary. Certainly Anglicans and Roman Catholics in the past have known better the language of separation than the language of agreement, and certainly "consensus" terminology was more appropriate to the results achieved than "convergence" language would have been. I would emphasize that the Final Report is, from an Anglican point of view, a laudable first attempt in the most serious international dialogue we have yet had to reach ecumenical agreement, even fundamental consensus, on matters that are themselves somewhat imprecise. By dividing the Commission's published contents of the Final Report into five chronological layers, moreover, I think I have demonstrated that the Commission itself grew, somewhat, in verbal wisdom as it moved from one stratum to the next. ARCIC is the first major appearance of such consensus terminology for Anglicans, and I think we have learned much from it.

But does the consensus of ARCIC I coincide with the consensuses currently, at this point in history, operative in either, or both, churches as to what is true? I turn to an evaluation of the terms for fundamental consensus in the post-ARCIC I process, and first to the questions for reception of the Final Report that were posed by the Anglican Consultative Council and by the Vatican's Unity Secretariat. Significant staff persons with some relation to each had also been participants in ARCIC I from both churches, and similar terminology appears again in the questions they posed. The churches were each asked to consider whether the contents of the ARCIC Final Report are "consonant in substance with the faith" (of Anglicans, of the Roman Catholic Church).[37] We note here a similarity with but also a difference from the terminology of the U.S. Lutheran-Episcopal Agreement that appeared about the same time, which said that "the basic teaching of each church is *consonant* with the *Gospel* and sufficiently *compatible* with the teaching of this church" to establish the partial agreement that was reached.[38]

The ARCIC reception phrase "consonant in substance" seems intentionally close to the ARCIC Final Report's terminology of substantial or basic consensus or agreement, but now of course the word "consonant" has been introduced, and I think this gives us some clue to the development of ecumenical thought in the reception process. The churches were not asked whether the Final Report expressed a "fundamental consensus" on the faith itself, but rather whether the contents of the Report were consonant in substance with the faith as each church currently understands it. My own church, the Episcopal Church in the USA, in its response chose to define its understanding of this phrase as meaning "in the first place, that no part of the Final Report explicitly contradicts the faith of Anglicans" and secondly as pointing "to an agreement in faith which does not exclude diversity of expression and emphasis,"[39] and its General Convention resolved that the

"Authority" sections of the Report were "sufficiently" consonant in substance with the faith of this church "to justify further conversations and to offer a basis for taking further steps" toward unity.[40] (By comparison, the Church of England in its response defined the phrase "consonant in substance" as meaning "substantially in harmony with the faith of Anglicans.") The published response of the U.S. Roman Catholic hierarchy found the Report "consonant in substance" with the faith of the Roman Catholic Church "regarding the role of the ordained minister in the eucharist" and concerning the Lord's real presence in the Eucharist.[41] Each church in the USA, Episcopal and Roman Catholic, was thus cautiously positive about the agreements reached by the Commission, perhaps aware that internationally each church expected to give a definitive response to the Final Report in 1988.

To dwell further on this reception process here might take me too far from the basic intention of this essay, but I can say that for Anglicans it illustrates the difficulty inherent in reaching fundamental consensus even among ourselves. This was apparently the first time in history that the entire Anglican Communion had undertaken to give an authoritative and binding answer on a matter of faith, and no one knew for sure how it would happen. The official responses of the twenty-eight churches or provinces of the Anglican Communion were collected by the Anglican Consultative Council, and a committee then drafted proposals for a possible response that were transmitted through the Anglican Consultative Council for debate and resolution by the Lambeth Conference itself. Thus it was understood that the Lambeth Conference of Anglican Bishops meeting in 1988 would "discern and pronounce a consensus"[42] on behalf of the Anglican Communion. Leaving aside the question of what degree of consensus or agreement or consonance or even convergence may have been reached with the Roman Catholic Church, we may ask whether or not the Lambeth reply of 1988 did really represent a definitive reply on behalf of Anglicanism. In one sense, morally and spiritually, it did, although legally or constitutionally of itself it did not. Recent volumes of the proceedings of the Lambeth Conferences now contain a warning near the front cover to the effect that, inasmuch as the Conference's function is "consultative and advisory," its Reports and even Resolutions carry no binding authority or legislative force until and unless they are endorsed by the canonical authority of particular national or regional churches. Will such endorsements follow in the case of the Lambeth response to the ARCIC Final Report? So far, to my knowledge, none has. Can those churches of the Anglican Communion that take no synodical action to bind themselves to the Lambeth reply be said to share at the formal level a "fundamental consensus" with it? Perhaps. At the very least they are already bound to the responses they have previously made, and the Lambeth reply carries the added weight of moral persuasion, but certainly some further synodical action would be necessary in every case where any formal change in relationship with the Roman Catholic Church is to be made.

To conclude: Still one other place where Anglican experience of the ecumenical terminology of fundamental consensus may be found is in what might be called the sixth ARCIC stratum, or the first stratum of ARCIC II, the agreed statement on *Salvation and the Church,* published in January of 1987, and here we find that the old terminology of ARCIC I has been largely (if not completely) avoided. In the Preface by the co-chairmen it is stated that the Commission's "concern has been to *state our common faith* on the issues in the doctrine of salvation which have proved problematic in the past,"[43] whereas by contrast the co-chairmen of ARCIC I has stated in 1971 that the intention had been "to reach a *consensus* at the level of faith."[44] The new Commission also does not itself use the old ARCIC I terminology, but, perhaps more modestly and I think more clearly, states that it is now "able . . . to affirm that the four areas of difficulty" (faith, justification, good works, and the church as each relates to salvation) "need not be matters of dispute between us,"[45] and it concludes (# 32) that as regards the doctrine of salvation no "remaining differences of theological interpretation or ecclesiological emphasis, either within or between our Communions, can justify our continuing separation. We believe that our two Communions are agreed on the essential aspects of the doctrine of salvation and on the Church's role within it."[46] No one determinative phrase is used here, like basic or substantial or fundamental consensus, but I believe the wording that was chosen is more directly descriptive of the agreement reached. The only word that may be difficult, as I review in retrospect the work of the new Commission of which I am a member, is the word *essential:* What does it mean to reach agreement on "the essential aspects"?

I offer a test case in answer, one that I raised in the Commission's deliberations. I cited as a possible problem canons 992 and 994 of the new 1983 Roman Catholic Code of Canon Law, which state that sins involve not only guilt but also temporal punishment, that the church "dispenses and applies authoritatively the treasury of the merits of Christ and the saints," and that therefore indulgences can be gained for the living or even "applied for the dead by way of suffrage," canons that might have also proved difficult for the compilers of the U.S. Lutheran-Roman Catholic Justification Statement at paragraph 143 and note

209,[47] had they been discussed at that time. But in reply the Roman Catholic members of ARCIC II seemed unanimous in upholding these canons as the current teaching of the Roman Catholic Church yet as not in any way invalidating our ARCIC II claim, which we were about to subscribe, that we had reached agreement on the *essential* aspects of the doctrine of salvation and on the church's role in it. These current canons on indulgences were not *essential* to the Roman Catholic doctrine of salvation, the Roman Catholic members seemed to say, and because of their answer I too felt able to subscribe to the ARCIC II statement at Llandaff in 1986. We had reached agreement on the *essential* aspects of the doctrine of salvation, including justification, and on the church's role within it. I think our use of "essential" here is not entirely clear, but neither do we claim unanimous verbal agreement. Would the Llandaff Statement have been more significant or impressive if we had claimed that it is a substantial or fundamental consensus or agreement? I think not.[48]

Roger W. Fjeld

J. ROBERT WRIGHT'S essay invites reflection because it is itself a reflection on our topic. This response will take the form of reflections, first about the function of terminology and then about the content of Wright's observations in relation to Lutheran ecumenical concerns.

Reflections about the function of terminology

The historian in me applauds Dr. Wright's careful rehearsal of the evolution of terminology in connection with some recent ecumenical discussions and action. If something similar were done in relation to the whole dialogue enterprise, we might better be able to see what has been happening as we seek to understand each other and to affirm unity where it appears to us to exist.

The debate about language can, of course, be simply a distraction from the ecumenical task. A preoccupation with terminology can lead by accident or design to unnecessary arguments or to empty agreements. But it need not be that way. If we understand the search for adequate terminology to be in reality a gradual definition of the task itself, attention to language can be very helpful. We are after all on ground quite new for our churches, and it should not be surprising that we grope for appropriate language. Until very recently we knew better the language for separation and caricature.

But it is more than the fact that we are on relatively new terrain. New initiatives sometimes require new language (symbols) because the old invoke old responses. Our communions have each developed in separate and often antagonistic ways. That separate development has included the adoption of separate vocabularies for key matters of faith and life, language which we have come to revere as the right way to express these matters. To attempt now to use that same language in ecumenical discussion is to doom the discussion from the start.

An example from another discipline may help make the point about the value of a search for new linguistic symbols to serve the ecumenical task. In the early 1960s sociologist Robert Bellah borrowed an old phrase from Rousseau and gave it particular meaning in modern American experience when he coined the phrase "American civil religion." The essay which he built around that phrase has significantly influenced the study of religion in America. A new phrase represented a new conceptual framework for studying cultural artifacts which were already well known. In retrospect Bellah laments the way his choice of language has been the occasion for much debate and wonders whether some other phrase than "civil religion" might better have enabled discussion about the substance of his concern. But at the same time he recognizes that the debate about terminology is in fact a debate about content and is therefore essential to an adequate understanding of the phenomenon which he chose to call "American civil religion." New descriptive language became the occasion for a new understanding of familiar data and experience.

Thus new language in ecumenical discussion has the potential to move us beyond the mindset and the stereotypes which accompany the old and separate language patterns (symbols). We will need new language, with agreed-upon meanings, to use in ecumenical encounter and especially in the search for ecumenical agreement.

Dr. Wright's essay illustrates the way the struggle for language mirrors a struggle for understanding. Even for those who are leaders in ecumenical matters, there is (or ought to be) a wholesome sort of uncertainty about how best to understand and proceed. Dr. Wright rehearsed the uncertainties in two sets of dialogues. One senses in those descriptions how the participants were more concerned about their developing common understanding than about consistency of language. The evidence suggests that various terms were tried, found satisfactory by the participants, then shared with the wider ecclesial communities. If they did not fare well there, the search began again, as dialogues continued or were reconstituted. That process seems to me to be altogether appropriate! It serves us well to acknowledge our limitations and to search together for better language to express what we want to say. I covet just such an atmosphere in which our churches and our individual egos allow us to say, "I'm not sure . . ." and "What if . . .?" That surely serves the gospel better than when we simply use traditional terminology to stake out traditional positions.

The search for adequate terminology cannot be completed until we know what it is that we seek to describe. It is difficult to label what has not been circumscribed, but it is also difficult to circumscribe what has not been at least provisionally labeled. This is not a catch-22, as someone suggested, but rather a creative tension by which the task can profitably proceed. It is useful to begin with substance and to seek out the points at which there is emerging agreement or clarity about disagreement. Then comes the necessity of describing the nature of the agreement or disagreement, first to the satisfaction of those who are engaged in the discussions and then with those who have not been dialogue participants. As people in that wider audience study these descriptions, they are led to affirm or to question the descriptive language and to ask the questions which renew the dialogue.

What language best serves the current stage of ecumenical dialogue and reporting? Dr. Wright suggests that "consensus" and "agreement" are used interchangably in the documents on which he reported and says he prefers the more direct word "agreement." I agree and think that "convergence" is the best current term for that which is approaching but is not yet agreement.

"Fundamental," "basic," and "essential" all try to say two things at the same time and in the process create doubt as well as offering information. On the one hand, they are used to modify the idea of agreement in such a way that there is apparently less complete agreement because they are modifiers. That leaves the readers wondering what was not agreed upon. On the other hand, they are used to suggest the centrality of certain subject matter and to suggest that agreement on such material is the agreement that counts. That leaves the readers wondering about the principle of selection, i.e., do we agree with their assessment about what is "fundamental" or "basic" or "essential"?

There comes a time when the accumulating evidence from dialogues and interchurch discussions makes it appropriate to survey the whole and determine whether agreement has been reached on all that the partners agree is central to fellowship. At that point it may be possible to report that there now exists "fundamental agreement" or better yet "sufficient agreement" and to test the possibility that the basis has therefore been established for closer interchurch relationships.

Thus it seems to me that we are well served at the present stage to use the simple language of agreement-disagreement-convergence to describe the results of particular dialogues. When we survey the accumulating results of many dialogues with a number of partners, it is appropriate to qualify agreement with some modifier which suggests that such agreement now covers a broad range of topics, including all of those considered necessary for fellowship.

Reflections about the content upon which we must agree

Upon what subject matter must there be agreement if there is to be declaration and practice of fellowship? What is the content of an agreement broad enough to call it "fundamental" or "sufficient"? To start ecumenical dialogue with such a question is in all likelihood to doom the discussion. But we are not at the beginning of this enterprise. We are in fact at a point where it is altogether proper to ask the question about sufficiency, about how much must be included in the sort of agreement which leads beyond dialogue to some manner of common life.

Dr. Wright points to the four criteria set forth for Anglican churches by the Chicago-Lambeth Quadrilateral, criteria "upon which agreement is necessary as a basis for an approach to ecumenical reunion with other churches." He suggests that the churches of the Anglican Communion are prepared to enter into "full *koinonia* or fellowship with other churches" which agree with the Anglicans on "those four points or articles or elements of the faith. . . ."

Other communions represented at this conference and in various ecumenical dialogues use other starting points and other sets of criteria for what is essential to fellowship. In fact, the Lutheran churches represented here do not all use the same criteria in making fellowship judgments. What that suggests, of course, is that we have no prior agreement about the subject matter upon which we must agree if we are to move from study to common declarations and consequent actions.

Given that fact, the way we approach this matter is quite important. We can either engage in a wholesome uncertainty about what should finally be required or we can start from fixed positions, risking the likelihood of an impasse. We are good at fixed positions, but these do not lend themselves to fresh inquiry and the search for unity with integrity. In the name of faithfulness to tradition or Confessions, we are tempted to insist that the only road to unity is the road mapped out by our particular criteria. Such an approach ensures that dialogue will never be more than a comparison of mutually exclusive requirements for unity.

It seems we will need to be commuters rather than people guarding fixed positions. That is to say, we need to start the process of discussion and discovery with particular topics that we believe are important for our possible life together. We are not able in advance to know whether agreement is possible on such topics nor are we able to know what will be the consequences of agreement or disagreement.

But there will also be times when we need to commute between the discrete topics of given dialogues and the broader question of what constitutes a fundamental or sufficient set of topical agreements necessary before there can be formal fellowship. This is more than simply incorporating the results of one set of dialogues into the succeeding ones. And it is more than simply accumulating agreements until there is a disposition to say we have agreed often enough to proceed to fellowship. It is rather that genuine dialogue must proceed on two levels: the one concerning a particular topic and the other concerning what the dialogue partners conceive to be the range and completeness of agreement needed before two or several churches are ready to declare themselves one in faith and mission. The latter level will never be simply the question, "Is this enough?" but rather "Are these the subjects upon which we must agree and do we agree with each other on these matters?"

There is another dimension to this matter of the content of our common study. Dr. Wright alludes to it in his paper when he suggests that some things are static and some are changing in the lives of our churches. Even as we present ourselves to each other for possible fellowship, our churches are changing in understandings and practices, sometimes in response to concerns internal to our own church life and sometimes to events and issues in the world around us. This matter of seeking common ground among churches which are simultaneously experiencing change is easier for some of us than for others. Churches which see faithfulness as a matter of unchanging doctrine and practice must be perplexed by changes occurring in dialogue partners. They wonder what other changes are just around the corner and what it might mean to be in fellowship with another church which might in the meantime change in unacceptable ways. Churches which see faithfulness as a matter of fresh inquiry and theological development with potential for practical change must be perplexed by dialogue partners who question whether faithfulness can countenance change.

The decision of some churches to ordain women can serve as a key example. Some Lutheran churches, as a matter of fresh biblical and theological understanding and of the freedom to revise practice accordingly, now welcome women as clergy. The day is not far away when the Evangelical Lutheran Church in America will celebrate the election of some ordained women as bishops. That development in the life of some Lutheran churches has caused much distress for other Lutheran church bodies. One senses that it has also complicated our developing relationships with Roman Catholic and Orthodox dialogue partners. At the same time it has been welcomed by other dialogue partners, such as the United Methodists, who already have long welcomed women as ordained clergy.

How will we deal with this matter? It is the sort of subject which admits of no "consensus," let alone "agreement," if we are to begin with the present practices of the several communions. Will we not need instead to engage each other at the level of discussion about the relationship between hermeneutic and practice so that differences in practice, if they are the result of careful study and interpretation, are not church dividing? This seems to be essential to our continued search for unity.

Moving from that extended example to the broad question which it was intended to illustrate, we need ways to deal with the generic issue of faithfulness and of the different ways we define and practice faithfulness. We must especially find ways to understand how faithfulness can encompass both change and changelessness. Within that generic understanding we then need to find ways to deal with specific changes as they occur or are proposed. The goal must be to be able to recognize and affirm faithfulness among us even when we have come to different conclusions about specific beliefs and practices.

If there is little by way of criticism in this set of reflections on Dr. Wright's paper, it is because I find little to criticize. His paper has made a real contribution by delineating the function of terminology in specific dialogues and by suggesting how Anglicans view the subject which has drawn us to this conference, the question about whether and what kind of fundamental consensus exists as a result of a generation of ecumenical dialogue.

Notes

WRIGHT

1. "Report on the Basis of Anglican Unity," *The Report of the Lambeth Conference 1978* (London: Church Information Office Publishing, 1978) 99.

2. Book of Common Prayer, section on "Historical Documents of the Church."

3. Ibid.

4. See further J. Robert Wright (ed.), *Quadrilateral at One Hundred* (Essays on the Centenary of the Chicago-Lambeth Quadrilateral 1886/88-1986/88; Cincinnati: Forward Movement; London and Oxford: Mobray, 1988; also published as Supplementary Series no. 10 of the *Anglican Theological Review*, March 1988).

5. LED I, 23.

6. LED II, 54.

7. Ibid., 57.

8. Ibid., 31.

9. Ibid., 41.

10. Ibid. Emphasis added.

11. Ibid., 43.

12. *Anglican-Lutheran Dialogue.* The Report of the Anglican-Lutheran European Regional Commission (London: SPCK, 1983) 8-22.

13. *The Lutheran-Episcopal Agreement.* Commentary and Guidelines (New York: Lutheran Church in America, 1983) 6.

14. Ibid., 8.

15. Ibid., 6.

16. Ibid., 13.

17. *Anglican-Roman Catholic International Commission. The Final Report* (Cincinnati: Forward Movement, 1982) iv.

18. Ibid., 11.

19. Ibid., 12, #1.

20. Ibid., 16, #12. Emphasis added.

21. Ibid., 30, #1. Emphasis added.

22. Ibid., 38-39, #17.

23. Ibid., 66, #25.

24. Ibid.

25. Ibid., 64, 66, ##24, 26.

26. Ibid., 49-50.

27. Ibid., 50.

28. Ibid., 64-66, #24.

29. Ibid., 17, #2.

30. Ibid., 24, #9. Emphasis added.

31. "ARC Response to ARCIC Canterbury Statement," *Documents on Anglican-Roman Catholic Relations (ARC DOC) III* (Washington: United States Catholic Conference, 1976) 84, #4.

32. ARCIC I, 44, #5.

33. Ibid.

34. "Observations on the ARCIC Final Report" (by the Congregation for the Doctrine of the Faith), *Origins* 11:47 (6 May 1982) 753.

35. ARCIC I, 5, #2.

36. Ibid., 99. Emphasis added.

37. "Report of the Standing Commission on Ecumenical Relations to the General Convention of the Episcopal Church, 1985," *Ecumenical Bulletin* 71 (May-June 1985) 19.

38. Lutheran-Episcopal Agreement, 8. Emphasis added.

39. "Report of the Standing Commission," 19.

40. *Ecumenical Bulletin* 74 (Nov-Dec. 1985) 13.

41. "Evaluation of the ARCIC Final Report" (by the National Conference of Catholic Bishops in the USA), *Origins* 14:25 (6 December 1983) 410, 412.

42. *The Emmaus Report.* A report of the Anglican Ecumenical Consultation which took place at the Emmaus Retreat Centre, West Wickham, Kent, England, 22 January-2 February 1987 in preparation for the Anglican Consultative Council-7, Singapore, 1987, and the Lambeth Conference 1988 (Cincinnati: Forward Movement, 1987) 73.

43. *Salvation in the Church* (London: Anglican Consultative Council and the Secretariat for Promoting Christian Unity, 1987) 7. Emphasis added.

44. ARCIC I, 11. Emphasis added.

45. *Salvation*, 13, #8.

46. Ibid., 26, #32.

47. L-RC 7, 65, #143, and 335-37, note 209.

48. Another document that pertains to this article is: *Towards a Church of England Response to BEM & ARCIC* (London: Church Information Office Publishing, 1985).

13

Doctrine, Opinions, and Christian Unity

A Wesleyan and Methodist Perspective

Geoffrey Wainwright

LIBERAL METHODISTS isolate Wesley's dictum that "we think and let think" and make him the patron of sentimental ecumenism or even religious indifferentism. They forget that Wesley's magnanimity was limited to "opinions that do not strike at the root of Christianity."[1] In his generous sermon on a "Catholic Spirit," in which he reached out to Baptists and Roman Catholics (to name only those) in a plea for mutual respect and love, Wesley declares that "a man of truly catholic spirit is fixed as the sun in his judgment concerning the main branches of Christian doctrine" and supposes that the practitioners of a catholic spirit have in common at least "the first elements of the gospel of Christ."[2] In his "Letter to a Roman Catholic" Wesley expressed the faith of "a true Protestant" in words that amount to an expansion of the Nicene-Constantinopolitan Creed.[3] At the anthropological end of the scale Wesley stated in "The Principles of a Methodist Farther Explained" that "our main doctrines, which include all the rest, are three, that of repentance, of faith, and of holiness,"[4] and behind these stood, as Wesley shows in a lengthy treatise on "The Doctrine of Original Sin," original sin and the gratuitous work of Christ and the Spirit:

> A denial of original sin contradicts the main design of the gospel, which is to humble vain man, and to ascribe to God's free grace the whole of his salvation. Nor, indeed, can we let this doctrine go without giving up, at the same time, the greatest part, if not all, of the essential doctrines of the Christian faith. If we give this up, we cannot defend either justification by the merits of Christ, or the renewal of our natures by his Spirit.[5]

In all this Wesley adhered wholeheartedly to the official teachings of the Church of England, and he expected his preachers and people

193

to do the same. As a simple presbyter of the Anglican Church he was not in a position either to declare or to break ecclesial communion. But he sought for Methodists both friendly association and practical cooperation, whether within the Church of England or beyond it. There were, however, certain conditions set on his side. Thus soon after his own "evangelical conversion" in which the Moravians had been instrumental, Wesley ceased to meet with them on account of their teaching on "stillness": the quietistic attitude that those awaiting full assurance of faith should meanwhile abstain from the means of grace. And in 1741 he broke off evangelistic collaboration with his younger friend George Whitefield on account of the latter's Calvinistic teaching on predestination. In his ferocious sermon of 1739-40 on "Free Grace" (which was never included among his "Standard Sermons"), Wesley berated predestination as "a direct and manifest tendency to overthrow the whole Christian Revelation."[6]

From the 1740s on Wesley was dealing with Methodism as an embryonic denomination, not yet out of the womb of Anglicanism. The separation took place slowly, and indeed it was not until the end of the *nineteenth* century that the British Wesleyans took to themselves the name of church as distinct from "connexion." By Christmas 1784, however, the Americans had constituted themselves the Methodist Episcopal Church. Besides the *Standard Sermons* and the *Explanatory Notes upon the New Testament* which Wesley by the law of England set up as doctrinal guidance for his conference and connexion, Wesley also gave to the American Methodists his reduction of the Thirty-Nine Articles to Twenty-Four and his own abridgment of the Book of Common Prayer ("The Sunday Service"). He bequeathed to both sides of the Atlantic, although it nowhere attained constitutional status, *A Collection of Hymns for the Use of the People called Methodists* (1780), which Wesley saw as containing "all the important truths of our most holy religion, whether speculative or practical."[7]

Since these documents belong to various literary and theological genres, it is not in fact easy to distill from them a single comprehensive statement that would declare what is necessary and sufficient Methodist doctrine. But it seems clear enough that Wesley intended to maintain and propagate the scriptural, creedal, patristic, orthodox, catholic faith as this had been reformed in the Church of England. As "essential" to Christianity (he used the word), he clearly held to God the Holy Trinity, origin and goal of human salvation; the work of Christ and of the Holy Spirit in our redemption and its application; and the human condition, need, and calling, involving original sin, the justification of believers, and their sanctification and glorification. If Methodist

194

denominations ever declined constitutionally from those doctrines, they could no longer legitimately claim to be Wesleyan.

That is the substantial heritage which Methodist denominations have had at their disposal for their life and mission and with which they have ever since Wesley had to negotiate, theoretically and practically, their own ecumenical relationships. Inherent in those substantive doctrines and in Wesley's understanding and practice concerning them are also certain distinctions and goals that come into play when the substance has to be dynamically interpreted in the ongoing life of the Methodist denominations and, which is our chief concern here, in their ecumenical interactions with other ecclesial bodies in the search for Christian unity.

The first of these is the distinction between doctrine and opinions. The former admits no difference; the latter may vary. Thus Wesley later admitted that at the time of his break with Whitefield he considered Calvinist teaching on predestination "not as an opinion, but as a dangerous mistake." It is, however, interesting that by the time of his letter of May 14, 1765, to John Newton, Wesley was prepared to rank it among those matters of "opinion" where Christians might vary as long as they were "compatible with a love to Christ and a work of grace." Wesley had been persuaded to reclassify the matter through acquaintance with Calvinists, including Newton himself, who "have real Christian experience." With fine evenhandedness, incidentally, Wesley was prepared to qualify as an "opinion" his own teaching on perfection, which he told Newton was "the main point between you and me."[8] These particular examples of predestination and perfection assume their full importance when it is realized that the most frequent partners with Methodists in church union plans and achievements have been denominations in the Reformed family. However particular negotiations turn out to distribute items between "doctrine" and "opinions" (and obviously a maximal consistency must be aimed at—that is why "multilateral" dialogues are so important), the distinction remains an important one of principle in the cause of Christian unity.

The second indication Methodists will be liable to take from Wesley concerns the importance of soteriological considerations. It is this, for example, which will cause Wesley to refuse his hand to Arians, semi-Arians, and Socinians, and to insist on full trinitarianism. Listen to his late sermon "On the Trinity":

> There are ten thousand mistakes which may consist with real religion; with regard to which every candid, considerate man will think and let think. But there are some truths more important than others. It seems there are some of which are of deep importance. I do not term them

"fundamental" truths; because that is an ambiguous word. And hence there have been so many warm disputes about the number of "fundamentals." But surely there are some which it nearly concerns us to know, as having a close connexion with vital religion. And doubtless we may rank among these that contained in the words above cited: "There are three that bear record in heaven, the Father, the Word, and the Holy Ghost. And these three are one. . . ."

The knowledge of the Three-One God is interwoven with all true Christian faith, with all vital religion. . . . I know not how anyone can be a Christian believer till "he hath" (as St. John speaks) "the witness in himself"; till "the Spirit of God witnesses with his spirit that he is a child of God"—that is, in effect, till God the Holy Ghost witnesses that God the Father has accepted him through the merits of God the Son—and having this witness he honours the Son and the blessed Spirit "even as he honours the Father." Not that every Christian believer *adverts* to this; perhaps at first not one in twenty; but if you ask any of them a few questions, you will easily find it is implied in what he believes.[9]

That example is not without substantive interest to us at a time when the doctrine of the Trinity is for various reasons under threat and bids fair to become once more, as in the fourth century (where the argumentation of Athanasius and Basil was also basically soteriological!), the *articulus stantis et cadentis ecclesiae*. In fact, in all issues of doctrine or opinion Wesley displayed a strong soteriological interest in the content of the gospel, its proclamation, its reception, and its end in that holiness without which no one shall see the Lord.

The third Wesleyan indication will encourage Methodists to stretch their tolerance to the limits for the sake of unity in evangelism and mission. That approach was shown by Wesley in his letter of April 19, 1764, to "various clergymen" of Calvinist persuasion in the Church of England, wherein he sought, though without success, to win them for a missionary alliance.[10] The same attitude governed his views on church order, as expressed in his letter of June 25, 1746, to "John Smith":

> What is the end of all ecclesiastical order? Is it not to bring souls from the power of Satan to God; and to build them up in his fear and love? Order, then, is so far valuable, as it serves these ends, and if it answers them not, it is nothing worth.[11]

Methodists have been sympathetic to the modern ecumenical motto *ut omnes unum sint*, "in order that the world may believe." It is above all this missionary motivation which has prompted Methodist participation, both British and American, in the World Council of Churches, and which has pushed churches of British Methodist origin in particular in the direction of organic unity with churches of other confessional traditions.

It would now be appropriate to examine how well Methodist bodies have used their doctrinal deposit and followed the Wesleyan guidelines in their application of it to ecumenical situations. If space allowed, we could look in detail at union schemes (failed, successful, and continuing), at the reports of bilateral dialogues between Methodists and others, and (though this may be premature) at initial Methodist responses to the Lima text on *Baptism, Eucharist and Ministry*. The most significant unions have probably been those of the United Church of Canada (1925), the Church of South India (1947), and the Uniting Church in Australia (1977). The first and the third brought Methodists together with Presbyterians and Congregationalists; the second joined Methodists of British origin not only to Christians of Reformed background but also to Anglicans. One would need to look at the "Basis of Union" in these three cases to see how the historically controversial matters of doctrine and order were dealt with. In England, in connexion with the finally unsuccessful plan of 1982 for a "covenant" between Methodists, Moravians, United Reformed, and Anglicans, the Church of England declared itself satisfied with the doctrinal assurances it had already received from the Methodist Church at the time of the earlier, and unadopted, plan of union in 1969 and 1972. In the United States all four Methodist denominations in the Consultation on Church Union have given affirmative answers to questions on the "theological basis" for a "covenant" put forward by COCU in 1984.

As to bilateral dialogues, the World Methodist Council's oldest is with the Roman Catholic Church, which began in 1967 and is now in its fifth quinquennial series. Whereas Wesley in the historical circumstances of the eighteenth century had looked upon individual Roman Catholics as Christians *in spite of* their allegiance to their church (and Wesley wrote several tracts against certain Roman Catholic doctrines, along the lines of the Anglican Articles of Religion), the Nairobi Report of 1986 (*Towards a Statement on the Church*) declares joint commitment to a "goal of full communion in faith, mission and sacramental life." The first twenty-eight paragraphs of the Nairobi text are a completely agreed statement on many matters of ecclesiology, and the succeeding long discussion on authority concludes that "in any case Catholics and Methodists are agreed on the need for an authoritative way of being sure, beyond doubt, concerning God's action insofar as it is crucial for our salvation." [12]

The "final report" produced in 1984 by the joint commission between the World Methodist Council and the Lutheran World Federation on "The Church: Community of Grace" was able to recommend that "our churches take steps to declare and establish full fellowship of Word and sacrament" and that "as a first and important step our churches officially provide for pulpit exchange and mutual hospitality at the table of the Lord." While recognizing continuing characteristic "emphases," the report reaffirms the "basic common convictions" present from the start. It "witnesses to important agreements and convergences" and "indicates the ways in which we express our common faith differently."[13]

Two points may be made in conclusion. The first is to admit the great internal variety within the United Methodist Church, in the United States in particular. The 1972 *Book of Discipline* sandwiched the "foundation documents" between a statement on their "historical background" and a reflection on "our theological task." It declared that the Methodist pioneers believed there to be "a 'marrow' of Christian truth that can be identified and that must be conserved. This living core, as they believed, stands revealed in *Scripture*, illuminated by *tradition*, vivified in personal *experience*, and confirmed by *reason*."[14] Since then there has been much debate concerning the relationships and respective functions of the four terms in this "quadrilateral." Unfortunately the 1972 text used the words "doctrine" and "theology" very loosely so that it is difficult to know where the church stands on the matter of a theological pluralism that does not sink into doctrinal laxity. The 1988 *Book of Discipline* contains a revised statement on "Doctrinal Standards and Our Theological Tasks" which the General Conference mandated for a four-year study in the church at large.[15]

The second concluding point returns to Methodist origins. For the Wesleys it was clear that Christian doctrine and Christian unity subserved the upbuilding of the church in truth and love. Therein resides human salvation, which is to the glory of God.[16]

Notes

1. John Wesley, *The Works of the Rev. John Wesley, A.M.* (ed. T. Jackson; London, 1829-31; reprint: Grand Rapids, MI: Baker, 1984) 8:340.

2. Ibid., 5:492-504.

3. Ibid., 10:80-86. See further G. Wainwright, "Methodism and the Apostolic Faith," *What Should Methodism Teach?* (ed. M. D. Meeks: Nashville: Abringdon, 1990) 96-112.

4. Ibid., 8:472.

5. Ibid., 9:429.

6. Ibid., 7:373-86.

7. *The Works of John Wesley*. Volume 7: *A Collection of Hymns for the Use of the People called Methodists* (1st ed. London, 1780; ed. F. Hildebrandt and O. A. Beckerlegge; Oxford: Clarendon, 1983) 73-74.

8. *The Letters of the Rev. John Wesley, A.M.* (ed. J. Telford; London: Epworth, 1931) 4:297-300.

9. J. Wesley, *Works* (ed. Jackson) 6:199-206. See further, G. Wainwright, "Why Wesley was a Trinitarian," *The Drew Gateway* 59 (1990) 26-43.

10. J. Wesley, *Letters*, 4:235-39.

11. Ibid., 2:77-78.

12. *Towards a Statement on the Church* (Lake Junaluska: World Methodist Council, 1986) 8, 20, ##20, 75.

13. Lutheran-Methodist Joint Commission, *The Church: Community of Grace* (Geneva: LWF; Lake Junaluska: World Methodist Council, 1984) 31, 9, 5; ##91, 14, 13, preface.

14. *The Book of Discipline of the United Methodist Church 1972* (Nashville: United Methodist Publishing House, 1972) 39-40, #68.

15. *The Book of Discipline of the United Methodist Church 1988* (Nashville: United Methodist Publishing House, 1988) 40-60, 78-90, ##66-67, 69. See further T. C. Oden, *Doctrinal Standards in the Methodist Tradition* (Grand Rapids, MI: Francis Asbury, 1988); J. L. Walls, *The Problem of Pluralism: Recovering United Methodist Identity* (Wilmore, KY: Bristol Books, revised edition, 1988); G. Wainwright, "From Pluralism towards Catholicity? The United Methodist Church after the General Conference of 1988," *The Asbury Theological Journal* 44 (1989) 17-27.

16. On Lutheran-Methodist relations in the U.S., see G. Wainwright, "Uniting what was never divided: The next steps for Lutherans and Methodists," *dialog* 29 (1990) 107-10.

14

Fundamental Consensus in the New Testament

James D. G. Dunn

Introduction

HOW CAN WE EXPECT the New Testament to help us in our discussion of Fundamental Consensus and Church Fellowship? Only if we bear in mind its twofold character as historical source for the beginnings of Christianity and as Christian Scripture.

1. We must use the NT as historical source for Jesus' own ministry and for the testimony of those closest to him. Not because we believe that "original is best" or cherish what has been fairly called "the myth of Christian beginnings," but by the logic of our theology of incarnation. We assert that the word of God came to its fullest and clearest expression in the life of Jesus, the most definitive expression of divine revelation that is possible or ever has been within human history. By that assertion we inevitably bind ourselves to the task of historical inquiry and to historical inquiry into the NT itself. For the NT is in simple fact the only real source within history which we have for that climactic period of divine revelation, the only historical access to that crucial midpoint of salvation history. And, as with all historical inquiry, that will require us to recognize the differences between the languages and idioms, thought forms and assumptions, conventions and social structures of that far distant time and our own. It will require us above all to remember the historical contingency of that revelation, the fact that the words preserved for us in the NT were addressed to particular situations and that they usually cannot be fully understood without taking that historical context into account. Just as the doctrine of the incarnation can never dispense with "the scandal of particularity," neither can exegesis ignore the historical conditionedness and contingency of any NT passage.

2. At the same time the NT is also Christian Scripture. To describe these documents as contingent and episodic in character is only part of the picture. For however local and specific in purpose and function they may have been in original intention, it is also a historical fact that they were recognized as much more than occasional by those to whom they were initially sent. These documents were evidently cherished from the first, presumably because they were recognized to bear a stamp of authority and relevance which transcended the immediacy of the local situation. They were heard to speak not simply with the voice of a Paul or a John, but as God's word. Other letters and tracts written by the first Christians did not survive. But these were preserved precisely because their continuing authority was valued. Canonization was only in very small part a bestowing of authority not previously possessed. Much more was it a process of recognition of authority already experienced and acknowledged by an ever widening circle of churches.

The point for us is that these two aspects of the NT must be kept together. We cannot confine the meaning of the NT as a whole or of any NT text in particular to the first and original meaning. The word of God which has been heard through the NT in diverse and developed forms down through the centuries has not been simply a repetition of that first word. The canon has been used to validate much more than ever appears in the NT itself. But neither dare we let the meaning read from the NT become separated from the original meaning. The meaning intended by the original author and heard by the first readers was the decisive impulse toward the acknowledgement of their canonical authority. More important, that original meaning is part of the first witness, the "apostolic witness" to the decisive revelation event of Christ which is the heart and foundation in history for Christianity as a whole. That first testimony in all its historical conditionedness and relativity is bound to serve as some sort of check or control or "canon" on the meanings subsequently heard by those who recognize that canonical authority.

It is here that the Christian NT scholar can hope to play his part in discerning the voice of the Spirit today in issues to which the NT also speaks. Not that the *"Neutestamentler"* can think to set himself or herself over against the teaching authority of the church in its diverse forms. But as a specialist in the foundational documents or constitutional articles of Christianity, the Christian *"Neutestamentler"* is part of the teaching ministry of the church, whose special task or charism is to recall the churches to fundamental features of the Christian tradition as attested in the NT. In evaluating claims to "word of God" authority today, the NT Scriptures must have a primary claim on our attention since all other claims to "word of God" authority in writing derive more or less immediately from them. And the one whose calling has been to enter as fully as possible into the original mind and purpose of these Scriptures is specially charged to remind others involved in that evaluation process of what the NT writers said in their own terms and their own times.

With this in mind, what then does the NT contribute to the issue of "Fundamental Consensus"?

Fundamental Consensus

In my study of *Unity and Diversity in the New Testament*[1] I came to a conclusion somewhat to my surprise, a conclusion which has bearing on our discussion. It can be expressed in the terms we are using, as follows. There is no fundamental consensus in the NT if by that is meant an agreed form of words consistently maintained across the spectrum of the NT documents. But there is an agreed heart or core of common faith which came to expression in different terms in different contexts and in which other elements of faith and practice cohere, with diverse and at times divergent emphases depending on context. At the beginning of the final chapter I summarized the position thus: "The integrating center" and "unifying element" in earliest Christianity was

> the unity between the historical Jesus and the exalted Christ, that is to say, the conviction that the wandering charismatic preacher from Nazareth had ministered, died and been raised from the dead to bring God and man finally together, the recognition that the divine power through which they now worshipped and were encountered and accepted by God was one and the same person, Jesus the man, the Christ, the Son of God, the Lord, the life-giving Spirit.[2]

This remains, I believe, a justifiable statement of "fundamental consensus" in the NT.[3] But let me attempt a brief restatement of the analysis which will speak more directly to our present discussion.

What do we mean by "fundamental consensus" in the NT? What are we looking for? What are the criteria for recognizing it? I would suggest two possible criteria, one which springs more from the NT as historical source for the beginnings of Christianity and the other from the NT as Scripture. The first puts some stress on the word *"fundamental"*: a fundamental consensus is one on which all of Christianity was united from the beginning, belonging to the historical foundation of

Christianity. The second gives a little more emphasis to the word *"consensus"*: a fundamental consensus is an element common to all the NT writings, a basic belief or practice affirmed or assumed by all the NT documents. When we ask what elements of Christianity meet both these criteria, we are driven toward the sort of answer that I gave above. It can be summed up in two words, "Easter" and "Pentecost."

Easter

There can be little doubt that the resurrection of Jesus is at the heart of Christianity, fundamental in terms of both the above criteria. Since the assertion is noncontroversial, I need not develop it in detail. Suffice to recall that belief in Jesus as raised by God from the dead belongs to the very earliest stages of Christian faith which we can trace (e.g., 1 Cor 15:3-7; Rom 1:3-4; 10:9)[4] and runs through the NT writings like a golden thread (e.g., Acts 4:2; 17:18; 1 Cor 15:14, 17; 1 Tim 3:16; Heb 13:20; 1 Pet 3:18; Rev 5:6).

Pentecost

Similarly, historical research points to the Pentecostal experience of the Spirit in Jerusalem (Acts 2) as an equally fundamental beginning for Christianity and to experience of the Spirit of God as an equally basic stratum of Christian faith as attested by the NT writers (e.g., John 7:39; Acts 10:47; Rom 8:9, 14, 23; 2 Cor 1:22; Gal 3:3; Tit 3:5-7; Heb 6:4; 1 Pet 4:14; 1 John 2:20, 27; 3:24).[5]

If, then, we are looking for fundamental consensus in the NT, in the twofold sense of elements which were part of Christianity from the first and which consistently feature as central to Christianity across the range of documents which make up the NT, we must start with Easter and Pentecost, Christ and the Spirit. Moreover, we should not ignore the fact that it was *the manifest correlation* of these two fundamental elements which lay at the heart of Christianity's initial distinctiveness and success. It was the proclamation of the resurrection of Christ which evidently resulted in the gift of the Spirit. And the gift of the Spirit was taken as proof that God had accepted the act of commitment to the risen Lord. The gift of the Spirit demonstrated that God had both vindicated Christ and accepted them. The experience of the Spirit was given definition by reference to Christ — as the Spirit of Christ, the Spirit of the Son who cries "Abba! Father!" (particularly Rom 8:9, 15; Gal 4:6). *Ecumenical conversation must never forget that it is the correlation and mutual interdependence of doctrine and experience which is at the heart of the fundamental consensus of the NT.*

Of course there are other elements which are bound up in the integration of these two fundamental elements: for example, it is implicit in what has already been said that *commitment* to this risen Christ was what brought these two together in the experience of faith from the first. And other elements cohere with these most basic features as soon as we begin to unpack them, or, speaking historically, as soon as the first Christians began to work out what they meant in the context of mission to Jew and Gentile. We will go on to look at the most important of these in the next section. But none other seems to be quite so fundamental in original expression or to be maintained with quite the same consistency of emphasis across the NT documents. These two are the *minimum core,* the *presupposition* for all the rest, the *touchstone* by which all the others can be seen to bear a Christian character.

There is, however, one exception, a further feature of earliest and NT Christianity which has only recently come to the fore in ecumenical discussion and which deserves a good deal more attention that it has so far received, what may perhaps best be described as the fundamental tension between Christianity and its Jewish origins.[6] Which brings us to our next main topic.

Fundamental Tension

It belongs to the essence of Christianity that it emerged from first century Judaism. Jesus was a Jew. The very first Christians were all Jews. Christianity began as a movement within Judaism, a messianic sect of Judaism. It did not understand itself as a new religion but rather as the eschatological expression of Judaism. This point is well enough known and need not be further elaborated. What has not been so much appreciated, however, is that this fundamental relation between Christianity and its original Jewish matrix set up within Christianity a tension, *a tension which is constitutive of Christianity by virtue of these origins.* It is the tension of continuity and discontinuity. The tension emerges from the fact of that continuity and discontinuity, from the fact that the continuity and discontinuity have to be held together and can never finally be resolved this side of the eschaton.

The point which needs to be made here is that this fundamental tension is as fundamental to Christianity as the elements of fundamental consensus already examined. *At the heart of fundamental consensus there is also a fundamental tension,* inescapable and unresolvable so long as Jew and Christian go their separate ways. Let me try to document this point and to demonstrate its importance by referring to the elements of fundamental consensus already outlined and the other elements of consensus which quickly became definitive for earliest Christianity.

Resurrection and outpoured Spirit are part of Israel's eschatological hope (e.g., Dan 12:2; Joel 2:28-32). The tension emerges even here because Christianity lays claim to that hope as having been fulfilled, but that hope interpreted in the light of the fulfillment which actually happened. The resurrection of Jesus as a discrete event, not part of the beginning of the final resurrection prior to the judgment, as the first Christians seem to have thought (Rom 1:4, the resurrection of Jesus = "the resurrection of the dead"). The outpoured Spirit on a limited range of "all flesh," not part of the climactic final events marked also by cosmic convulsions. It is this element of reinterpretation of Jewish hope which stemmed immediately from the experience of Christ risen and Spirit given, which also sets up the tension not only between Christianity and its parent faith, but within Christianity itself as fulfilled Judaism. The tension is between the "already" and the "not yet," [7] the tension of a fulfillment only partial, of a continuity which has sufficient discontinuity for the Jewish observer to have reasonable grounds for questioning whether it is indeed fulfillment at all.

In other words, in order to make sense of its fundamental consensus, Christianity has to understand these two most basic of Christian beliefs as the eschatological fulfillment of Jewish hope. But in making this very claim it has to reinterpret that hope in the light of what actually happened at Easter and Pentecost. The problem of the delay of the parousia, the ever lengthening gap between Jesus' first and second comings, is simply an expression of this fundamental feature of Christianity. Likewise, the problem of formulating satisfactory doctrines of sanctification, Christian perfection, fullness of the Spirit, and so on, when Christians started with the claim that they were already in the new age, already part of the new creation, already enjoying the Spirit outpoured in eschatological fullness. *This eschatological tension is constitutive of the Christianity which we meet in the NT.* What its consequences are for the expression of fundamental consensus requires a good deal more thought.

What is even more striking is that, as soon as we broaden out the area of consensus beyond Easter and Pentecost, we find that the same tension between continuity and discontinuity with Christianity's Jewish matrix is integral and inescapable. Let me illustrate.

(a) Christianity and the *people of God*. The belief that Christianity is the continuation and eschatological fulfillment of Israel, the people of God, is widespread within the NT, the conviction that those who believed in Christ, Gentile as well as Jew, constituted a renewed or even a new Israel. It is particularly important in Matthew, Paul, and Hebrews, and is prominent also in different ways in the writings of Luke, the Fourth Gospel, 1 Peter, and Revelation. But the discontinuity, and in historical terms the discord, emerges with the claim that Gentiles are part of this Israel and are so simply by virtue of their faith in the risen Christ. The tension at this point enters into the very heart of our conception of the people of God.[8] Who are "the people of God"? Those to whom the promise to the patriarchs was given? (They have a promise and "calling" which Paul tells us are "irrevocable" [Rom 11:29]). Or only those Jews who believe in Jesus as Messiah? And if Gentiles are members purely by faith, what then of the Jews who do not (yet) believe in Jesus as Messiah? This tension remains unresolved in the NT, even despite Paul's efforts (Rom 9-11), and was to bear fruit in the anti-Semitism which has been such a dreadful stain on Christian history. It is unresolved because it is at the heart of Christianity. *The greatest schism in salvation history was not between Catholic and Protestant, or between East and West, but between Judaism and Christianity.* Even if all our current ecumenical efforts are successful, this tension will remain unresolved. Even at the level of fundamental consensus the question as to how Jew and Christian relate to each other within the purposes of God remains open and unanswered.

(b) The same is true with regard to *Scripture*. A fundamental paradox at the heart of Christianity is its claim that the Old Testament is also part of its sacred writings. There is no need to document the degree of continuity which the NT claims with the Old. Even if the Johannine Epistles never quote the Old Testament, it still remains true that the OT is the substructure of NT theology.[9] But here too the fact of discontinuity between Judaism and Christianity is inescapable and indeed even more pronounced. For Christianity takes over the Jewish Scriptures only in a selective way. By reference to Easter and Pentecost large tracts of the OT come to be disregarded by the increasingly dominant Gentile churches. The laws of sacrifice so central to the Pentateuch are set aside. So too food laws and even one of the ten commandments, the law of the Sabbath. And perhaps most striking of all, the law of circumcision, even though it was given to Abraham as a sign of God's covenant with him, an "everlasting covenant" (Gen 17:11-13). This appeal to the OT as Scripture, which at the same time discounts so much of that Scripture, sets up a tension within Christianity which has never been resolved and indeed never will be resolved until Jew and Christian come together in common worship of the one God. Not only so, but to take over so many chapters as Scripture by ignoring their obvious

206

meaning and import is to legitimate a hermeneutic fraught with problems for our own interpretation not only of the OT but of the NT as well. Here again at the heart of Christianity are questions which permit no simple or final answer.

(c) A somewhat similar point can be made with regard to *worship and order*. Characteristic of the NT writers here too is the sense of eschatological newness, of a reality of worship which transcends the forms and structures of the old age and which belongs to the age of spiritual immediacy. Worship no longer a matter of sacred place, Gerizim or Jerusalem, but a worship in Spirit and truth (John 4:20-24). Worship as the congregational act together, one body in charismatic integration and interdependence (1 Cor 12; Rom 12; Eph 4). Worship as no longer of the old age, where priests must offer the same sacrifices year after year, but now of the new age, where each worshiper can enter immediately into the very presence of God with only Christ as priest and mediator (Hebrews). The language of priesthood is still used, but in its eschatological fulfillment, Christian congregations as a whole as "a holy and royal priesthood" (1 Pet 2:5, 9; Rev 1:6). The language of sacrifice and of priestly ministry is still used, but it is the sacrifice of each Christian in the social relationships of every day (Rom 12:1),[10] the ministry of committed service, whatever that service might be (Rom 15:16; Phil 2:17, 25).

In this case the tension expresses itself in the fact that despite this consistent NT emphasis on discontinuity with the forms and ordering of Jewish worship, Christianity began soon after to reassert a much stronger degree of continuity by readopting the categories of priest and sacrifice which the NT writers had left behind. Here a *"Neutestamentler"* has the uncomfortable responsibility of asking the question: Did the reacceptance of an order of priesthood, essentially different from the priesthood of all believers,[11] signal a crucial loss of that eschatological perspective so fundamental for NT Christianity? Or to put the issue more sharply: Would the NT writers not have regarded the reemergence of such an order of priesthood, more like that of Aaron than that of Melchizedek, as a return to what Hebrews certainly regards as the age of imperfection and shadow? Here it would very much appear that the tension is not to be found within the NT itself, where the discontinuity is much more marked than the continuity. Or to put it the other way, the tension now seems to lie between the NT on the one hand and Christian tradition as it developed subsequently on the other. Is it too bold for a *"Neutestamentler"* to suggest that any attempt of Christianity truly to come to terms with the eschatological character of its beginnings cannot avoid addressing even this issue?

(d) Similar points can be made with regard to other fundamental features of earliest Christianity, for example, *"justification by faith."* As Krister Stendahl pointed out a quarter of a century ago, justification by faith came to expression as a way of saying that Gentiles as much as Jews are fully and equally accepted by God through Christ as members of his people.[12] As the proclamation of God's saving righteousness, it is actually part of Christianity's heritage from the OT (particularly the Psalms and Second Isaiah). But in its distinctiveness as a Christian doctrine, justification by faith emerged precisely on the interface of Jewish/Christian continuity/discontinuity. So too the later tension between Lutheran and Catholic on the issue of faith and works is rooted in the tension caused by the early Christian reinterpretation of the covenant with Israel, a tension already there within the NT, between Paul and James, a tension unavoidable within Christianity because of its roots in the revelation given to Israel.

We might just note that a consequent tension focuses on the centrality of *the love command in Christian ethics.* The issue between Judaism and Christianity was not about whether "Love your neighbor as yourself" was a legitimate summary of the law regarding human relationships. There were plenty within Judaism who would have agreed with Jesus and Paul that Leviticus 19:18 encapsulated such social obligations and that "the neighbor" could include a Gentile. The real dispute was whether love of neighbor could only properly be exercised by bringing the neighbor within the law[13] or could be offered to the neighbor without condition. The twentieth century tension within Christianity between the older-style "evangelical" gospel and the so-called "social gospel" has its roots here.

We can even include *the doctrine of God* at this point. The tension within Christian understanding of God emerges precisely because of the compelling need for Christians to give adequate significance to the revelation event of Christ *within* the Jewish doctrine of God as one.[14] The Christian doctrine of the Trinity is not so much a resolution of that tension as a way of living with it, a heuristic definition of God, an acknowledgement that the mystery of God can never be contained within the inadequacies of human formulations. The Christian doctrine of incarnation emerges initially as a way of asserting that God's self-revelation has come to definitive and final expression not in written Torah but in the human person Jesus of Nazareth, a revelation much less capable of being reduced to any particular form of words.

(e) Finally, we should simply instance the two (undisputed) *sacraments.* Here we are about as close to the elements of fundamental consensus as anywhere in the NT. For baptism in the name of Christ was evidently a distinctive feature of Christianity from the first and is taken for granted by the NT writers. And the words spoken by Jesus on the night in which he was betrayed were evidently cherished, passed on, and remembered by regular repetition from the first. But here too it is not possible to escape the fundamental tension of Christianity's Jewish origins. Is baptism like circumcision, a mark of family, tribal, or national belonging? Or is the new covenant equivalent "the circumcision of the heart," the Pentecostal gift of the Spirit, given to faith in the risen Christ?[15] The tension which still afflicts the Christian understanding of baptism, particularly in relation to faith, arises out of the continuity/discontinuity of new covenant with old and is inescapable as such. And how does the Lord's Supper relate to the Passover meal and to the table fellowship which was such a hallmark of Jesus' ministry, not least his ministry among "tax collectors and sinners"?[16] To what extent are the tensions which still afflict our understanding of the Eucharist the direct result of our abstracting it from its original context within a meal and aligning it more to the ritual act of priest and sacrifice? Here again questions arise which seem inescapable because of the fundamental tension which results from Christianity's beginnings in Judaism.

To sum up: *at the heart of the fundamental consensus which we find in the NT we also find a fundamental tension.* Christianity understands itself in continuity with the faith of the OT and cannot understand itself otherwise. At the same time it has to assert a degree of discontinuity with the OT in order to make sense of its own distinctive claims, a fulfillment which transforms some basic Jewish categories and nullifies others. That continuity and discontinuity are forces which pull Christianity in different directions and create a tension which is part of Christianity. The tensions which in subsequent generations were in danger of rending Christianity into two or more pieces were there from the beginning because they are constitutive of Christianity as offspring of Judaism as it was before Christ.

In short, when we lift our eyes beyond the core elements of fundamental consensus we find ourselves still at a fundamental level of Christian self-understanding. But we also find that that self-understanding contains a tension which runs all through it because it involves an incomplete dialogue with the Judaism from which Christianity sprang, an unresolved ambiguity regarding Christianity's continuing relationship with the Jewish Scriptures and the faith and people they bear testimony to. And the clear implication seems to be that as long as this dialogue remains incomplete, as long as this ambiguity remains unresolved, Christianity itself can never hope to achieve final expression of its faith and worship as the people of God.

This brings us to our final main section.

Fundamental Diversity

The phenomenon of fundamental diversity in the NT is a direct consequence of two features to which we have already drawn attention. One is the diversity of situations and human contexts in which the gospel came to expression from the first and the fact that every expression of the gospel was conditioned by its particular situation and context in some degree or other. Diversity of expression was an inevitable consequence. The other feature is the fundamental tension just described and illustrated. And both, of course, are consequences of the fact that any attempt to speak of God is bound to be provisional, any attempt to encapsulate divine reality within human speech and act is bound to be inadequate to a greater or lesser degree, however 'adequate' we may find it for the purposes of common confession and worship.

This is true even of our *normative statements* in the NT or anywhere else. As I pointed out in *Unity and Diversity in the New Testament,* there is no single formulation of the *gospel* which is maintained unchanged throughout the NT. In different contexts and writers we find the gospel taking different forms, containing different elements. Easter and Pentecost remain more or less constant: the call for faith in the risen one accompanied by the promise of the Spirit. But even they come to diversity of expression. To achieve a more universal formulation we would have to abstract it from the diversity of forms, to summarize it in words which may never actually have been used by any NT writer, in slogan summaries like "Easter" and "Pentecost." We are sufficiently confident that we can speak of the same gospel coming to expression in all these specific proclamations, but at the same time we have to accept the uncomfortable fact that there is no final or finally definitive expression of that gospel.[17]

The diversity within the NT can be illustrated readily enough. For example, the fact of *the four Gospels.* No single connected exposition of Jesus' life and ministry, death and resurection, was considered sufficient. And that diversity is broad enough and flexible enough to contain, for example, two significantly different portrayals of Jesus' attitude to the law, in Matthew and Mark. Mark can readily assume that Jesus by his words and actions undercut and did away with a whole tract of law (the law on clean and unclean foods in Mark 7:15, 18-19). But

Matthew in contrast feels it necessary to portray Jesus as denying any such intention (Matt 5:17-20).[18] Here the fundamental tension pulls strongly in quite sharply opposed directions, presumably because the Gospels were written to quite different groups of Christians who also differed in their understanding and practice of the law, but who could *both* look to Jesus' ministry for guidance on the point.

Another example would be the different concepts of *apostleship* within the NT. There is agreement that apostleship stems from a commission by the risen Christ during the limited period of his resurrection appearances (Acts 1:21-22; 1 Cor 15:8). But beyond that, diversity becomes more prominent. Paul regards successful establishment of new churches as of the essence of apostleship (1 Cor 9:1-2), and in consequence he can speak of each church having its (own) Apostles, the ones who brought it into existence (1 Cor 12:27-28). Moreover, he regards the authority of Apostles as limited by their divine commission, limited to the sphere to which they were appointed (2 Cor 10:13-16; Gal 2:7-9), so that he never thinks to exercise his apostolic authority in Jerusalem while violently resisting any apostolic encroachments on his own territory (Gal 1:6-9; 2 Cor 11:1-15). Luke, however, seems to think of "the Apostles" as more or less synonymous with "the twelve" (e.g., Acts 1:21-26; 6:2) and attempts in some measure to show the Jerusalem apostolate as permanently resident in Jerusalem, with only one or two of their number engaged in mission and otherwise exerting a supervisory role over the (initial) expansion (e.g., Acts 8:1, 14-15; 11:22).[19] Here again we have an expression of diversity which emerges directly from the fundamental tension within Christianity, with Luke using the concept of apostleship to emphasize the continuity of Christianity with its Jewish antecedents while Paul emphasizes the element of discontinuity with his strong insistence in his apostleship to the Gentiles. We might simply remind ourselves how these different concepts of mission have given rise to some of the fiercest language in the NT, with Paul wishing that those who demand circumcision would castrate themselves (Gal 5:12) and denouncing other missionaries as false apostles and servants of Satan (2 Cor 11:13-15). Not what we might wish to call the language of friendly ecumenical dialogue![20]

The point could be illustrated further by reference to the subjects dealt with under the heading of "Fundamental Tension."[21] But perhaps we need do no more than recall the diversity of the NT documents themselves, *the diversity within the canon.* We may count it part of the wisdom of the early Fathers of the church that they recognized both that Christianity can only exist in a diversity of forms and the importance of this insight by enshrining it in a diverse canon: the openness to new revelation and charismatic emphasis of Paul; the strongly Jewish character of James; the appreciation of church office and "routinizing of charisma" in the Pastorals; the enthusiasm of Luke; the mystical depths of John; and the apocalyptic visions of his namesake. The canon contains all these types of Christianity, presumably in recognition that Christianity can only exist in diverse forms, and always has. The canon canonizes diversity as well as unity![22]

The point then is that diversity is not some secondary feature of Christianity, not just a sequence of temporal husks which can be peeled away to leave a virgin, pure, unchanging core. *Diversity is fundamental to Christianity,* as fundamental as the consensus and the tension. Christianity can only exist in concrete expressions and these concrete expressions are inescapably different from each other.[23] In order to *be* Christianity it has to be diverse. This is a point which has been well taken in ecumenical discussions, particularly in the last ten years or so, that diversity coexists with unity, coheres with unity, that unity exists in diversity.[24] But what perhaps needs to be given more attention is the fact that the NT contains the archetypal model of "unity in diversity," i.e., *the body of Christ.*

The metaphor of the church as a body is used in three different Pauline letters and in three different ways. In Romans Paul speaks of "one body in Christ" (Rom 12:5); in 1 Corinthians of Christ as "one body" (1Cor 12:12); and in Ephesians Christ is the head of the body (Eph 4:15). But on each occasion Paul stresses that the unity of the body is a unity in diversity. For the point to be made so often to different audiences is sufficient indication of its importance. The point is that *the body only exists as a unity by virtue of its diversity.* In the famous twelfth chapter of 1 Corinthians Paul pours ridicule on the idea of a body which had only a single organ: "If the whole body were an eye, where would be the hearing? If the whole body were an ear, where would be the sense of smell? . . . If all were a single organ, where would the body be? As it is, there are many parts, yet one body." (1 Cor 12:17-20). The point is clear: without diversity the body could not exist as a body. Diversity is not a regrettable rationalization of a basically unsatisfactory state of affairs nor a decline from some higher ideal for which repentance is necessary. On the contrary, diversity is integral to the pattern of community which God has established. Without diversity there cannot be unity, the unity which God intended.

Paul also provides some indication of how he saw this ideal of unity in diversity working out in practice. I am thinking here of Romans 14:1–15:6.[25] There he deals with the problem of disagreement within the church and gives advice on how to cope with it. The disagreement was over food, what is permissible for the believer to eat (14:2), and also over holy days, whether some days should be given special significance (14:5). It should not be thought that these were minor matters, merely over vegetarianism or some particular feast day. On the contrary, what we have here is almost certainly a further expression of the fundamental tension. For those who would not eat meat and who wished to observe some days as special would certainly have at least included Jewish Christians. And for devout Jews the observance of the food laws and the sabbath law was at the very heart of the obligation laid upon them by their membership in the covenant people of God. They could not yield in these matters without calling in question their history and their traditions, without dishonoring the blood of the (Maccabean) martyrs who had died for these very beliefs (1 Macc 1:62-63: "Many in Israel stood firm and were resolved in their hearts not to eat unclean food. They chose to die rather than to be defiled by food or to profane the holy covenant; and they did die"). What was at stake was their very understanding of the covenant and of the obligations laid upon the people of God, deep and fundamental issues.[26]

The advice Paul gives is clear and straightforward. It is that these two opposed views could *both* be acceptable to God. There could be disagreements over issues which were *fundamental* for the different parties and yet *both* be upheld by God. It was not necessary for the one to be wrong in order for the other to be right. The consequence was that each should accept the other, despite the diversity of views. Each should respect the other, that is, respect his right to go on holding a sharply distinct opinion, not use his own conscience as a stick to beat the other, and not see it as his duty to convince the other of error (Rom 14:3-13). Here we might say is a model of "reconciled diversity"[27]: the willingness to *defend* the right of the other to hold an opinion different from my own on issues which I regard as fundamental to a proper understanding of the faith and the acceptance of that other as *one* with me in the diversity of the *one* body of Christ.

Romans 14 refers, of course, to the local church or, to be more precise, the various house congregations in Rome. But Ephesians 4 shows that the body imagery transposes into the church as universal. On the universal scale the disagreements would be of the same order: Jewish Christian congregations who understood the gospel and its outworkings in terms of strong continuity with earlier Judaism; largely Gentile congregations who emphasized discontinuity by disregarding the law and more traditional patterns of Jewish worship and order; and mixed congregations, like the ones in Rome, who had to work out the tensions internally as best they could. The point is that Paul's advice in

213

Romans 14 would seem to be equally applicable: be clear in your own mind about what's right for your congregation; but do not insist that every other congregation agree with you in everything, even on points which you hold to be of central significance; accept that the other is equally Christian, equally accepted by your common Lord, and continue to worship together. Only if there is diversity is there a body, but only if the diversity is harmonious diversity is the body one.

One other thought might follow from Paul's conception of the church as Christ's body. Paul, of course, uses the term "body" in other ways than in reference to the church, local or otherwise. His most common usage is in reference to the body of the individual. The body of the believer is the "mortal body," the body of flesh. As such it belongs to this age, is part of the eschatological "not yet." As such it will waste away, a perishable body, "dust to dust," to be "put off" in death and transformed or "redeemed" at the resurrection (e.g., Rom 8:11; 1 Cor 15:42-50; Phil 3:21). If the physical body is the embodiment of the individual believer in this age, so we might say the structure of the church is the embodiment of the corporate body of believers. In which case the forms taken by the church as body in this age must share the character of the physical body, perishable, corruptible, "dust to dust." The point is that this would be true for Paul even for the church as Christ's body. For the church as Christ's body is *not* the risen body of Christ;[28] that transformation, as in the case of the individual, awaits the resurrection. The church in this age is Christ's body crucified, his body broken, not yet his body of glory. Consequently we may say that the diversity of the members of the universal body of Christ is also an expression of the transitory nature of all bodies in this age, the incompleteness of the eschatological "not yet."

Whether this final line of thought is followed or not, the chief point of this last section is that *diversity is inescapable when we look at the Christianity which we see attested in the NT*. In *historical* terms we cannot ignore the diversity of first century Christianity, particularly of Jewish Christians and Gentile Christians, with all the differences involved of emphasis and attitude, of confessional and liturgical form. Christians disagreed with one another, often over issues which were central to one or the other, and often passionately. The sophisticated analyses of the "fundamental differences" which are a feature of contemporary Christianity[29] could be applied equally to the fundamental differences within apostolic Christianity: the divisions between East and West, in the final analysis, are no more profound than those between Paul and James; the challenge to Luther, "Are you alone right and a thousand years wrong?" was in effect first put to Paul by Jewish Christians.

In *theological* terms we cannot ignore the significance of the body imagery. The unity of the body comes to expression by means of the diversity of its members. Only by their functioning in harmonious diversity does the body function as one. In short, *diversity is as fundamental to the Christianity of the NT as is the consensus of Easter and Pentecost and the tension caused by Christianity's Jewish origins.* It is the way in which the consensus comes to expression in the unity of the body. It is the way the tension is lived out in the reality of the eschatological "not yet." Without it the church cannot exist as Christ's body.

Conclusions

(a) There is a *fundamental consensus* given us in the NT which is the basis of Christianity and therefore the source of Christian unity, the consensus of Easter and Pentecost. It is not capable of a single or finally satisfactory expression in human language, but it can be confessed in word and worship with a unifying power which no controversy over mere words can prevent. This consensus alone is not all that belongs to the "essence" of Christianity, for there is also what it inherits from its parent faith, but this is where the distinctiveness of Christianity's self-understanding begins.

Also fundamental is the fact of Christianity's emergence from first century Judaism. In this OT and *heilsgeschichtliche* heritage are contained much that is integral to the fundamental consensus of Easter and Pentecost, including, we may say, the "one hope, one faith, one baptism, and one God" of Ephesians 4:4-6. But Christianity's claim to that heritage also set up a *fundamental tension* which is an inescapable part of Christian faith and which came to most tragic expression in the schism between the Israel of old and the eschatological Israel of Jew and Gentile. This means that the consensus can be expressed in fuller terms, which continuity between the Old Testament and the New makes possible. But the more the consensus is elaborated in terms of Christian distinctives, the more it is caught in the tension of continuity/discontinuity which can never be finally resolved in this age. The tension is fundamental because divine revelation has stretched human logic and categories beyond their capacity. The new wine of Christ has burst more than the wine skins of early Judaism.

Diversity of expression of truth and of life, individual and corporate, is therefore inevitable as different generations and cultures strive to express both the consensus and the tension in their different *Sitzen im*

Leben. The gospel of Christ can never come to adequate expression in the abstract, only in the concrete. So with the body of Christ. There can be agreement on the gospel even without agreement on the words which express it. There can be oneness of Christ's body without agreement on the forms taken by the body in its concrete existence. *Fundamental diversity* is an inevitable expression of fundamental consensus within the imperfections of this age.

Then: "Does the idea of fundamental consensus have biblical grounds?" If there is anything at all in what I have tried to say, the answer must be "Yes." Just as long as (1) we do not try to pack too much into the consensus, for then we quickly come to issues where emphases are bound to differ and questions need to be left more open than in most of our churches. As long as (2) we do not insist that the consensus can be expressed in one and only one set of words, for that is to make an idol of our formulations. And (3) as long as we do not attempt to hold only to the consensus and ignore the tension or suppress the diversity. A consensus without the tension and without the diversity is one-dimensional and of little lasting value.

(b) It is worth reflecting a little further on *the fundamental role of experience* in the fundamental consensus, particularly with reference to the Spirit. The Spirit in the NT is characteristically a power that inspires and engages the emotions at a deep level. For example, John speaks of the Spirit as "a fountain of water bubbling up into eternal life" (John 4:14); Luke consistently depicts the Spirit as a power which falls upon and catches up individuals in eye-catching action and ecstatic speech (Acts 2:4; 8:18; 10:45-46; 19:6); and Paul thinks of the gift of the Spirit as the means by which "the love of God has been poured out in our hearts" (Rom 5:5) and as bearing witness with our spirits by inspiring our cry "Abba! Father!" (Rom 8:15-16). For Paul in particular it is this experience of the Spirit which is the foundation and formative influence in their common life as Christians. The phrase "the fellowship of the Spirit," *koinonia tou pneumatos* (2 Cor 13:13-14), does not denote an objective entity, a congregation or community created by the Spirit.[30] Rather, it should be translated "participation in the Spirit," as referring to *the shared experience of the Spirit.* It is this shared experience of the Spirit which is the source of what we now more usually think of as "fellowship." That is why the word *koinonia* first occurs in the description of the Christian congregation after Pentecost; a new experience of community was the consequence of this foundational experience of the Spirit which they had shared (Acts 2:42). In the same way Paul in warning the Philippians against selfishness and conceit appeals in emotive terms precisely to their shared experience of the Spirit as providing the source and motivation for a common mind (Phil 2:1-11).

The point is that at the heart of the fundamental consensus of the NT is not just a *doctrine* of Christ's resurrection, but the *experience* of God's acceptance through his Spirit. The fundamental unity of the earliest Christian churches was a unity of spirit *which grew out of the shared experience of God's Spirit*. It was by being baptized in one Spirit, by having the one Spirit poured out on them, that they became members of the one body: the oneness of the body was a consequence of their sharing the one Spirit (1 Cor 12:13). The unity of the Spirit was not something created or contrived by them. On the contrary, it was something they experienced as the outworking of God's gift of the Spirit. The same point can be made with reference to the eucharistic elements in 1 Corinthians 10. The cup and the bread are described as a *sharing* (*koinonia*) in the blood and body of Christ; "because the bread is one, we the many are one body, for we all participate in the one bread" (10:16-17). The oneness of the body is the consequence not only of the oneness of the bread but of the common participation in the one bread. Here too the reality of oneness is something which is dependent upon, something which arises out of the shared experience of communion.

All this seems to me to be a matter of fundamental importance. Inevitably we direct our attention to agreed statements and common liturgies. But in so doing it is all to easy to forget that the unity of the Spirit is something experienced as a gracious gift of God. It is easy to forget even that the common statement which usually results from the wrestlings of conferences like this is as much an expression of the unity experienced by the conference participants as of anything else. And what is true at this level will be as true at the level of denomination and congregation, house group, local ecumenical project, or base community. According to the Apostle Paul, the unity of the body arises out of the shared experience of one Spirit and one bread. It is not something structural as such, nor something which we can create or impose by our ecumenical labors. The fellowship of the Spirit is something discovered, something given, and, unless structural unity grows out of the shared experience of the Spirit, it surely cannot hope to succeed.

(c) The eschatological character of Christianity's beginnings gives rise to a further potentially important line of reflection. Christianity began as *a renewal movement within first century Judaism*. It began as an experience of liberation, as a breaking through of boundaries and recasting of traditions, as a movement of the Spirit clothing itself in *new* forms and expressing itself in *new* structures. Moreover, that self-understanding of Christianity, as a movement of liberation and renewal, often enthusiastic in character, has been enshrined within our foundation documents, the NT. It is integral to the canonical portrayal of Christianity.

This remains true even though there are clear indications of fading enthusiasm and increased patterning of faith and order also within the NT, especially in the Pastoral Epistles and even though Christianity has often taken on the same sort of structural solidity and exclusiveness as the Judaism against which Jesus and the first Christians reacted. The point is that Christianity retains in its sacred Scriptures not only the tension between Old Testament and New, but also the inspiration and resources for renewal *within* the structures of the church provided they are flexible enough, *outside* them if they are not!

It is all the more important, therefore, that the structural unity which grows out of the shared experience of the Spirit be sufficiently open-ended to let the diversity of that experience come to fullness of expression. All the more important that *consensus* should be broad enough to embrace all those who rejoice in and confess Easter and Pentecost, open enough to leave *tensions* unresolved and ever subject to new insight and revelation, and flexible enough to allow the *diversity* of Christ's body to express itself in its full range. Only so can the diversity be expressive of the unity without allowing the tensions to pull it apart.

(d) In short, if we may hazard a few final epigrammatic summaries of what the NT seems to offer to our deliberations: The fundamental consensus of risen Christ and shared Spirit is the source of Christian unity; fundamental tension means that there are basic issues in Christianity which do not permit of resolution within Christianity itself or within Christianity alone; fundamental diversity means that uniformity is not only unrealizable but theologically wrong-headed since it would only result in the fundamental diversity expressing itself in new and schismatic forms. A continuing obligation within the ecumenical movement is to maintain a biblical and realistic balance among these three fundamentals.

Of course much more needs to be said on all the points made above. Each issue needs much more careful analysis than is possible here. Moreover, there are important aspects of the topic I have been unable to go into — for example, the limits of acceptable diversity[31] and the tensions which earliest Christianity found on the other front as it entered more fully into the wider Greco-Roman world (some of which lie behind the great prayer for unity in John 17). And I am fully aware that the NT is by no means the only factor in the whole discussion. But it is itself a "fundamental" factor in these discussions, and these seem to me to be "fundamental" considerations which it presses upon us.

Notes

1. James D. G. Dunn, *Unity and Diversity in the New Testament* (London: SCM; Philadelphia: Westminster, 1977).

2. Ibid., 369.

3. Ibid., 378-79. I also note that this *center* also determined the *circumference,* the limits of acceptable diversity; but I cannot go further into that aspect of the subject in this essay.

4. See further, e.g., W. Kramer, *Christ, Lord, Son of God* (London: SCM, 1966) 19-26; J. D. G. Dunn, *The Evidence for Jesus* (London: SCM; Philadelphia: Westminster, 1985) ch. 3.

5. See further J. D. G. Dunn, *Baptism in the Holy Spirit* (London: SCM; Philadelphia: Westminster, 1970), and *idem, Jesus and the Spirit* (London: SCM; Philadelphia: Westminster, 1975), ch. 6, esp. 136-46.

6. I am thinking here of the Rome Report, 1983, "The Apostolic Faith in the Scriptures and in the Early Church," *Apostolic Faith Today* (ed. H. G. Link; Geneva: WCC, 1985), particularly 259-60, 265.

7. I use the terms which have become familiar in talk of the eschatological tension classically described by O. Cullmann in his *Christ and Time* (London: SCM, revised 1962). The importance of this tension between East and West is highlighted by J. M. R. Tillard, "We Are Different," *Mid-Stream* 25 (1986) 279, 281.

8. See particularly M. Barth, *The People of God* (Sheffield: JSOT, 1983); earlier version in *Paulus — Apostat oder Apostel?* (Regensburg: Pustet, 1977).

9. Using the imagery offered by C. H. Dodd, *According to the Scriptures* (London: Nisbet, 1952).

10. The point has been given justifiable emphasis by E. Käsemann, "Worship in Everyday Life: A note on Romans 12." *New Testament Questions of Today* (London: SCM, 1969) 188-95.

11. I am, of course, echoing Vatican II, LG 10: "There is an essential difference between the faithful's priesthood in common and the priesthood of the ministry or the hierarchy and not just a difference of degree." The ARCIC I Report, "Ministry and Ordination" (1973), echoes this view (##13-14). But I note the important qualification argued by E. Schillebeeckx, *Ministry* (London: SCM, 1981), that "in the ancient church the whole of the believing community concelebrated, albeit under the leadership of the one who presided over the community" (49).

12. "The Apostle Paul and the Introspective Conscience of the West," *Harvard Theological Review* 56 (1963) 199-215; reprinted in his *Paul Among Jews and Gentiles* (London: SCM, 1977).

13. Cf. two of the sayings attributed to Hillel: "That which you hate, do not do to your fellow; this is the whole law; the rest is commentary; go and learn it" (b Shab 31a); "Be of the disciples of Aaron, loving peace and pursuing peace, loving mankind and bringing them nigh to the Law" (m Aboth 1.12).

14. I have attempted to reflect at greater length on this theme in a sequence of publications: *Christology in the Making* (London: SCM; Philadelphia: Westminster, 1980) particularly chs. 5-7; a debate with Maurice Wiles in *Theology* 85 (1982) 96-98; 326-30; 360-61; "Was Christianity a Monotheistic

Faith from the Beginning?" *Scottish Journal of Theology* 35 (1982) 303-36; "Let John be John—A Gospel for its Time," *Das Evangelium und die Evangelien* (ed. P. Stuhlmacher; Tübingen: Mohr, 1983) 309-39.

15. An issue at the heart of my *Baptism* (above n. 5).

16. See, e.g., J. Reumann, *The Supper of the Lord* (Philadelphia: Fortress, 1985) 4-5.

17. *Unity and Diversity* (above n. 1) 29-31.

18. For details see *Unity and Diversity* (above n. 1) 246-49, and the fuller treatment of the Mark 7 tradition in my "Jesus and Ritual Purity: A Study of the Tradition History of Mark 7.15," *A Cause de L'Evangile* (Festschrift J. Dupont; Lectio Divina 123; Paris: du Cerf, 1985) 251-76.

19. See further *Jesus and the Spirit* (above n. 5) 110-14, 272-80; also *Unity and Diversity* (above n. 1) 106-7, 111-12, 354-56.

20. See also *Evidence for Jesus* (above n. 4) ch. 4.

21. I perhaps do not need to deal more fully with the example of Christology itself since points such as I expressed in *Unity and Diversity* (above n. 1) 33-59 and 216-31, and in *Christology* 265-67, have been well taken in the Odessa Report, 1981, "The Ecumenical Importance of the Nicene-Constantinopolitan Creed," *Apostolic Faith Today* 251-53.

22. The famous (or infamous) assertion of E. Käsemann: "The New Testament canon does not, as such, constitute the foundation of the unity of the Church. On the contrary, as such (that is, in its accessibility to the historian) it provides the basis for the multiplicity of the confessions," "The New Testament Canon and the Unity of the Church," *Essays on New Testament Themes* (London: SCM, 1964) 103, was perhaps stated too provocatively, though it contains a recognition of NT diversity whose challenge dare not be ignored. But it certainly should not be taken to justify "a plurality of totally separate or opposed churches," as Congar (below n. 24) rightly observes (*Diversity* 6).

23. Cf. Bonhoeffer's words: "The Confessing Church does *not* confess *in abstracto*. . . . It confesses *in concretissimo* against the 'German Christian' church. . . ," quoted by U. Duchrow, "The Confessing Church and the Ecumenical Movement," *Ecumenical Review* 33 (1981) 214.

24. See, e.g., the Leuenberg Agreement, in *Apostolic Faith Today* 45; the theme of "reconciled diversity" introduced by H. Meyer, with Y. Congar's reflections on it in his *Diversity and Communion* (London: SCM, 1984) 149-58, and his plea for recognition that "diversity has always been accepted in the unity of faith" (*Diversity,* ch. 3); P. Avis, *Ecumenical Theology and the Elusiveness of Doctrine* (London: SPCK, 1986), particularly ch. 7.

25. Of course the body imagery has particular reference to ministry, but Rom 14 is also concerned with mutual relations within the Christian congregation, and by placing the body imagery at the beginning of the whole section on relationships (ch. 12-15), Paul probably intended the image of the Christian community as body to be determinative also for the later passage; cf. particularly Rom 12:3 with 14:4, 22-23.

26. The importance of the food laws for Jewish self-identity is also indicated by three of the most popular of the "intertestamental" writings, Daniel, Judith, and Tobit, all of which give special prominence to the heroes' and heroine's faithfulness in this matter (Dan 1:8-16; Tob 1:10-13; Jth 12:1-4). As for the central significance of the Sabbath, we may note especially Ex 31:13, 16; Isa 56:6; Jubilees 2:17-33.

27. See n. 24 above.

28. Against J. A. T. Robinson, *The Body* (London: SCM, 1952), ch. 3, who makes a highly questionable synthesis of different strands of Paul's thought.

29. See particularly, H. Meyer, "Fundamental Difference—Fundamental Consensus," *Mid-Stream* 25 (1986) 247-59.

30. This is a mistaken exegesis which my much esteemed "doctor father," C. F. D. Moule, quite often warned against.

31. See above, n. 3.

15

Incremental Ecumenism

William H. Lazareth

IN THE DIALECTICAL interaction between theology and doxology, how far may we go and with whom, amid the many ambiguities on all sides of the "already-not yet" state of insufficient consensus and incomplete communion in the churches' ecumenical relations? Speaking from the perspective of a pastor associated with the mission and ministries of the new Evangelical Lutheran Church in America, I want to affirm the ecumenical strategy of an incremental or "step by step" (rather than an "all or nothing") approach to "levels of fellowship."

To be sure, I know the ecclesiological advantages of the "all or nothing" alternative. If "fellowship" means *koinonia* and *koinonia* means participation in Christ, then strictly speaking there can be no quantitative "levels" or "degrees" or "stages" in reaching an admittedly qualitative goal. Indeed, how can you "reintegrate" an indivisible integer?

Nevertheless, when our responsibility (*Aufgabe*) in manifesting the gift (*Gabe*) of church unity falls short, as in our present state of "mutually condemning," "reciprocally excommunicating" divided churches, then theologians are generally reduced to one of two alternatives, neither of which is totally defensible for evangelical catholics called "Lutherans":

1. Either we claim to be *the* organizational expression of the *Una Sancta*, whether in its totality or at least in its fullness;
2. or else we claim to be *wholly* the church but not the whole church and conscientiously commit ourselves "to speak the truth in love" as it has been given to us with other separated Christians who also confess the blessed name of the triune God and the saving lordship of Jesus Christ.

I believe that most Lutherans are sincerely ecumenical precisely because they mean to be scriptural and Confessional. Thereby they commit themselves to a cautious but confident pilgrimage to manifest, in and for the world, more God-pleasing expressions (ecclesial, sacramental, and missional) of that unique spiritual unity for which Jesus Christ prayed to the Father in the Spirit on his last night here on earth.

It follows that this "cautious but confident" journey is fraught with obstacles on all sides, not least for an ecclesial body that views itself as a "Confessional movement within the church catholic." We reject unionism no less than separatism. We disavow syncretism as readily as triumphalism. Ours is a *theologia crucis*, a "theology of the cross" that demands a cruciform discipleship, corporately as well as personally, that is in but not of this world.

The formation of the new Evangelical Lutheran Church in America provides us with a providential opportunity to evaluate past steps and to project future ones that are both Confessionally permissible and ecumenically advisable in our dealings with other Christian communities. Lutherans have been rather an ecumenical enigma, alternately blowing hot and cold in our official involvements and causing no little concern to our ecumenical friends about our internal coherence or external consistency.

I intend now to place an ecumenical mirror before ourselves in order to guide us to engage in that blessed means of grace that the Lutheran Reformers called "the mutual conversation and consolation of the faithful" (SA 3,4; BC 310). Much more clarity is needed as we face some of the key decisions that will likely have to be made in the next decade alone as the new Evangelical Church in America evaluates its corporate involvement in a number of preferred "levels of ecumenical fellowship."

I will argue that we should approach these opportunities conscientiously and incrementally, attempting to speak the truth in love with other orthodox Christians on a "case to case" basis, going as far as we are able with whomever we can. However, all these challenges deserve to be governed by a wholistic and integrated approach that is far more worthy of a Confessional church than a series of spasmodic starts and stops and alleged "tilting" in incompatible directions simultaneously. Should we not be able to say doctrinally the same to all, however and whenever it is addressed to some? This demands that we gain far more Confessional consistency on two basic issues: our ecumenical motivation and our ecumenical destination. Why and where are we going?

I

I turn first to review our ecumenical commitment as documented in the present constitutional foundations of the Evangelical Lutheran

Church in America, reflecting the official positions of the uniting bodies. Here "evangelical in depth" and "ecumenical in breadth" are developed in organic interdependence.

The position statement of the Lutheran Church in America is called *Ecumenism: A Lutheran Commitment* (1982). It is divided into a preface and six major sections. The preface states: "This unity is God's gift in the life of the Church under Christ and the Spirit. Ecumenism is the experience and on-going task of expressing this unity." The first section deals with scriptural, Confessional, and constitutional foundations. (It might be added that this foundational section was likewise endorsed completely by the Church Council of the American Lutheran Church in its own official statement entitled, *Ecumenical Perspective and Guidelines,* 1985.)

It declares that the vision of the Lutheran Church in America as an ecumenical church is dependent on an understanding of Scripture and the Lutheran Confessions which is also found in the constitution of this church. Then follows an overview of New Testament teaching on unity, a unity in diversity pictured realistically within the context of human inclinations against unity and fellowship. The Lutheran Confessions are seen as products of an effort at evangelical reform which contrary to its intention resulted in divisions within the Western church. They are viewed as evangelical writings, stressing justification by grace through faith, concerned for the oneness of the church, the preservation of the catholic heritage, and the renewal of the whole church. Indebted to recent scholarship, the statement presents the Confessions not as denominational charters but as ecumenical proposals to the entire church. This is true of its interpretation of the Augsburg Confession, especially Article 7, which according to the statement has as its underlying intention not the adoption of the Lutheran reforms by others but their recognition as legitimately Christian. The ecumenical potential of the Confessions is affirmed. Because the Confessions insist that agreement in the gospel suffices for Christian unity, Lutherans are free to enter into church fellowship without insisting on doctrinal or ecclesiastical uniformity. When there is consensus on the gospel, there can be room for living and experiencing fellowship within the context of seeking larger theological agreement.[1]

Since this is a relatively new emphasis within American Lutheranism, I should like to quote the relevant material in its totality:

> The primary Lutheran confessional document, the Augsburg Confession of 1530, claims to be a fully catholic as well as evangelical expression of Christian faith. It states that nothing here departs from Scripture or

the Catholic Church. The confessors at Augsburg asked only for freedom to preach and worship in accordance with the Gospel, and were willing, provided this freedom was granted, to remain in fellowship with those who did not share their theological formulations or reforming practices. It is in this historical context that the *satis est* of Article VII is to be understood: "For the true unity of the church, it is enough (*satis est*) to agree concerning the teaching of the Gospel and the administration of the sacraments." What was asked for as a condition of church unity was the recognition of the Lutheran reforms as legitimately Christian, rather than the adoption of these reforms by others.

The historical situation is now different. The question is no longer that of preserving an existing church unity, but that of re-establishing a communion which has been broken. Yet Article VII of the Augsburg Confession continues to be ecumenically liberating because of its insistence that agreement in the Gospel suffices for Christian unity. This interpretation of Article VII frees Lutherans, as they seek to promote the proclamation of the message of God's saving action in Jesus Christ, and to enter into church fellowship without insisting on doctrinal or ecclesiastical uniformity. Lutherans still place considerable emphasis on common formulation and expression of theological consensus, yet they recognize from this article that, where there is consensus in the Gospel, there is room for a living and experiencing of fellowship within the context of seeking larger theological agreement.[2]

This affirmation of incremental ecumenism is corroborated by the Church Council of the American Lutheran Church in a related section of its official statement, *Ecumenical Perspective and Guidelines* (1985). That position is formulated as follows:

An ecumenical breakthrough in 1982, following a series of Lutheran-Episcopal dialogs, was the American Lutheran Church's authorization of interim eucharistic sharing with the Episcopal Church. This action, a departure from the long-standing Lutheran practice of requiring complete doctrinal agreement, was based on the understanding that the *satis est* of Article VII of the Augsburg Confession allowed the two churches to recognize one another as "true churches where the Gospel is truly preached and the sacraments duly celebrated. . . ."

We believe that varying degrees of fellowship will be exercised as churches find their way in new circumstances and relationships. Traditional "altar and pulpit fellowship" is therefore not the only option for establishing forms of fellowship with other churches.

The gift of unity which God has already given in Jesus Christ impels Christians toward fellowship in worship, including altar and pulpit fellowship. No expression of fellowship, however, should be understood as a stage on the way to organizational unification of the churches involved. Organic merger is not the immediate objective of dialog and fellowship, nor, of course, does fellowship preclude this possibility.[3]

An ecumenical specialist of the Lutheran Church in America, William Rusch, has lucidly interpreted for Episcopalians the current significance of these official Lutheran commitments:

"Although Lutherans assert a highly significant role for article 7 in an understanding of church unity, they have come to recognize certain limits inherent in the article. These strictures are caused in part by the fact that the context of the article in the sixteenth century no longer exists today. The practice of fellowship and physical unity, while in extreme danger in 1530, had not yet been lost. The task of the church in our century is not to maintain visible unity but to attempt to regain it.

"Naturally, article 7 of the Augsburg Confession does not directly address our situation. But even with this acknowledgement, Lutherans have continued to identify with the ecumenical commitment of this article. However, they recognize that the framework of familiarity and practical fellowship, taken for granted by article 7, is not now present. Therefore, some Lutherans today admit that unity cannot be limited to the quest for theological agreement only, but must also be sought in the midst of familiarity and fellowship, and that this context must be developed alongside efforts aimed at theological concord. This means that different forms of worship and church order, which were not obstacles until the sixteenth century, but have been burdens in the centuries of division, must be part of the ecumenical endeavor today. Such items include the Anglican tradition's stress on episcopal succession from the apostles and on communion with the archbishop of Canterbury.

"This approach, giving attention to theological and non-theological factors, can be seen in two documents of the Lutheran World Federation: "More than Church Unity" and "Guidelines for Ecumenical Encounter." They reflect a theological understanding resulting from involvement by Lutherans in the ecumenical movement. Both documents are worthy of careful study. They do not surrender as a goal the attempt to formulate a theological consensus, but they recognize multiple expressions of doctrine, life and action as valid. Dr. Harding Meyer of the Strasbourg Institute for Ecumenical Research has spoken of this new theological understanding expressed in these documents as follows:

Today it is possible to say that the traditional principle "doctrinal conversation and doctrinal agreement first, and only then church fellowship" has, even on the Lutheran side, been recognized as too rigidly one-sided and has therefore been considerably modified. . . . On the Lutheran side considerable emphasis is still placed on the importance of a common formulation and expression of theological consensus of confession. There is no doubt that today this is still a characteristic and important facet of the Lutheran understanding of the church, of ecumenical endeavor and of church unity. But, at the same time, it is recognized that there is a clear interrelation, a sort of "circle", between the fact of living and experiencing fellowship on the one hand, and explicit agreement on faith and doctrine on the other.

"Meyer reflects the most recent position of many Lutheran theologians, who would argue today that for Lutherans the most satisfactory concept of church unity is one of a fellowship in which confessional particularities and differences are not blended but reconciled as legitimate pluralism."[4]

II

These words bring us to our second major area of concern, namely the ecumenical destination or goal. This focus does not repudiate the incremental approach of "step by step" attempts to gain convergences here or to effect interim arrangements there. However, tentative guidelines or projected visions are also necessary to provide us with some doctrinal direction without canonical directives for making needed periodic "course corrections."

It is not a matter of course that the divided churches can agree on a description of the goal which they are committed to achieve in the ecumenical movement. This is because they differ in the understanding of the nature of the church and consequently also in their understanding of the so-called "unity we seek." On the basis of their varied ecclesiologies, they also propose different ways of achieving the goal. Within the variety of concepts is it possible to offer a common description of the goal? The need for such a description is obvious. Only agreement on the goal can prevent the dispersion of unity efforts in conflicting, different directions, a critical problem which has faced the ecumenical movement from the beginning and has become more recently the painful experience of some American Lutherans.

To highlight the urgency of the issue, I quote some recent words from Bishop Lesslie Newbigen, a respected ecumenical veteran, on his response to the query, "What is the ecumenical agenda?"

> The greatest need is a serious theological effort to reaffirm the good news of God's saving action in Jesus Christ in terms which are dictated neither by a blind adherence to the so-called requirements of "modern" thought, nor by a blind rejection of it. . . .
>
> Along with this theological task, which I regard as primary, there is need for fresh thinking in the field of structure. In this matter we are polarized between the advocates of full "organic union" and the advocates of "reconciled diversity." The latter slogan often seems to be a polite way of agreeing to do nothing. The former arouses understandable fears of "monolithic structures." This fear is understandable when one contemplates the structures to which we have become accustomed. I think that there is room for more vigorous exploration of the middle ground between these extremes, looking to visible forms of ecclesial life which would combine the variety of different forms of discipleship and spirituality manifested in our divided churches, with a degree of mutual commitment and shared ecclesial life much greater than is provided in our existing council of churches.[5]

It may prove helpful for our discussion to trace the ways in which the goals of "organic union" and "reconciled diversity" have developed in recent decades of ecumenical dialogues, not least through the efforts of the World Council of Churches and the Lutheran World Federation, respectively.

Turning first to "organic union," we recall that the earliest method used in the modern ecumenical movement was that of comparative ecclesiology.[6] Both the divisive and the unifying points of doctrine were carefully identified. By the time of the Faith and Order Commission meeting in Lund (1952), this comparative approach had reached an unproductive dead end. It was therefore replaced by a new "christological method" according to which the qualitative unity of the church is based on the indivisibility of Jesus Christ himself. The churches are called to make this given unity in Christ visible in history. The closer the churches come to Christ, the closer they will also come to each other in Christ. The Commission at Lund concluded:

> The nature of the unity towards which we are striving is that of a visible fellowship in which all members, acknowledging Jesus Christ as living Lord and Saviour, shall recognize each other as belonging fully to his body, to the end that the world may believe.[7]

The WCC General Assembly in Evanston (1954) further deepened this christological approach by emphasizing eschatology:

> The unity of the Church even now is a foretaste of the fulness that is to be because it already is; therefore, the Church can work tirelessly and wait patiently and expectantly for the day when God shall sum up all things in Christ. . . . It is certain that the perfect unity of the Church will not be totally achieved until God sums up all things in Christ. But the New Testament affirms that this unity is already being realized within the present historical order. . . . In the upheavals of the present hour, Jesus Christ is gathering his people in a true community of faith and obedience without respect for existing divisions.[8]

The theological conception of unity appeared in a more concrete form at the WCC General Assembly at New Dehli (1961). The ecumenical model of "organic unity" was affirmed. According to this model, the goal of ecumenism is the "one fully committed fellowship" of all Christians "in each place." The assembly declared:

> We believe that the unity which is both God's will and his gift to his church is being made visible as all in each place who are baptized into Jesus Christ, and confess him as Lord and Savior, are brought by the Holy Spirit into one fully committed fellowship, holding the one apostolic faith, preaching the one gospel, breaking the one bread, joining in common prayer, and having a corporate life reaching out in witness and service to all, and who at the same time are united with the whole Christian fellowship in all places and all ages in such wise, that ministry and members are accepted by all, and that all can act and speak together as occasion requires for the tasks to which God calls his people.[9]

The WCC General Assembly at Uppsala (1968) further developed the model of organic unity with the addition of the concept of "catholicity." The Assembly stated:

> The purpose of Christ is to bring people of all times, of all races, of all places, of all conditions, into an organic and living unity in Christ by the Holy Spirit under the universal fatherhood of God. This unity is not solely external; it has a deeper, internal dimension, which is also expressed by the term 'catholicity'. . . . The Church is constantly on the way to becoming catholic. Catholicity is a task yet to be fulfilled.[10]

The concept of "catholicity" also highlighted a further kind of ecumenical approach: the realization of catholicity also reaches out to the world, aiming at nothing less than the unity of all of God's creation in humankind. One of the major documents of Vatican Council II

("The Dogmatic Constitution on the Church," *Lumen Gentium*, 1964) had declared in its opening section: "By her relationship with Christ, the Church is a kind of sacrament or sign of intimate union with God, and of the unity of all humankind. She is also the instrument for the achievement of such union and unity." In positive reaction to this text's christocentric and pastoral orientation, Uppsala chose to speak in similar—though sacramentally more guarded—tones:

> The Church is bold in speaking of itself as the sign of the coming unity of humankind. . . . This unity of man is grounded for the Christian not only in his creation by the one God in his own image, but in Jesus Christ who "for us men" became man, was crucified, and who constitutes the Church which is his body as a new community of new creatures.[11]

The model of organic unity in catholicity acquired an even more precise formulation at the Faith and Order meetings of Louvain (1971) and Salamanca (1973). The new ecumenical goal was referred to as the model of "conciliar fellowship." Conciliarity was the main topic of discussion at Louvain:

> By "conciliarity" we mean the coming together of Christians—locally, regionally or globally—for common prayer, counsel and decision, in the belief that the Holy Spirit can use such meetings for his own purpose of reconciling, renewing and reforming the Church by guiding it towards the fulness of truth and love.[12]

According to this model each "truly united" local church, which is an expression of organic unity attained on the local level, possesses in conciliar fellowship with other organically united local churches "the fulness of catholicity" and "the fulness of truth and love." Thus united, each local church participates in the full conciliarity of the Christian church. (For episcopally structured churches, of course, "local church" designates an episcopal diocese.)

A final goal of conciliar fellowship is to prepare the way for a "genuinely ecumenical council" that would represent and serve all Christians and all churches. It was the Uppsala Assembly that had first called the churches "to work towards the time when a genuinely universal council may once more speak for all Christians and lead the way to the future."[13] It has been twelve hundred years since the convening of the last of the first seven great councils of the early church (Second Nicaea, A.D. 787). This council is generally acknowledged in both East and West to be not merely regional but authentically "ecumenical" or "universal." The Louvain meeting went on to request the churches to question "whether their life and work are helping to prepare the way for such a 'genuinely ecumenical council.' "[14]

After extended debate, the WCC Nairobi Assembly (1975) ratified this decade-long theological development by adopting the following statement as a comprehensive description of the unity to be realized in the ecumenical movement:

> The one Church is to be envisioned as a conciliar fellowship of local churches which are themselves truly united. In this conciliar fellowship each local church possesses, in communion with the others, the fulness of catholicity, witnesses to the same apostolic faith, and therefore recognizes the others as belonging to the same church of Christ and guided by the same Spirit. They are bound together because they have received the same doctrine, and share in the same eucharist; they recognize each other's members and ministries. They are one in their common commitment to confess the gospel of Christ by proclamation and service to the world. To this end, each church aims at maintaining sustained and sustaining relationships with her sister churches in conciliar gatherings whenever required for the fulfilment of their common calling.[15]

Other decisions made at the Nairobi Assembly are also relevant in this context. A new constitution was adopted that states the functions and purposes for which the World Council of Churches exists. The formulation concerning the unity of the church reads as follows: "To call the churches to the goal of visible unity in one faith and in one eucharistic fellowship expressed in worship and in common life in Christ and to advance towards that unity in order that the world may believe."[16] Nairobi went on to clarify the concept of "conciliar fellowship":

> [It] does *not* look towards a conception of unity different from that full organic unity sketched in the New Delhi Statement, but is rather a further elaboration of it. The term is intended to describe an aspect of the life of the one undivided Church *at all levels*. In the first place, it expresses the unity of churches separated by distance, culture, and time, a unity which is publicly manifested when the representatives of these local churches gather together for a common meeting. It also refers to a quality of life within each local church; it underlines the fact that true unity is not monolithic, does not override the special gifts given to each member and to each local church, but rather cherishes and protects them.[17]

The Bangalore meeting (1978) of the Faith and Order Commission was able to enumerate in its report three essential elements of the conciliar fellowship of a reunited church: "There was broad agreement that, in order to reach visible unity, three fundamental requirements must be met. The churches must reach (a) common understanding of the apostolic faith; (b) full mutual recognition of baptism, the eucharist and the ministry; (c) agreement on common ways of teaching and decision-making."[18]

A major climax was then reached at the Faith and Order Commission meeting in Lima (1982) when over one hundred theologians (Roman Catholic, Eastern and Oriental Orthodox, Anglican, and Protestant) unanimously voted to transmit to the churches a convergence document, which later appeared as *Baptism, Eucharist and Ministry*, for the churches' official responses and spiritual reception. After a half century of research and collaboration, that action marked an ecumenical milestone toward meeting one of the three cited criteria for the calling of a truly universal council.

Highly significant for the "evangelical catholic" self-understanding of Lutheran Christians is the reassuring realization that it has been ecumenically possible to affirm together, as authentic expressions of the church's *sensus fidelium* and as potential bases for the churches' *communio in sacris*: (1) the sacraments as living and effective signs of God's saving grace; (2) infant/believers' baptismal regeneration and unrepeatable incorporation into the body of Christ; (3) the Eucharist as real presence, sacrifice of praise, actualized memorial (*anamnesis*), Spirit-invoked (*epiclesis*), communion (*koinonia*), and normative weekly celebration in Christ; and (4) the apostolic tradition, episcopal-presbyteral succession in the church's order and faith, the threefold ministry of bishop, presbyter, and deacon as the fulsome sign (*plene esse*) of the church's visible unity and continuity, and the universal priesthood of all its baptized members in the church's participation in God's inclusive mission to the world.

Many Lutherans, both theologians and church leaders, were deeply involved for decades along with Protestants, Anglicans, Orthodox, and Roman Catholics in the gradual development of this model of "organic union" in terms of "conciliar fellowship" as an ecumenical goal consonant with the Lutheran Confessions. At the same time other Lutherans were far less sanguine about this general development and raised either objections or serious qualifications in the name of an alternate model first labeled "reconciled diversity" and later modified to "unity in reconciled diversity." That the first model became associated popularly with the multilateral dialogues of the World Council of Churches, and the second model with the bilateral dialogues of the Lutheran World Federation, did not easily help mutual reconciliation of churches, such as the American Lutheran Church and the Lutheran Church of America, that were involved simultaneously in both sets of endeavors by virtue of their joint memberships.

Let me rapidly highlight the alternate approach of "unity in reconciled diversity." Here we will be helped by referring to the major address by Oslo's Bishop Andreas Aarflot to the Sixth Assembly of the Lutheran World Federation (Dar es Salaam, 1977). In speaking of the ecumenical intentions of the Lutheran Reformation, Aarflot first identified four dimensions: 1) The principle of going back to the Holy Scriptures. The Lutheran Reformers were willing to discuss any doctrinal questions with anyone who was willing to submit to the authority of Scripture; 2) The principle of going back to the ancient church. Luther, Melanchthon, and others wanted to express their deep conviction of consistency with the writers of the early church. Note the inclusion of the three ancient creeds and patristic quotations in the Book of Concord; 3) The principle of willingness to enter into discussion and dialogue. The spirit is reflected in the entire Augsburg Confession. In the sixteenth century Lutherans sought dialogue with Catholics and the Reformed; 4) The principle of discriminating between the fundamental and nonfundamental articles of faith. For Lutherans the key question was: Is there the same understanding of the gospel as expressed in justification by faith? This was the only fundamental; polity, liturgy were nonfundamental.[19]

Bishop Aarflot then went on to contrast what he called "two tendencies within the modern ecumenical movement":

> The one aims at a unity in which traditional confessional identities are transcended and left behind, giving place to a new all inclusive identity. The model striven for here is that of "organic union." Churches of different confessional traditions and styles in a given locality or country unite in such a way that they surrender their previous confessional identity in order to constitute a new church with new norms and a new identity. Particular emphasis is placed on the necessity for faithfulness to the calling of the church to be the sign, instrument and foretaste of Christ's purpose to draw all people to himself.
>
> The other tendency [represented by "reconciled diversity"] seeks an ecumenical fellowship in which each confessional heritage and confessional identity is still maintained. The emphasis here is on faithfulness to the truth as it has been confessed in the past, and as it is embodied in the received tradition.[20]

Much of the language of Bishop Aarflot's address was picked up officially at the Dar es Salaam Assembly (1977) in its report, "Lutheran

Churches in the Ecumenical Movement." I would again like to recall the most significant material for our comparative purposes.

> We believe that at the present stage of the ecumenical movement, the following deliberations on "reconciled diversity" could function as guiding principles;. . .

> In this study, expression would be given to the abiding value of the confessional forms of the Christian faith in all their variety, but also to the fact that this diversity, when related to the central message of salvation and Christian faith, far from endangering this center, actually loses its divisive character and can be reconciled into a binding ecumenical fellowship in which even the confessional elements have an essential role to play. This concept of a "reconciled diversity"—which can be applied in principle even to confessionally compact churches (as, for example, the Lutheran churches themselves), since each church has to face the problem of plurality and diversity within itself—is not altogether new. It picks up and develops what already used to be said about an ecumenical fellowship which preserves and integrates confessional traditions within itself in all their distinctiveness and diversity.

> It is not claimed that the concept of "reconciled diversity" itself provides a detailed and final description of the goal of our striving for the unity of the church. Nor could it be said that, at this present juncture, when various concepts of unity are being considered, the LWF has officially adopted this concept of unity. Nevertheless, this concept is well suited to provide us with valuable help in pointing the way in the present phase of the ecumenical struggle, since it describes a way to unity which does not automatically entail the surrender of confessional traditions and confessional identities. This way to unity is a way of living encounter, spiritual experience together, theological dialog, and mutual correction, a way in which the distinctiveness of each partner is not lost sight of but rings out, is transformed and renewed, and in this way becomes visible and palpable to the other partners as a legitimate form of Christian existence and of the one Christian faith. There is no glossing over the differences. Nor are the differences simply preserved and maintained unaltered. On the contrary, they lose their divisive character and are reconciled to each other.

> In all our endeavors for unity, this element of reconciliation needs to be strongly emphasized. For unity and reconciliation do not mean mere coexistence. They mean genuine church fellowship, including as essential elements the recognition of baptism, the mutual recognition of church ministries, and a binding common purpose of witness and service.

Church unity means unity and diversity, not uniformity. To the extent that the concept of "reconciled diversity" takes this seriously, it comes very close to the concept of "conciliar fellowship" as recently developed by the World Council of Churches (see Nairobi 1975, Sect. II, paras. 3ff.), and cannot be put forward as a rival to this concept. There is indeed a difference between the concept of "reconciled diversity" and the concept of "conciliar fellowship," in that the latter seems to take insufficiently into account the legitimacy of the confessional differences and therefore the need to preserve them. Insofar as the concept of "conciliar fellowship" also allows room for the diversity of confessional traditions and for church fellowships as custodians of these traditions, the difference which still separates the two concepts will disappear. The result would be a concept of church unity in which both tendencies mentioned at the beginning of this section could exist side by side within the ecumenical movement.[21]

At a subsequent assembly of the Lutheran World Federation held in Budapest (1984), a working group on "The Unity We Seek" offered this statement: "Since the Dar es Salaam Assembly (1977), these questions have repeatedly been discussed thoroughly in meetings of representatives of the Christian World Communions and the World Council of Churches, in the context of Faith and Order, and by other groups in the churches. These discussions both deepened and clarified the concept of "unity in reconciled diversity" [in relation to "conciliar fellowship"] and led to the insight that these two concepts of unity are complementary."[22]

Having been involved intimately in both the bilateral work of the Lutheran World Federation and the multilateral work of the World Council of Churches, I can personally testify that while the concepts may certainly be theoretically complementary, their practical fulfillment often generates a good deal of ecumenical tension. Therefore I want the internal reception process of the Evangelical Lutheran Church in America to increase the light and lessen the heat as much as possible in the ecumenically challenging first years of our new life together.

To conclude: Since 99.9% of the people of God have absolutely no idea where we are supposed to be ecumenically heading, it is totally understandable that they will react either in defensive rejection or in ignorant support when they are suddenly challenged to respond to unexpected convergences, consensus statements, or proposals which have been worked out assiduously for decades without the benefit of any meaningful involvement of the laity in any prior or subsequent local reception process.

In the new Evangelical Lutheran Church in America ecumenism must become far more than the esoteric hobby of a few conference-attending jet setters. As the ecclesial corollary of the gospel ecumenism should become a Confessionally safeguarded, corporate life style of ongoing receptivity, a conscientious pattern of give and take within the body of Christ that is nourished by a doctrinal memory and an ecumenical tenacity that will sustain us over likely a very long haul ahead.

Consequently I have addressed myself to the twin foci of ecumenical motivation and destination as they face the Evangelical Lutheran Church in America at its inception. Churchwide clarity on "why and where we're heading" will be imperative as the new church faces incrementally a plethora of practical decisions regarding "levels of church fellowship" in terms of what is both Confessionally permissible and ecumenically advisable. Here as always we are normatively guided by the catholic intent and evangelical content of the Augsburg Confession.

Notes

1. This summary is provided by William G. Rusch in *Ecumenism: A Movement Toward Christian Unity* (Philadelphia: Fortress, 1985) 103-4.

2. *Ecumenism: A Lutheran Commitment*, an official statement of the Lutheran Church in America adopted by the Eleventh Biennial Convention, Louisville, Kentucky, September 3-10, 1982, 3-4.

3. *Ecumenical Perspective and Guidelines*, an official statement of the American Lutheran Church adopted by the Church Council, June 1985, 10, 13.

4. William G. Rusch, "The Vision of Unity Held in the Lutheran Churches," *A Communion of Communions; One Eucharistic Fellowship* (ed. J. R. Wright; New York: Seabury, 1979) 133-35; the quotation from Meyer is Harding Meyer, "The LWF and Its Role in the Ecumenical Movement," *Lutheran World* 20 (1973) 20.

5. Lesslie Newbigen, "What is the Ecumenical Agenda?" *Ecumenical Trends* 16 (1987) 6.

6. This historical survey is excerpted from my earlier study on "Evangelical Catholicity; Lutheran Identity in an Ecumenical Age" in Carl E. Braaten (ed.), *The New Church Debate; Issues Facing American Lutheranism* (Philadelphia: Fortress, 1983) 22-25.

7. *Faith and Order; The Report of the Third World Conference at Lund, Sweden, August 15-18, 1952* (London: SCM, 1953) 37.

8. *The Evanston Report. The Second Assembly of the World Council of Churches*, 1954 (ed. W. A. Visser t' Hooft; New York: Harper, 1955) 84, 88.

9. *The New Dehli Report. The Third Assembly of the World Council of Churches, 1961* (New York: Association Press, 1962) 116.

10. *The Uppsala Report. 1968. Official Report of the Fourth Assembly of the World Council of Churches, Uppsala, July 4-20, 1968* (Geneva: WCC, 1968) 13, 78.

11. Ibid., 17-18.

12. *Faith and Order, Louvain, 1971* (Geneva: WCC, 1971) 226.

13. *Uppsala*, 17.

14. *Louvain*, 228.

15. *Breaking Barriers, Nairobi 1975. The Official Report of the Fifth Assembly of the World Council of Churches, Nairobi, 23 November-10 December 1975* (ed. D. Paton; London: SPCK, 1976) 60.

16. Ibid., 295.

17. Ibid., 60. Emphasis in text.

18. *Faith and Order, Minutes, Bangalore, 1978* (Geneva: WCC, 1979) 40.

19. The address of Bishop Andreas Aarflot is included within *In Christ, a New Community*. Official Proceedings of the Sixth Assembly of the Lutheran World Federation (Geneva: LWF, 1977) 35-37, ##2-11.

20. Ibid., 43, #50.

21. Reprinted in *From Dar es Salaam to Budapest*. Reports on the Work of the Lutheran World Federation, 1977-1984 (LWF Report 17/18; Geneva: LWF, 1984) 19-20.

22. *In Christ—Hope for the World*. Official Proceedings of the Sixth Assembly of the Lutheran World Federation, Budapest, 1984 (LWF Report 19/20; Geneva: LWF, 1985) 219. Further cited ecumenical research: Günther Gassmann and Harding Meyer, *The Unity of the Church. Requirements and Structures* (LWF Report 15; Geneva: LWF, 1983); *Kundgebung der Bischofskonferenz der VELKD zum Thema "Einheit der Kirche," Texte aus der VELKD* 26 (1984).

16

Levels of Fellowship

A Missouri Synod Perspective

Samuel H. Nafzger

WERNER ELERT, in the opening chapter of his book *Eucharist and Church Fellowship in the First Four Centuries,* describes the contrasting conceptions of fellowship which he finds in the thinking of Luther and Schleiermacher. Luther, says Elert, was uneasy about the theological use of the German word *Gemeinschaft* for the Greek term *koinonia* and the Latin *communio.* Attributing his opponent's misunderstanding of the Lord's Supper, at least in part, to this word, Luther writes in his *Large Confession of the Lord's Supper* (1528): "It is not the genuinely German equivalent as I would like to have it, for to have fellowship is ordinarily understood as meaning to have something to do with a person. Here (1 Cor. 10:16), however, it means, as I have explained earlier, many using, enjoying, or having part in a common thing. I have had to translate 'fellowship' because I simply could not find a better word."[1] According to Elert the distinction between having "something to do with a person" and having "a part in a common thing" was vital for Luther. Fellowship, as Luther understands this concept, is not something produced by a human act. On the contrary, it precedes human efforts. It is that which actually binds people together.

Schleiermacher, on the other hand, understands fellowship quite differently, says Elert. He writes in his *Glaubenslehre:* "The general concept of the church, if there is to be such a thing, must be derived from ethics because the church at all events is a fellowship created by the voluntary actions of men, and only through these does it continue to exist."[2] Instead of drawing his understanding of fellowship from the nature of the church, as had Luther, Schleiermacher derives the nature of the church from the concept of fellowship as understood in the realm of ethics. For Schleiermacher, therefore, the church is a special instance of the general category of fellowship. Concludes Elert: "What Luther meant is, then, diametrically opposed to what Schleiermacher meant by fellowship when he spoke of the church. For Schleiermacher fellowship 'is created by the voluntary actions of men.' This is precisely what Luther rejected when he denied that fellowship means 'to have something to do with a person.'"[3]

My assignment is "to look at the basic challenge of Fundamental Consensus and Fundamental Differences in the light of 'Levels of Fellowship' as seen from your place in the Lutheran tradition."[4] I understand this to be an invitation for me to discuss this topic from the perspective of the position of The Lutheran Church—Missouri Synod on fellowship, since this is the "place" where I stand. In the first part of this essay I shall therefore sketch out Missouri's traditional understanding of the doctrine of church fellowship on the basis of two sets of theses prepared by two of its most formative theologians, C. F. W. Walther (the first president of the Synod and of Concordia Seminary in St. Louis) and his successor, Francis Pieper (also president of the Synod and the Seminary and author of *Christian Dogmatics*, a three-volume work still used as a basic text at the Synod's seminaries). We shall then review the most recent statement on fellowship of the Synod's theological commission. Having done this, we will be in a position to take up the topic "Levels of Fellowship" from within the context of the Missouri Synod's doctrinal stance on this issue.

As we take a look at Missouri's understanding of fellowship, let us keep in mind the distinction which Elert has drawn between Luther's understanding of this concept as "having part in a common thing" and that of Schleiermacher as "the voluntary actions of men." This distinction, it seems to me, can be most helpful to us as we consider "Levels of Fellowship." I want to suggest that Missouri's understanding of fellowship takes into account both of these conceptions. It is also my contention that by clearly distinguishing, but not separating, these two ways of thinking about fellowship, it becomes not only possible but also perhaps even necessary to talk about "Levels of Fellowship" as a possible response to the "basic challenge of Fundamental Consensus and Fundamental Differences."[5]

C. F. W. Walther's Altenburg Theses

Questions concerning the doctrine of the church and the meaning of fellowship surfaced in crisis fashion very early among the Saxon Lutherans who were instrumental in founding The Lutheran Church — Missouri Synod. Under the leadership of Bishop Martin Stephan these

German immigrants had arrived in Missouri in 1839 with some rather definite ideas about the nature of the church and their relationship to it. One of Stephan's followers described their views about the church in this way: "We announced to all Europe that Christ was leaving the old world with us, and to America that Christ was coming to her . . . we made our debut in St. Louis as the true Church."[6]

But when they felt it necessary, scarcely weeks after their arrival in this country, to depose their bishop because of charges of immorality, they were forced to come to grips with questions which touched the heart of their endeavor and of their very existence as Christians. What is the church? Were they still the church apart from their bishop? Were the office of the ministry and the sacraments still present among them? What was their relationship to the universal church and to other Christians? On the basis of the Holy Scriptures and the writings of Martin Luther and the Lutheran Confessions, a twenty-nine-year-old pastor by the name of C. F. W. Walther drew up eight theses for presentation at a debate held in Altenburg, Missouri, in April 1841, which he later refined and expanded in his books *The Voice of Our Church on the Question of Church and Office* (1852); *The Correct Form of a Local Congregation Independent of the State* (1863); and *The True Visible Church* (1867). The understanding of the church presented in these theses has been very influential in forming Missouri's position on fellowship.

According to Walther the true church in the most proper sense of the term is the totality of all believers of all times and places.[7] Because those truly having faith are known only by God (2 Tim 2:19), this church, which is the spiritual body of Jesus Christ, is invisible. The name of the true church belongs also to all visible companies or societies (*Haufen von Menschen*) in which God's word is purely taught and the holy sacraments are administered according to Christ's institution. The name church, and "in a certain sense also the name the true church," belong also to such visible companies which, although guilty of a partial falling away from the truth, nevertheless retain so much of the word of God and the holy sacraments that children of God can be born through them. According to Scripture the "high name church" may also be applied to heterodox companies (*irrglaübigen Haufen*), for outside the church there is no salvation. The outward separation of a heterodox company from an orthodox church (*einer rechtgläubigen Kirche*) is not necessarily a separation from the universal Christian church. Also heterodox companies have church power (*Kirchengewalt*) and in them the preaching office (*Predigtamt*) may be established and the sacraments validly administered. Taking this into account, heterodox companies are not to be dissolved but reformed. Finally, the orthodox church is to be judged chiefly by the common, orthodox, and public profession of faith to which its members are pledged.

In defining the church, properly speaking, as the sum total of all those who truly believe in Christ and therefore invisible, Walther was deliberately rejecting the notion that the one, holy, Christian, and apostolic church could ever be identified with an external organization or institution, and he expressly states: "The Evangelical Lutheran Church is not that one Holy Christian Church outside of which there is no salvation."[8] But while the one, holy, Christian church cannot be seen, there are "infallible outward marks by which its presence can be known . . . the unadulterated preaching of the divine Word and the uncorrupted administration of the holy sacraments."[9] A church which possesses these marks, says Walther, may be called "a true visible Church in the real strict sense of the term."[10] And he concludes that "the Evangelical Lutheran Church has all the essential marks of the true visible Church of God on earth."[11]

On the basis of this understanding of the doctrine of the church, Walther says: "Everyone is obligated by his salvation to flee all false teachers and avoid fellowship with heterodox congregations or sects."[12] Association with a visible, orthodox congregation is not a matter of indifference. Those who think that accommodations to perversions and distortions of the gospel are permissible make the same error as those who think that, just because Christians continue to commit sins of weakness after they come to faith in Christ, they can therefore knowingly and maliciously continue to do that which is contrary to God's will. Walther therefore, after presenting a series of theses on "the written Word of the apostles and prophets as the sole and perfect source, rule, and norm, and the judge of all doctrine,"[13] and after concluding that "the Evangelical Lutheran Church is sure that the doctrine set forth in its Confessions is the pure divine truth, because it agrees with the written Word of God on all points,"[14] says, "the Evangelical Lutheran Church rejects every fraternal or ecclesiastical fellowship with such as reject its Confession, either in whole or in part."[15]

But Walther also says that God is at work gathering for himself "a holy Church of elect persons" also there "where His Word is not taught in complete purity and the sacraments administered according to the institution of Jesus Christ, if God's Word and the Sacraments are not denied entirely."[16] In keeping with this conviction Walther also strongly advocates openness for contacts with heterodox churches and warns the members of the Synod against the dangers of falling into the clutches of an arrogant, separatistic spirit:

If those who by God's grace have come to recognize the glory of all our churchly confessions timidly withdraw from those who have the same faith and not the same knowledge, an equally. . .dreadful danger would threaten, namely that the one part would become guilty of a pharisaic carnal, spiritually proud, loveless insistence on its strict confessionalism, while the other part, instead of being filled with confidence and love for the continued building and further fortification of our confessional castles, would more and more be scared off as from a prison tower of the spirit and of faith. In consequence, the work of rejuvenating our church in America on the old tried foundation, a work so obviously begun by God, would be halted even though there was the best intention to further it.[17]

Walther, in keeping with this spirit, was instrumental in promoting a series of "free conferences" for the purpose of working toward the "eventual formation of an evangelical Lutheran Church of North America united in faith, doctrine and confession."[18]

Francis Pieper on "Unity of Faith"

The free conferences promoted by Walther were not successful in leading to the formation of one Lutheran church in America, but they were instrumental in bringing together in 1872 the Missouri Synod, the Ohio Synod, the Wisconsin Synod, the Norwegian Synod, the Illinois Synod, and the Minnesota Synod into the Evangelical Lutheran Synodical Conference. The purposes of this conference included giving external expression to the spiritual unity of its members, mutual strengthening in faith and confession, the promotion of unity in doctrine and practice, united action for common aims, the geographic delimitation of member synods except for necessary language divisions, and the consolidation of all Lutheran synods in America into one orthodox American Lutheran Church.[19]

In 1888 Francis Pieper, Walther's successor as president of Concordia Seminary, delivered an essay entitled "Unity of Faith" to the twelfth convention of the Synodical Conference. Pieper begins this essay by stating that there was general agreement that there should be unity in the Christian church. Everyone, he says, complains about the divisions in the church, and as a result there have been energetic efforts to effect unity. This would be a happy development, he says, were it not for the fact that "a closer look shows that most efforts toward unity are made in total ignorance regarding the nature of Christian unity." He then proceeds to list five theses which present "the correct, Christian God-pleasing unity, the unity of faith."[20] Referring to Augsburg Confession 7 and Formula of Concord 10 and 11, he defines unity of faith as "agreement in all articles of Christian doctrine as revealed in Holy Scripture." Unity of faith is possible, he says, because "all articles of Christian doctrine are clearly revealed in Holy Scripture." God desires unity of faith "because He both commands the acceptance in faith of His entire revelation and strictly forbids every deviation therefrom." Those who "stand in the unity of faith" necessarily give "outward testimony" to it by professing each other to be "brethren in the faith." And those who are united in the unity of faith, recognizing it "as a glorious blessing of God's grace, should diligently seek to nurture and preserve it."

In short, for Pieper unity of faith means agreement in all articles of doctrine revealed in Scripture, and this is the necessary requirement for church fellowship. He writes: "We cannot practice church fellowship with them [the erring] for thereby we would be approving their errors and partaking of the sins of others."[21] The Lutheran Church, he maintains, understands "the God-desired unity as agreement in *all articles* of Christian doctrine," and it has "consistently refused to foster church fellowship with the heterodox in order not to give a false idea regarding church unity as if agreement in all articles were not necessary, as if it were not necessary to accept God's Word in its entirety."[22]

But in this same essay Pieper, like Walther before him, strongly rejects the notion that the Lutheran Church is the only saving one. He writes: "We do not claim that children of God are born only in the Lutheran Church. Rather we acknowledge that there are Christians where the essentials of the Word of God are to be found."[23] However, says Pieper, when a fellowship has "completely abandoned" the essentials of God's word, then saving faith can no longer be effected there, and it is then "a body standing outside the church." He gives as an example of such a group those who no longer confess the Holy Trinity. This necessarily implies that a distinction needs to be made between the various articles of faith revealed in Holy Scripture. There are doctrines which every Christian must know and believe "without whose knowledge and acceptance saving faith cannot exist."[24] But, he continues, "there are doctrines which one, in weakness, may not know or regarding which he may even harbor error and yet remain a Christian."[25] Moreover, Pieper, referring to Romans 15:1, holds that it is certainly God's will that we "bear with the weak" and that "they should not be cast aside in a loveless manner and be declared non-Christians."[26]

Pieper summarizes his thoughts in these words:

> If we wish to preserve unity in faith we dare not surrender any article
> of revealed doctrine. But it is also to be noted that the apostle says in
> Eph. 4:3, "Make every effort to keep the unity of the Spirit *through the*
> *bond of peace.*" The unity of the Spirit can only be preserved through
> the bond of peace. If those who stand in unity of faith are not truly
> peaceable but quarrelsome, if they do not allow love to govern in
> everything that does not pertain to faith, then unity of faith will not long
> remain. Luther: "Where there is no love, doctrine cannot remain
> pure."[27]

To be sure, Pieper is here talking about the necessity of expressing love
between those "who stand in the unity of faith," that is, who are in
"agreement in all articles of Christian doctrine which are revealed in
Holy Scriptures." But he also recognizes the need to manifest love
toward true Christians in heterodox fellowships. He writes:

> What is our position toward those who are true Christians within
> heterodox fellowships? Is it sufficient that we simply acknowledge the
> fact that there are Christians in such fellowships? Or should we not give
> expression to this conviction in our outward conduct? We conduct
> ourselves, it appears, toward the erring as toward the children of the
> world.[28]

Pieper responds to these questions by immediately rejecting the implied
charge that the Lutheran Church, with its position on fellowship, treats
erring Christians the same as it does "children of the world." He says:

> We already distinguish between erring fellowships and the children of
> the world when we acknowledge that there can be true Christians among
> the former. . . . However, we cannot practice church fellowship with
> them. . . . It is simply impossible to practice fellowship with the Chris-
> tians in the sects because we do not know who the Christians are among
> the errorists; they are hidden from us. These are two different questions:
> (1) Who is a member of the invisible church, that is, a true Christian
> who sincerely believes in Jesus Christ? And (2), whom must I acknowledge
> as an orthodox Christian so that I can establish church fellowship with
> him? Here I must determine that he together with me submits to the total
> Word of God. Only then can I recognize him as a brother in the faith.[29]

Pieper himself at this point seems to sense an inconsistency with what
he had said previously with this refusal to recognize an erring Christian in heterodox fellowships as "a brother in the faith" simply on account of the hidden nature of the invisible church, for he immediately

proceeds to acknowledge that "there are hypocrites also in the true visible church." Rather than address this problem, however, he merely asserts: "We must view as Christians all those who profess the Christian doctrine and lead a godly life. Love requires that. But love does not require that we declare as Christians all who are in heterodox fellowship."

While few today would find themselves in agreement with Pieper's position regarding the recognition of members of heterodox churches as "brothers in the faith," the important point for us to recognize here is that he, like Walther, clearly distinguishes between fellowship in the body of Christ and recognition of an orthodox Christian with whom "I can establish church fellowship."

The CTCR's "The Nature and Implications of the Concept of Fellowship"

The Missouri Synod at its 1969 synodical convention adopted the following resolution: "We, the members of The Lutheran Church— Missouri Synod, rejoice over the existing unity of faith and confession, as stated in the doctrinal position of The American Lutheran Church and The Lutheran Church—Missouri Synod, and we embrace the opportunities and assume the obligations of altar and pulpit fellowship."[30] However, in the years that followed this declaration, several points of doctrinal disagreement between these two church bodies became manifest.

One of the things the ALC and the LCMS disagreed about was the meaning of fellowship. Missouri's representatives to the ALC-LCMS Commission on Fellowship reported to the Synod in 1977:

> The Missouri Synod has always believed and taught that "agreement in doctrine and practice" is the necessary basis for altar and pulpit fellowship. On the basis of discussions with the ALC officials and theologians within the Commission on Fellowship, LCMS representatives have reached the conclusion that "consensus in the Gospel" means for The American Lutheran Church a certain freedom with respect to agreement in doctrine beyond the central teaching of the Gospel itself. It is clear that commissioners from the ALC and the LCMS view the basis for altar and pulpit fellowship quite differently.[31]

At the same time the Synod's Commission on Theology and Church Relations (CTCR) reported to the convention that there was evidence of a lack of agreement within the LCMS itself on the meaning of fellowship. It stated: "At both local and church body levels, there is considerable evidence of theological disagreement and confusion in understanding the nature and implications of the concept of fellowship itself." The CTCR therefore suggested that it would be well for the Synod, before taking up the question of continuing altar and pulpit fellowship with the ALC, to clarify such questions as the following:

> Practically speaking, what does altar and pulpit fellowship mean when the church bodies establishing it have different understandings of its nature and basis? Is it consistent with confessional principles to recognize the legitimacy of local expressions of fellowship while insufficient doctrinal agreement exists at the church body level? . . . Given the doctrinal diversity and variance in practice within church bodies today, what is the significance of church body fellowship per se? What kinds of relationships can be established with other church bodies that will avoid both doctrinal indifference, on the one hand, and separatism and aloofness, on the other?[32]

In response to these reports the convention declared the Synod to be in a state of "fellowship in protest" with the ALC, formally requested its CTCR to prepare "a comprehensive study and report on the nature and implications of the concept of fellowship" for study throughout the Synod, and resolved to reconsider its relationship to the ALC in 1979.[33]

In response to this assignment the CTCR prepared a report entitled "The Nature and Implications of the Concept of Fellowship." In this report the CTCR first of all presents a summary of the use of the word *koinonia* in the New Testament. Noting that this term and its cognates are used in a variety of ways by the New Testament writers, e.g., for the offering taken up in Macedonia (2 Cor 9:13), for the relationships existing between the wine and the blood and the bread and the body of Christ in the Sacrament of the Altar (1 Cor 10:16-17), for the relationship existing between James, John, and Simon in the fishing business (Luke 5:10), and even for participating in the sins of others (1 Tim 5:22), the Commission's report observes that this is a term which has as its root meaning "having part in a common thing."[34]

Turning specifically to the use of the term *koinonia* in the context of inter-Christian relationships, the CTCR reports that this word is most frequently used in the New Testament in "connection with that spiritual unity which exists in the body of Christ (e.g., 1 Cor. 1:9; 1 John 1:3)." It also finds that this same word is sometimes used "to refer to the attempts of Christians to manifest this unity externally (e.g., Acts 2:42; Gal. 2:9)."[35] But the Commission calls attention to the fact that the

Scriptures have much to say about "each of these two distinct (but not separate) relationships without making specific use of the term *koinonia* at all." Neither Paul's discussion of spiritual unity in the body of Christ in Ephesians 4:1-6 nor John's account of Christ's High Priestly Prayer (John 17:20f.) makes any use of this word, for example. Nor do many of those portions of Scripture which exhort Christians to guard the truth and to live together in the church in an external relationship of peace and love. This necessarily implies that the nature of fellowship understood both as spiritual unity with Christ and as external relationships with fellow Christians cannot be limited to a mere "word study" of the term *koinonia*.

The Commission summarizes the results of its study of fellowship in nine Scriptural Principles.[36] The first three of these principles take up "spiritual fellowship" with Christ. This spiritual unity is a matter of "faith in the heart (*fides qua*)," a relationship which binds Christians together with Christ and each other in the one, holy, Christian church which transcends time, space, and denominational divisions. This relationship comes into being through the power of the Holy Spirit working through the scriptural gospel in word and sacrament. It is therefore a gift from God and not the product of human efforts.

The Commission's next three principles turn to a consideration of the role of the confession of the apostolic faith in connection with a discussion of the nature of fellowship. Just as faith (*fides qua*) is to manifest itself in acts of edifying love, so those who have been incorporated into the spiritual unity of the body of Christ by divine mandate are to confess and teach the faith (*fides quae*) as it has been recorded by the prophets and apostles so that the body of Christ may be edified and extended. Edifying love will manifest itself in a variety of ways, depending on the circumstances, but never by compromising the means by which the spiritual unity of the church comes into being in the first place.

The Commission's final three theses talk about church fellowship understood as external unity in the church. Unlike spiritual unity, which is a matter of faith in the heart, church fellowship is constituted by agreement in the faith which is confessed. Where the faith is not confessed in conformity with the prophetic and apostolic Scriptures, external unity does not exist in the church, and church fellowship has no basis. But by the same token the Scriptures command those who have been made one in Christ by virtue of Spirit-wrought faith in the heart to seek agreement in the confession of the faith with all those who profess faith in him, those whom they recognize in Christian love as fellow members of the body of Christ. In other words, the quest for external unity in the church and its acknowledgment when agreement in Confession has been attained are not optional matters but divine mandates. Church fellowship, therefore, understood as external unity in the church is not "a given." Although the achievement of church fellowship is also a gift from God, it is also a matter of Confession and therefore involves human efforts.

The Commission summarizes its understanding of the nature of fellowship this way:

> Our study has reached the conclusion that in the Scriptures fellowship is understood in the sense of its root meaning as having part in a common thing. . . . The writers of the New Testament use this term to refer both to spiritual unity in the Body of Christ and to external unity in the church. Each of these relationships, therefore, may properly be referred to by the use of the English word "fellowship." But neither of them is the result of human achievement, nor "are they matters about which people are free to make their own arrangements."[37]

Levels of Fellowship: A Theologically Possible Response

What is meant by the phrase "levels of fellowship"? Several possibilities exist. Some may understand this to refer to degrees of consensus in the confession of the apostolic faith. Others may think of this concept in terms of stages of intimacy in expressing degrees of consensus in doctrine through participation in a variety of activities such as prayer, public worship services, and the Lord's Supper.[38] Still others may find in this proposal reference to variety in "witness value" of joint activity, depending on whether it is carried out by an individual lay person, by a pastor, or by official representatives of a local congregation or church body.

Each of these ways of thinking about "levels of fellowship," it seems to me, provide important insights into this concept, and there are no doubt also many others, all of which are worthy of discussion. Important for us to note here, however, is not so much the variety of interpretations that might be given to "levels of fellowship," but rather that *all* ways of understanding this concept necessarily fall into the category of "having something to do with a person." They have to do, to a certain extent at least, with "the actions of men."

At this point we need to recall Elert's statement: "What Luther meant is, then, diametrically opposed to what Schleiermacher meant by fellowship when he spoke of the church. For Schleiermacher fellowship 'is created by the voluntary actions of men.' This is precisely what Luther rejected when he denied that fellowship means 'to have something to do with a person.'"[39] The question therefore arises: Is a "levels of fellowship" approach a theologically viable response to "the challenge of basic consensus—fundamental differences" by those who agree with Luther that fellowship means "having part in a common thing"?

As we have demonstrated above, Walther, Pieper, and the report of the Synod's Commission on Theology all understand fellowship as the spiritual unity which unites all believers with Jesus Christ and with each other. They all understand this unity to be something effected by God, a gift, and therefore not produced "by the voluntary actions of men." This spiritual unity is, moreover, invisible, hidden from human eyes, a matter of faith in the heart. It is dynamic in character, knowing no space or time limitations. In short, fellowship understood in this way is a qualitative concept and therefore by definition incapable of a "levels" conceptualization.

But we have also seen that Missouri, at least as illustrated in the writings examined above, understands the concept of fellowship *not exclusively* in terms of spiritual unity in the body of Christ. *Church* fellowship, as we have seen, denotes in each of the sets of theses examined a relationship to be distinguished (but not separated) from unity in the body of Christ. As Pieper says: "These are two different questions: (1) Who is a member of the invisible church . . . And (2), whom must I acknowledge as an orthodox Christian so that I can establish church fellowship with him?"[40]

"Levels of fellowship" is not compatible with fellowship understood *only* as spiritual unity in the body of Christ. But to the extent that the Missouri Synod distinguishes spiritual unity in Christ from church fellowship, "levels of fellowship" is a theologically possible response to "the basic challenge of fundamental consensus and fundamental differences."

Levels of Fellowship: A Contextually Necessary Response

Not only is a "levels of fellowship" approach to the challenge of fundamental consensus and fundamental differences theologically possible, but it seems to me that it is also contextually necessary today.

To a certain extent, to be sure, "levels of fellowship" concerns are implicit in the very distinction between spiritual unity in Christ and membership in a visible, external institution. Accordingly, questions about "levels of fellowship" have been present from the very beginning, as Elert's *Eucharist and Church Fellowship in the First Four Centuries* amply illustrates. But this matter acquired new urgency with the emergence of schismatic groups and especially with the Donatist controversy in the fourth century. Hermann Sasse describes the unanswered questions which this schism provoked:

> In what sense can those who are excommunicated be said to be members of the church, whose members they remain? When schismatic churches possess the priesthood and episcopal consecrations, when even the baptisms performed by heretics, if they are done properly, are valid, and when today heretics are called "separated brethren," where is then the exact boundary of the church? Already Optatus of Mileve [fourth century] bestowed the name of brother upon the Donatists, with exhaustive theological grounds for doing so in his seven books on the Donatist schism.[41]

Similar questions immediately confronted the Lutheran church following the Reformation. Nicolaus Hunnius (1585-1643), for example, offered this response to the question whether pastors of "erring churches" could perform legitimate baptisms:

> Some false teachers there are who retain the mode of baptism entirely unchanged. Such have a full right to administer the sacrament of baptism, without depriving the receiver of the benefits this act is able to confer; always understood that such people, who know this minister to maintain errors, should not go to him, nor bring their children to him for receiving baptism, except in cases of utmost necessity.[42]

A few years later in 1633 this same orthodox Lutheran theologian wrote an article in response to the question concerning the possibility of a Lutheran pastor conducting a funeral for a Calvinist who happened to die in a Lutheran territory where there was no Reformed church. His answer was that such individuals were not to be buried with the normal rites and ceremonies.[43] Numerous other questions concerning relationships with members of heterodox churches arose. But as long as church membership was largely a matter of Lutheran, Reformed, and Roman Catholic territorial churches, the question of "levels of fellowship" could generally be relegated to the realm of casuistry. The rise of denominationalism in the nineteenth century, however, made this an increasingly unsatisfactory way of dealing with these questions.

David B. Barrett's *World Christian Encyclopedia* reports that in 1980 there were 20,780 distinct Christian denominations in the world, 2,050 of which are to be found in the United States alone. Not only is there a growing number of church bodies and movements in existence today, but we are increasingly confronted by wide differences in theology and doctrine not only between but also within denominations of the same name,[44] a phenomenon which has led the Missouri Synod's theological commission to refer to the present day as an age of ambiguous denominationalism. The multiplicity of denominations and movements, the high degree of mobility in the modern world, and the proliferation of ideologies and beliefs complicate the efforts of Christians to be faithful to the biblical mandates to preserve the pure gospel and at the same time to exercise edifying love for fellow members of the household of faith. The CTCR states in the introduction to its report on the "Nature of Fellowship":

> Members of The Lutheran Church—Missouri Synod are not exempt from the effects of these developments. Lay members of the Synod are seeking guidance regarding participation in numerous kinds of joint activities with members of other Christian churches in Bible study groups, mass evangelism programs, interdenominational workshops and retreats, and a variety of religious associations. Pastors are increasingly confronted with requests to take part in ecumenical weddings, funerals, and occasional services and rallies of every description. Many congregations are discussing their policy for admission to Holy Communion and the question is frequently asked: "How much agreement with another church body is necessary before altar and pulpit fellowship can be declared?" Some today are even questioning whether ecclesiastical declarations are workable in this age of "ambiguous denominationalism."[45]

Such a context as we find ourselves in today, I believe, demands a consideration of a "levels of fellowship" approach to "the basic challenge of fundamental consensus and fundamental differences."

In its report the CTCR evaluates four contemporary models which seek to manifest external unity in the church: conciliarity, reconciled diversity, selective fellowship, and ecclesiastical declarations of altar and pulpit fellowship. The Commission concludes that only altar and pulpit fellowship declarations, although "neither divinely ordained nor scripturally mandated," offer at least the possibility for being able to take into account all of what the Scripture has to say about the nature of fellowship.[46] But noting the contemporary context and also the tendency that often accompanies ecclesiastical declarations of altar and pulpit fellowship to follow an "all or nothing" approach to inter-Christian relationships, the Commission concludes its report with the recommendation that the Synod continue to study the topic of fellowship "by giving special attention to the implications of the principles of fellowship presented in this report for relationships and activities between

Christians at the congregational, pastoral, and individual levels."[47] This is an assignment which has subsequently been given by the Synod to the CTCR and which it is presently in the process of completing.

Conclusion

In this essay we have examined a "levels of fellowship" approach to the basic challenge of fundamental consensus and fundamental differences from within the perspective of The Lutheran Church — Missouri Synod's understanding of the doctrine of fellowship. Our conclusion is that this approach is theologically possible and also that our contemporary context makes its consideration and development imperative. But now the question arises: "How can such an approach actually be worked out in practice?" This, of course, is a topic for another essay. At this time it is possible only briefly to sketch out the basic implications of our conclusions for the development of such an endeavor.

In the first place, a "levels of fellowship" approach to the search for Christian unity must always keep in view the fact that its viability is based on the possibility of distinguishing spiritual unity in the body of Christ from external unity in the church. If it is not possible to make this distinction, then a "levels of fellowship" approach is not possible. By definition "levels of fellowship" talk is quantitative in nature and therefore inappropriate and inadequate to refer to fellowship understood as a qualitative concept. Peter Brunner writes:

> The unity of the church is unquestionably constantly given. The unity of the spiritual body of Jesus is indestructible. . . .When we take this seriously, we cannot formulate our task in the ecumenical consultations to be the establishing of the unity of the Church of Jesus Christ. Contrariwise, we must derive our ecumenical obligation from the unity of the church that is continually given. We should not formulate our task in such a way as to say that we have to make the unity of the Church of God visible on earth. For we cannot visibly draw the lines of division which truly separate the living members of the body of Jesus from those who will not inherit the kingdom of God. This line of separation is seen now only by the eye of God. Therefore the unity of the Church of God will only first be manifest for our eyes in the apocalyptic revelation of the kingdom of God.[48]

Unity in the body of Christ is the presupposition, not the goal, of the ecumenical endeavors of the church. A "levels of fellowship" approach to the challenge of fundamental consensus and fundamental disagreements can assist us in avoiding the temptation to think that we can somehow or other by our own actions bring about the unity of the church.

In the second place, a "levels of fellowship" approach to the quest for unity in the church can help us remember that spiritual unity in the body of Christ can never be separated from external unity in the church. Precisely because Christians are already one in Christ, external unity can never be a matter of indifference to them. Recognition of this fact will preserve us from a separatistic failing to recognize that denominational divisions do not divide the body of Christ and also from a lack of concern for "right doctrine" which undermines the very means by which unity in the body of Christ is brought into being.

Finally, a "levels of fellowship" approach to the basic challenge of fundamental consensus and basic disagreements can help us avoid an "all or nothing" posture to the quest for unity in the church. "There is an inner dynamic to faith in Jesus Christ which works toward an external unity embracing all those who confess faith in Jesus Christ (1 Cor. 1:10)."[49] If this is true, and I believe that it is, then those who are one in Christ will necessarily be on the constant lookout for ways to give some manifestation of this unity. It is therefore simply imperative that we find ways to do this, but always so as not to compromise the truth of the gospel. I for one regard this conference itself as an opportunity for us to model one way brothers and sisters in Christ in a divided Christendom can give visible expression to a level of fellowship which we share in our Confession of the gospel of the one who suffered, died, and rose again for us. But also here the pain of our differences cannot be avoided. We in the Missouri Synod understand the Scriptures to teach the necessity of agreement in the Confession of the apostolic faith as the prerequisite for church fellowship. Here again Peter Brunner's words are to the point:

> For the sake of men's salvation, the church stands under the command to preserve clearly the apostolic Word, and thereby, the mark of apostolicity at its center. In obedience to this principal ecclesiological command, the church must repudiate all false doctrine. In obedience to this command, it must refuse to grant church fellowship where agreement cannot be reached on the content of the Word which is to be proclaimed as the apostolic message and faithfully administered in its sacraments.[50]

Although those of us gathered here at this conference recognize each other as fellow members of the body of Christ, let us pray that the "scandal of divided altars," as one theologian has put it, can "prod us on to reach consensus."[51] May God bless our efforts to this end.

Notes

1. Werner Elert, *Eucharist and Church Fellowship in the First Four Centuries* (tr. N. E. Nagel; Saint Louis: Concordia Publishing House, 1966) 4.

2. Ibid., 2.

3. Ibid., 5.

4. Letter of Assignment on file from Dr. Joseph Burgess, December 12, 1986.

5. Elert himself hints at this when he says in a footnote: "In his *Glaubenslehre* he (Schleiermacher) speaks of another concept of fellowship (*Lebensgemeinschaft mit dem Erloeser, Gemeinschaft mit Christo,* and this in connection with the Lord's Supper), but in discussing the church he holds unwaveringly to the concept derived from philosophical ethics: 'The Christian church is formed by the coming together of regenerated individuals for ordered interaction and cooperation.' (Par. 115)." See *Eucharist and Church Fellowship,* 12.
Hermann Sasse delineates the various ways the word fellowship is used as follows: " 'They devoted themselves to the apostles' teaching and fellowship.' Also in this word 'fellowship' something of the deep, divine mystery of the church lies hidden. For this word means something else than what we human beings otherwise call fellowship. Of human fellowship we have two kinds. There is the natural fellowship into which we are born. This is there before we are, and we are born into it without our consent. Such is the fellowship of our family and people. Then there is the fellowship which occurs because we wish it to, a fellowship we enter voluntarily. There is such a fellowship when we more or less voluntarily join a gymnastics club, a party, an association that has a purpose with which we sympathize.
"But the fellowship which binds together the members of the church never arises in such a way. We are not born into the church, nor can we join it. These are two very serious misunderstandings. 'Those who received his word'—the words of Peter's Pentecost sermon having gone into them working faith—'were baptized, and there were added that day about three thousand souls.' They 'were baptized'— passive voice. They 'were added'—passive voice. The One who added them was the One who called them by the Gospel and kindled the light of faith in their hearts.
"In this way, and in no other, did we also become members of the church." *We Confess the Church* (tr. N. E. Nagel; Saint Louis: Concordia Publishing House, 1986) 133. See also Thomo Mannermaa's treatment of the qualitative and quantitative bases for church fellowship in *Von Preussen Nach Leuenberg* (Hamburg: Lutherisches Verlagshaus, 1981) 103ff.

6. Quoted by Carl S. Mundinger in *Government in the Missouri Synod* (Saint Louis: Concordia Publishing House, 1947) 210.

7. See *Lutheran Cyclopedia* (ed. E. L. Lueker; Saint Louis: Concordia Publishing House, 1975) 22, for the complete text of Walther's Altenburg Theses.

8. C. F. W. Walther, *The True Visible Church* (tr. J. T. Mueller; Saint Louis: Concordia Publishing House, 1961) 45.

9. Ibid., 8.

10. Ibid., 35.

11. Ibid., 134.

12. C. F. W. Walther, "The Voice of Our Church on the Question of Church and Ministry," 1875, in *Walther on the Church* (tr. John Drickamer; Saint Louis: Concordia Publishing House, 1981) 52.

13. *The True Visible Church*, 50.

14. Ibid., 121.

15. Ibid., 128.

16. Walther, "The Voice of Our Church," 45-46.

17. C. F. W. Walther, "Foreword to the 1857 Volume" in *Editorials from 'Lehre und Wehre'* (tr. H. J. A. Bouman; Saint Louis: Concordia Publishing House, 1981) 41.

18. Ibid., 39-40.

19. See *Lutheran Cyclopedia*, 749.

20. Francis Pieper, "Von der Einigkeit im Glauben," in *Verhandlungen der zwölften Versammlung der ev. — luth. Synodalconferenz von Nord-Amerika*, 1888, 5ff. These theses read as follows: 1) Unity of faith is agreement in all articles of Christian doctrine as revealed in Holy Scripture; 2) This unity of faith is possible because all articles of Christian doctrine are clearly revealed in Holy Scripture; 3) God desires outward testimony of the unity of faith because He both commands the acceptance in faith of His entire revelation and stoutly forbids every deviation therefrom; 4) The necessary outward testimony of the unity of faith consists in this that those who stand in the unity of faith profess each other to be brethren in the faith; 5) Those who stand in the unity of faith, recognizing this unity as a glorious blessing of God's grace, should diligently seek to nurture and preserve it.

21. Ibid., 10-11.

22. Ibid., 8. Emphasis in the text.

23. Ibid., 7.

24. Ibid.

25. Ibid., 10.

26. Ibid., 25-26.

27. Ibid., 34. Emphasis in the text.

28. Ibid., 10.

29. Ibid., 10-11.

30. *Convention Proceedings, 48th Regular Convention of The Lutheran Church—Missouri Synod*, 1969, 98.

31. *Convention Workbook, 52nd Regular Convention of The Lutheran Church—Missouri Synod*, 1977, 70.

32. Ibid., 44.

33. Ibid., 126.

34. In reaching this conclusion regarding the root meaning of the term *koinonia*, the CTCR makes reference to a number of in-depth studies, including those of J. V. Campbell, "Koinonia and Its Cognates in the New Testament," *Journal of Biblical Literature* 51 (1932) 352-80, and Heinrich Seesemann, *Der Begriff Koinonia im Neuen Testament* (Giessen: Töpelmann, 1933).

35. "The Nature and Implications of the Concept of Fellowship," A Report of the Commission on Theology and Church Relations of The Lutheran Church—Missouri Synod, 1981, 9.

36. Ibid., 13-16. These theses read as follows: 1) Spiritual fellowship with Christ and with all believers is given with faith in the heart (*fides qua*); 2) Faith in the heart (*fides qua*) comes into being through the power of the Holy Spirit

working through the Gospel; 3) For the church today Holy Scripture is the only judge, rule, and norm of the Gospel; 4) Good works flow out of faith and are responses to the Gospel; 5) Love, which heads the list of "the fruit of the Spirit," always seeks the edification of the members of the body of Christ; 6) The confession of the apostolic faith (*fides quae*) as it is taught in the Scriptures is mandated by God for the sake of the edification and extension of Christ's body, the church; 7) Church fellowship (in the sense of external unity in the church) is constituted by agreement in the faith which is confessed (*fides quae*) and not by faith in the heart (*fides qua*); 8) The refusal to affirm church fellowship (in the sense of external unity in the church) with those who do not confess the faith (*fides quae*) as it is taught in the Scriptures is not an optional matter but a Scriptural mandate; 9) The quest for church fellowship (in the sense of external unity in the church), as well as its acknowledgement when agreement in the confession of the faith has been achieved, are not optional matters but Scriptural mandates.

37. Ibid., 40.

38. The Third World Conference on Faith and Order at Lund in 1952, for example, distinguishes the following different practices regarding admission to the Sacrament of the Altar: Full Communion; Intercommunion and Intercelebration; Intercommunion; Open Communion; Mutual Open Communion; Limited Open Communion; and Closed Communion. See Vilmos Vajta, "The Unity of the Church and Communion," *Church in Fellowship* (ed. V. Vajta; Minneapolis: Augsburg Publishing House, 1963) 225-26.

39. See pp. 238-39 above.

40. See p. 244 above.

41. Sasse, *We Confess the Church,* 48. Cf. J. M. R. Tillard's "We Are Different," *Mid-Stream* 25 (1986) 280; he writes: "The Roman Catholic Church affirms that the limits of the Church of God on earth are not identical with the limits of the Roman Catholic community."

42. Nicolaus Hunnius, *Epitome Credendorum* (tr. P. Gottheil; first ed. 1625; Nuremberg: Sebald, 1847) 290.

43. Nicolaus Hunnius, "Ob ein offentlicher Calvinist in einer Lutherischen Kirche mit den gewoenlichen Kirchen-Ceremonien zu begraben" *Consilia Theologica Witebergensia* (Frankfurt/Main: B. C. Wust, 1664) 486-87.

44. See, for example, Joan Chittister and Martin Marty's *Faith and Ferment* (ed. Robert Bilheimer; Minneapolis: Augsburg, 1983).

45. "The Nature and Implications of the Concept of Fellowship," 4.

46. Ibid., 42.

47. Ibid., 43.

48. Peter Brunner, "The Realization of Church Fellowship," *The Unity of the Church* (ed. V. Vajta; Rock Island, IL: Augustana Press, 1957) 13.

49. "The Nature and Implications of the Concept of Fellowship," 11.

50. Brunner, "The Realization of Church Fellowship," 20.

51. John H. Tietjen, "Holy Communion: Goal or Means for Church Unity," *Liturgy and Renewal*, Proceedings of the Institute for Liturgical Studies, February 4-6, 1964 (ed. Hans Boehringer; Valparaiso, IN: Valparaiso University, 1968) 40.

List of Participants

Rev. Lowell G. Almen, *The Lutheran Standard*, Minneapolis, MN

Prof. Arthur H. Becker, Trinity Lutheran Seminary, Columbus, OH

Prof. W. Beinert, University of Regensburg, Regensburg, West Germany

Prof. André Birmelé, Institute for Ecumenical Research, Strasbourg, France

President Ralph Bohlmann, LCMS, St. Louis, MO

Prof. Carl Braaten, Lutheran School of Theology, Chicago, IL

Dr. Keith R. Bridston, Vesper International Society, San Leandro, CA

Dr. Joseph A. Burgess, LCUSA, New York, NY

Rev. Juris Calitis, Latvian Evangelical Church in America, Toronto, Ontario, Canada

Mr. Daniel Cattau, LCUSA, New York, NY

Prof. Henry Chadwick, Oxford University, Oxford, England

Bishop Edelmiro Cortés, LCA, San Juan, PR

Bishop James R. Crumley, LCA, New York, NY

Prof. Karl Donfried, Smith College, Northampton, MA

Prof. James Dunn, University of Durham, Durham, England

Father Pierre Duprey, Secretariat for Promoting Christian Unity, Vatican City

Prof. Mark Ellingsen, Institute for Ecumenical Research, Strasbourg, France

Bishop Paul Erickson, LCA, Chicago, IL

President Roger W. Fjeld, Wartburg Theological Seminary, Dubuque, IA

Prof. Gerhard Forde, Luther Northwestern Theological Seminary, St. Paul, MN

Prof. Paul Fries, New Brunswick Theological Seminary, New Brunswick, NJ

Dr. Franklin D. Fry, St. John's Lutheran Church, Summit, NJ

Prof. Robert Goeser, Pacific Lutheran Theological Seminary, Berkeley, CA

Prof. Eric Gritsch, Lutheran Theological Seminary, Gettysburg, PA

Prof. A. Heron, University of Erlangen, Erlangen, West Germany

Bishop Will Herzfeld, AELC, Oakland, CA

Dr. John R. Houck, LCUSA, New York, NY

Prof. Horace Hummel, Concordia Seminary, St. Louis, MO

Prof. Robert Jenson, Lutheran Theological Seminary, Gettysburg, PA

Rev. Jerald C. Joersz, LCMS, St. Louis, MO

Prof. John F. Johnson, Concordia Seminary, St. Louis, MO

Dr. Jonas Jonson, LWF, Geneva, Switzerland

Prof. Theodor Jørgensen, University of Copenhagen, Hellerup, Denmark

Prof. Walter Kasper, Tübingen University, Tübingen, West Germany

Bishop William Keeler, Bishop of Harrisburg, Harrisburg, PA

Rev. Leonid Kishkovsky, Orthodox Church in America, Syosset, NY

Prof. Eugene Klug, Concordia Seminary, Fort Wayne, IN

Prof. Georg Kretschmar, University of Munich, Ottobrun, West Germany

Prof. Ulrich Kühn, University of Vienna, Vienna, Austria

Dr. William Lazareth, Holy Trinity Lutheran Church, New York, NY

Prof. H. Legrand, Institut Catholique de Paris, Paris, France

Bishop Clifford R. Lunde, ALC, Seattle, WA

Dr. George Madsen, ALC, Minneapolis, MN

Rev. Margaret Madson, ALC, Minneapolis, MN

Dr. Daniel Martensen, Washington Theological Consortium, Washington, DC

Archbishop Methodios, Archbishop of Thyateira and Great Britain, London, England

Prof. Harding Meyer, Institute for Ecumenical Research, Strasbourg, France

Dr. Samuel Nafzger, LCMS, St. Louis, MO

Prof. Norman E. Nagel, Concordia Seminary, St. Louis, MO

Prof. Peter Neuner, University of Munich, Munich, West Germany

Prof. Todd Nichol, Luther Northwestern Theological Seminary, St. Paul, MN

Prof. Carl Peter, Catholic University of America, Washington, DC

Dr. Christian K. Preus, Laporte, MN

Dr. J. A. O. Preus, Rogers, AR

Rev. Thomas Prinz, LCA, New York, NY

Father John A. Radano, Secretariat for Promoting Christian Unity, Rome, Italy

Prof. Michael J. Root, Lutheran Theological Southern Seminary, Columbia, SC

Dr. Walter Rosin, LCMS, St. Louis, MO

Dr. William G. Rusch, LCA, New York, NY

Dr. Edward Schneider, Good Shepherd Lutheran Church, Champaign, IL

Prof. Trygve Skarsten, Trinity Lutheran Seminary, Columbus, OH

Dr. Michael J. Stelmachowicz, LCMS, St. Louis, MO

Dr. Reuben Swanson, LCA, New York, NY

Father John Travis, Greek Orthodox Church of North and South America, New York, NY

President Vilis Varsbergs, Latvian Evangelical Lutheran Church in America, Chicago, IL

Prof. Geoffrey Wainwright, Duke University, Durham, NC

Bishop Wayne E. Weissenbuehler, ALC, Denver, CO

Prof. Dean O. Wenthe, Concordia Seminary, Fort Wayne, IN

Prof. Robert Wright, General Theological Seminary, New York, NY